MW00415050

This entire book and all of the contents are inspired by and dedicated to my little boy Jackson Erik Akers – my companion and steadfast helper in the garden, the woods and wherever else we may venture!

Hunt Gather Grow Eat

Your Guide to Food Independence

Jason Akers

Table of Contents

3

Introduction

One does not truly grasp the full meaning of the phrase "Putting food on the table" until failing to do so is a real and foreseeable proposition. For me that occurred during my drive home one morning in May of 2009. I had just been laid off from a job I'd held for four years. My wife's teaching job was effectively ending as well – leaving both of us unemployed and with no way to provide food for our one year old son Jackson. I had absolutely no idea how I'd explain this to my wife or what we'd do. We were just entering "The Great Recession".

Now rewind to 1984 – the titular year of the book by George Orwell. According to it, the government was supposed to initiate "big brother" and everyone was going to use a language called "newspeak", but if they were doing that in the cities we had no idea. I was 6 years old and I lived with my parents on an 80-acre farm just south of Louisville, Kentucky. In the spring we planted a huge garden and broke out the fishing poles. We raised rabbits, turkeys, chickens, pigs and cattle. In the summer we gathered blackberries. In the fall we gathered persimmons. Through the fall and winter we hunted deer, rabbit, squirrel, ducks and turkeys among other things. We canned our own food. We were happy.

Dad and I (age 2) in the Garden

How had I moved so far from my roots?

I had a large garden and I took the occasional weekend trip to a local wildlife management area to hunt. I fished for trout in park ponds and I still canned, but it was in a modern kitchen with a flat-top stove and to the sounds of television and suburban life.

Like most people I had ceded a lot of responsibility for feeding my family and myself. I had become reliant upon unreliable things – a job in the city, modern conveniences and unfortunately – the grocery stores.

The truth, is back then it was clear to me (as it is now) that a lot of people are in this situation. Some are oblivious, but others would like to take the red pill and slip back into reality – to a world where we feed ourselves and live off of what the land provides.

In 2009 I started a podcast called The Self-Sufficient Gardener (www.theselfsufficientgardener.com) to not only document my reawakening, but also to teach others what 33 years of living on and off the farm had taught me about hunting, gathering and growing my own food. Over 170 episodes later I've come to the conclusion that people not only want this information, but they need it.

I've interviewed great guests like Joel Salatin of Polyface Farms and Diane Ott Whealy co-founder of Seed Savers Exchange. I've been featured on LewRockwell.com. I blog for Mother Earth News Magazine and I presented at their 2011 Mother Earth News Fair in Seven Springs, PA.

Joel Salatin sitting with me in 2011

I was fortunate. I found a job quickly with only a small cut in pay. I took the generous severance package I was given and bought our eventual homestead – 4 acres in Western Kentucky. All in all I had come out better for the whole situation. I also promised to never let myself get complacent again or to take for granted where my next meal comes from.

Our culture has changed over the years. We went from absolutely creating almost all of the food we ate to not even being able to identify the origination or originator of our food. We see it as virtuous to "know your farmer". A hundred years ago we certainly knew our farmer – we had to look no further than a mirror! We define sustainability not as the amount of food we can provide for ourselves, but rather on what someone else in a distant field is doing. It's no longer good enough to name-drop Salatin or Judy or Pollan or Berry. What are you doing to increase your food production?

Fortunately there is a growing movement to get back to the land to pure food and to pure living. There are people who have never grown anything or set foot on a farm or in a garden who want to know where to start. And there are a lot of people like myself who lost their way along the path. Hopefully this book is the first step onto or back on that path - toward self-sufficiency and independence.

A Threatened Food Supply

In the US and abroad our food supply is under constant and persistent threat.

If you ate (or are on your way to) eating three square meals today and you will leave those meals with a full stomach you may have trouble believing my statement, but that doesn't make it any less true. There's a reason the saying is "Fat, dumb and happy".

Food Safety

For one thing our food supply is frequently tainted. Living under a fascist government model has put smaller food processors out of business and left us with large food processors that can't properly monitor their operations and are better equipped to fight legal battles than to produce healthy food.

The latest outbreak – Listeria from a cantaloupe farm in Colorado has claimed 61 lives and that number is by no means a final count. The CDC estimates that each year roughly 1 in 6 Americans (or 48 million people) gets sick, 128,000 are hospitalized, and 3,000 die of foodborne diseases.

If that number doesn't make the hair on the back of your neck stand up I'm not sure what will. Humans have an inherent fear of things entering our bodies and taking control of our functions. It's why we wear facemasks during minor flu outbreaks that serve no real purpose. It's why we wipe alcohol-based sanitizers on our kids' hands to kill germs. We need to feel in control.

Well there's no way to feel more in control than by securing your own food, but most of us can't secure everything. We have to pick and choose what we grow, raise, hunt or gather more of in any one season, but there are ways to pick what you can take responsibility for to ensure the most food safety for you and your family.

Processing

The real issue isn't the growing of food, but rather the industrialization of food. In every major case of large food recalls regarding vegetables it's the same old tune, different lyrics.

The 2006 recall of Spinach tainted with E.Coli from a California farm. The cause was found to be industrial beef production nearby (which is an E.Coli production machine!) tainting the fields.

The Listeria infected cantaloupes I mentioned previously were linked to a Colorado packaging shed. The conveyor belts and other uncleanable equipment were found to harbor listeria, probably tracked in by workers.

The 2009 recall of 2100 products from 200 companies using peanuts from a processing plant in Georgia (after eight people died) was caused by the lack of cleanliness and care in the roasting plant. Workers later recalled scenes of rodent infestations, failed tests and dishonest management.

The list goes on and on. The more foods are processed the more likely contamination will occur. In many instances it just takes one head of lettuce or a single tomato. The old adage is true: one bad apple ruins the bunch.

Risks

That's not the end of the story. Some foods are simply riskier than others. Leafy greens for instance are number 1 on that list. The fact that it's hard to clean something so fragile plays into the risk. You can't scrub a lettuce leaf or scour a piece of spinach.

Regulation

Many food safety advocates point to lax regulations and a fundamental lack of oversight and toughness regarding food laws. The real truth is this: Food regulations do well up to a point. Then they become self-fulfilling prophecies. The regulations become so stringent and broad that smaller companies simply cannot keep up. Those companies cease operations or become part of a larger company. Meanwhile the larger company has no trouble keeping up with the regulations. So why is this a bad thing? Well large companies can afford to get around the regulations.

Then there's the fact that PEOPLE WILL LIE, cheat, steal to get what they want. The regulations and testing did no good at the Georgia processing plant. Why would more help?

So the small company with an owner who cares and runs a tight ship fails and the large company with a profit first attitude buys their way past regulations and testing.

What Can We Do?

Very simply we must grow more of our own food and do it now. Grow the things that are deemed the most risky and that require the most processing. Grow things that travel long distances. The longer the distance the more chances of loss of containment or extra processing. Let's take the risk to our family out of other's hands. Those people don't care about our children. Let's take back responsibility for providing food for our families and us. Even a small garden will help. Anyone can grow lettuce!

What you can't grow will have to be purchased, but make informed decisions. Buy local when you can for risky items that you can't grow. Ask the grower about the product. If he/she can't answer then you should walk away, but nine times out of 10 they'll tell you all about their farm and how the product was grown. Ask them about processing and the methods used to grow. If they take issue with your questioning walk away. That's why we pay more at a farmer's market! To get connected with the farmer!

9

For some people, buying local food, or growing their own may not be options due to cost or availability. We shouldn't demean those people and be food snobs. All that does is create people who feel they are unable to make proper choices. There are good companies out there despite the unwise methods they use.

Know the good companies from the bad. Keep abreast of recalls and don't take chances (http://www.fda.gov/Safety/Recalls/). If you don't know – throw it out. Ten dollars worth of produce is not worth the life of a family member.

Whether you buy food from a local grower or the megamart, learn to wash the food thoroughly before use. You'd be surprised at how much more dirt you can pull away with a quick rinse. It's just a good habit to get into.

The GMO Threat

As I saw it recently (and chillingly) put, you and I are part of one of the largest experiments in the history of humankind. You did not sign up for this experiment and you are probably not aware of it. You get no benefit from this experiment in fact someone else is benefiting off of this experiment perpetrated onto you. You are part of it, so are your kids and the only thing you can do about it is to stop buying about 75% of the foods at the grocery store and right away.

I am, of course, talking about GMO food. GMO stands for Genetically Modified Organism. Though it sounds somewhat benign – similar to using a hybrid plant seed - it certainly is not. Genetically modified organisms are in the biosphere and more are introduced all the time. Many countries in Europe and Africa will not allow GMO foods to be imported, but the sad truth is pollens blow everywhere and eventually a good deal of the food supply around the world will be GMO whether we want it to be or not.

GMOs are also called transgenic organisms. Simply put, this is the result of taking the genes from one organism (such as a fish) and inserting them into the genetic makeup of another organism (a plant perhaps). The spliced genes are picked because of a certain feature that they are capable of turning on. The host organism then follows the instructions of the spliced genes. At first this was done by attaching the genes to gold films and shooting the gold particles into the host genes, but now it's done through a tame form of E.Coli bacteria (which in itself isn't all that harmful).

The harmful part is that the effects are simply not known. The companies that use GMO foods refuse to label their foods as such for fear that the public would not accept them. They are happy to keep us in the dark.

There have been unusual allergic reactions from GMO foods. GMO corn created to produce the insecticidal bacteria BT or *Bacillus thuringiensis* has resulted in the presence of the bacteria in the blood of fetuses which was passed from the mother to child. No one knows what the effects are or might be, but the real problem is that whatever the effects, the government and these Big-Ag companies are not content with waiting and seeing. Most GMO efforts are rubber stamped with little testing. And what testing completed by the producer is essentially forced into strict confines where the tests reveal nothing, but good news.

Some of the most popular GM crops such as corn and soy have been manipulated to resist the spraying of insecticides such as Roundup (and coming soon – 2,4-D). Though the plants themselves do not die with the application the proper studies have not been conducted to determine how much of the pesticide the plant absorbs and passes to the end consumer.

As early as 1998 Dr.Árpád Pusztai – one of England's top biochemists released finding he had conducted on a strain of GMO potatoes. His findings were shocking. The GMO potatoes were found to have damaged the immune and digestive systems of laboratory rats. His findings have been disputed, but afterward he was censored by director of the institute where the study was conducted 31 US and European scientist reviewed the data and supported the conclusions. It is for this reason much of Europe remains highly resistant to GMO products and introduction.

The environmental implications are still more difficult to discern. We simply do not understand all of the ways that nature works nor can we see down the chain more than several steps. In 1983 Advanced Genetic Sciences received authorization to release an ice-minus version of the bacterium *P. syringae* on fields of strawberries. The ice-minus bacteria would prevent the formation of frost crystals and thus allow the fruit to survive frosts without cell wall breakdown.

That field was at least partially destroyed by anti-GMO activists. However, there is some worry that if the bacteria had mutated and/or spread into the ecosystem the consequences could have been dire. For one thing, frost formation in the upper canopies of trees relates to water vapor capture that helps provide trees with the water they need. The bacterium (in normal form) is also responsible for killing out "agricultural weeds" such as pigweed. With a neutered form of the bacterium, pigweed would run rampant in farmer's fields.

So as you can see, GMO foods pose many questions that remain to be answered. If you don't relish the idea of being someone's science experiment it is important that you learn to hunt, gather, grow and eat food that you produce.

Permaculture

As a certified Permaculture Design Consultant everything I do is colored by permaculture and my understanding of it.

When I mention the word permaculture a small segment of the people I talk to understand exactly what I am talking about and why I mention it. However a large part of the populace either believe permaculture to be a "hippy" endeavor or they simply do not understand it.

Permaculture is simply a collection of sustainable agricultural ideas put under one umbrella. Its prime directive (from founder Bill Mollison) states: The only ethical decision is to take responsibility for our own existence and that of our children. The three ethics are Earthcare, Peoplecare and Fairshare.

The prime directive is the perfect explanation of permaculture and justification for getting back to the land. It is our responsibility to do these things. Besides for what other reason do we secure a food supply other than to ensure the wellbeing of us and our children?

Earthcare asks us to look at the effects of what we do to the land. This to me does not mean carbon emission or global warming, but it might to you. To me it means that if you ruin your own land you will not be growing things there in a healthy manner.

Peoplecare asks us to do what benefits us the best while still maintaining Earthcare. We should live off the land, but we have to do it responsibily and in a way that is beneficial to all involved. If we rape the land neither the land nor its occupants benefit.

Fairshare is often twisted by some crowds. Fairshare does not mean we have to share our rewards. It means that we take only what we need from the land. Being a hunter I understand this perfectly. Kill too many of the creatures on a given piece of ground and there will be none left for the future. We take only what we need.

Permaculture principles influence every section of this book. If you look you will find the 12 principles interlaced in everything I speak of.

Those 12 principles are:

1. Observe and interact - We are part of the system. We have to monitor, maintain and be responsible. By watching the systems in nature we learn efficient ways of doing things. By watching our own systems we learn better ways.
2. Catch and store energy – Sunlight is heat and energy for plants. Water has inherent energy in its flow. Even calories from food when properly preserved is stored energy.
3. Obtain a yield – We do things that provide a return on our investment. Doing things that do not make sense provide no benefit.
4. Apply self-regulation and accept feedback – Before we take too much from the land we have to be able to stop ourselves and understand when changes are needed.
5. Use and value renewable resources and services – We simply have to see the benefit in things and learn how to utilize them.
6. Produce no waste - There is no waste we need to utilize everything.
7. Design from patterns to details – We replicate the patterns in nature because they work!
8. Integrate rather than segregate –We bring in help from wild and domestic animals. We look at the flow of goods through the system.
9. Use small and slow solutions – We change things slowly to make sure the effect is one that is desired.
10. Use and value diversity - Food systems such as gardens are only sustainable when they run as a whole ecosystem.
11. Use edges and value the marginal – When we realize what fits we realize there are no suboptimal situations, only ones we must adapt to.
12. Creatively use and respond to change – Understanding that change is a normal part of anything we have to be prepared to deal with it.

Process Oriented System Design

Permaculture can help us be more conscious of how to develop sustainable, carefree systems to feed us. Each particular way of producing your own food should be considered an element. Once you know which elements you want to include in your design the next goal is to make it all work as a system. I call this next phase of design – which is heavily guided by permaculture - Process Oriented Systems Design. By doing this we can better realize how to make things interact in the way we want that will be the most productive. I consider this to be a practical and practicable application of permaculture.

Statement of Goals

At this point you are essentially deciding one small element's goal. It's best to focus it as narrow as possible. This often times is as simple as saying **I want eggs for me/family**. Don't worry about the larger goals. As the system builds around this one mini-system you'll begin to realize larger goals are being met as well.

Analyze

The next step is to determine what creates desired output most efficiently. The goal is **I want eggs for me/family**. Obviously birds **create eggs**, but what type is most efficient and desirable? You might choose **chickens**, ducks, turkeys or ostriches depending upon your particular situation and need. No one can analyze your situation for you. Looking to someone else to tell you what YOU want is a recipe for disaster.

Research

Examine nature and/or similar systems. Determine what system creates desired output. Is there a bird in nature that I can use? Well I can't use a bald eagle, it's illegal and it may peck my eyes out, but birds do this in nature all the time.

15

They find forage and water and lay eggs. So it's not a stretch to build a system as close to nature as possible. The goal here is to observe and interact.

Process Specification

System designs are populated with supplier, inputs, process, outputs and customer.

- Suppliers should be eliminated when possible.
- Inputs shall be durable when not and originating as close to point of use as possible. Use and value renewable resources and integrate rather than segregate.
- Inputs should be as limited as needed.
- Processes should utilize talents of components whenever possible.
- Outputs should either benefit you/family indirectly or directly or feed back into one or more systems to maintain or improve.

Considerations for the process design include:

- Sweating the details – colors, sizes, small features, materials, breeds, etc. all matter!

- There are no suboptimal situations, land, and objects – only things in different states of potential. There is no waste, there are no pests, and there are no weeds. Waste is matter that you haven't figured out how to utilize yet. Pests are beneficial insect snacks; invite the beneficials to the party. There are no weeds, only nutrient bioaccumulators. If you have land you don't like, make it better. Produce no waste/use edges and value the marginal.

- Every element should have multiple benefits when possible.

A chicken tractor provides shelter, pest control and soil improvement

- Some (if not all) elements should interact with other systems. Integrate elements rather than segregating them.

The grape trellis at the back of my garden gives me an opportunity to integrate birdhouses and insect habitat

- Simple is always better.

Development

Create a small version of the system (prototyping). In this case we might build a small **chicken tractor to house our chickens that create our eggs for my family and me.** Prototypes are simply individual, one off test models. We can make improvements as needed in future models.

Testing

Let the system run and monitor it. **Use and test the chicken tractor.** Does it make eggs efficiently for us? In this way we are ensuring that we use small and slow solutions to tweak the system to optimal.

Implementation

Once we are happy we can build the full-scale system (**build the final system**). By accepting that the system required changes and implementing those changes we are applying self-regulation and accepting feedback.

Evaluation and conclusion

Determine if the system meets customer needs. This must be answered with measureables. Did we get the **eggs** we wanted? Is there a system that has been tested or could be tested that might be more efficient? The measureables that should be accounted for are as follows:

- Efficient – Amount of man-hours and calories spent as a necessary component of said system. The goal is to obtain a yield.
- Responsible – Amount of different life forms (introduced or otherwise into the system). We must use and value diversity.
- Sustainable – Ability of the system to resist either your absence or your reasonable meddling. Also measured by the number of outside inputs needed to keep it running and their proximity to system location.

Redesign

When the system doesn't live up to expectations or things change we can adapt the system until it begins to fulfill its purpose again. By doing this we are creatively using and responding to change.

Processes and systems designed around a problem must realize that there is no problem. The problem is not a problem once the root cause becomes apparent.

<u>Systems</u>

18

Thinking about systems is a good thing. There are tons of systems in everyday life, modern and natural and we may take advantage of some of these systems and not even know it.

On the modern life side we have a public transportation system. The system is designed by humans to get humans from one place to another safely, cheaply and quickly. And whether the transportation systems you have encountered worked well or not, that is the purpose. Personally I've been to cities where they did and did not work well.

If we break down the whole system we see that it's really a conglomeration of smaller systems. For instance, many city public transportation systems rely on a central railway, but the users have to get to the railway to begin with so sometimes they take their cars on public roads. Other times they take a public bus on public roads to get to the train.

It's important we recognize the individual systems and their limitations. Buses could work for the entire system, but buses are inefficient, carrying a smaller amount of people for more energy than a train. Trains also have their limitations, they require rails and power and as such they can't reach outlying areas, but working together, the bus system and the train system make up the public transport system, which (if properly managed) is efficient and beneficial.

It's also important that we recognize and see the interactions between two systems. You can hop a bus in Alexandria, VA and that bus will take you to (among other places) a rail station that will lead you to Washington, D.C. The reason is quite simple. Most people living in Alexandria or staying there wish to at some point visit D.C., but what if the bus stopped one mile short of the rail station? It's the interaction that makes the bus part of the whole system.

On the natural side we cannot force, only encourage and propagate these interactions in a way that benefits the natural system and us. A rabbit husbandry system is great. It provides us meat, but the meat comes at a calorie cost. So if we feed the rabbit garden waste or weeds we pluck from the garden or clover and grain we grow in our pasture or crop field area we can cut the calorie cost. In addition, the waste from the rabbits can actually help the soil we grow their feed in by replenishing the nutrients lost.

So you can see very easily how the livestock system not only interacts with the garden or farming system, but also actually nearly integrates where it becomes impossible not to think of the whole system they create.

Just as the transport system has its limitations so can the natural systems when we force interaction or ignore needs. In many cases, the natural system will reject your attempts to force it. You can't feed a rabbit oak leaves. The rabbit will reject them as food. Just as we know what the bus and train is good at and capable of so must we know what the rabbit is good at and its capabilities. We ignore these at our own (and the rabbit's) peril.

In a similar vein we should pursue the best and least radical interactions possible. We might find that rabbit waste is not the best soil rejuvenator for one area in lieu of a second area. Just like a rickshaw might not be an appropriate public transport in a certain city. So we should not ignore interactions, but rather pick the best interactions to nurture within our systems.

Individual Systems

Though it is important to think of the whole system and the interactions within, it's equally important to set up the smaller system first and work outward from there. You'll notice that as you work through the smaller system you'll realize interactions from the whole system.

For instance you will notice as you set up the rabbit system you'll start thinking: How do I feed the rabbit? House it? Do I really want rabbits? What benefit do rabbits provide?

At least you should start thinking these things. Unfortunately we can't deny human nature and human nature is to sometimes act on impulse and many people will plant a garden full of a crop they hate eating because someone said it was a good crop and the gardener acted on impulse. So at the very least it's important to think about and decide if a particular system is one you want to or need to propagate.

The SIPOC approach (we will talk about in the next section) will help you identify the way the system moves energy and concrete substances throughout, but it is important also to identify the individual components of the system.

A rabbit system consists of rabbits, feed, housing, you, waste, feeders, waterers, space and other components that would we tough to all list here, but the point is that buying rabbits and then asking what you need is the wrong manner of propagating the system. For one, a lot of money or at the very least resources are spent quickly. Secondly, we tend to do things inefficiently when we aren't given adequate time to work out the details.

SIPOC

Any individual system (and thus a system of systems) can be thought of as a series of steps through which material, energy, time or money flows through in a set sequence. A quick and easy way to break down the flow of things through is the SIPOC method.

SIPOC is an acronym, which stands for:

Supplier – the process, person or thing supplying the element entering into the system.
Input – the actual thing entering the system.
Process – the method of getting the thing through the system.
Output – the result of the system on the thing.
Customer – the system or person who is receiving the output of the system.

Since we've been talking about rabbits in this section, let's continue and work out a rabbit system through the SIPOC model.

For a rabbit system you will have multiple suppliers and inputs (most times the S and I are thought of together). Rabbits (owned by other people or by you) supply new stock. The local hardware store is the supplier for cage materials. You get the idea.

The process is the general day-to-day upkeep maintenance and labor involved in raising rabbits. Anything that gets things through the process counts.

The output and customer sections are where things get tricky. First of all, any output must be counted, not just what is desired. Like S and I, O and C are counted together. The customer is linked to the output and vice versa. Where an output exists without a customer it is your job to find one. For instance, the desired output is meat and you and your family are the customer. A little more difficult is waste, which a person with even limited intelligence can use as fertilizer or compost fodder, but then we dig into more ethereal things. What about heat? Can we find a customer for heat? Perhaps the plants in a greenhouse could use heat.

Finding customers for all outputs is necessary for two reasons. The first reason is that an output without a customer can, but not always, become pollution – excess that is not consumed or taken up by the system quickly enough.

Secondly, killing an animal for food or resources – no matter how small – is not a thing to do lightly. Now don't get me wrong. We shouldn't feel guilt for it. The food chain dictates this role and evolution makes it concrete. However, killing an animal and not doing its life justice (I hate the term "honoring it") mean using every resource there; hide, meat, bones, waste and all.

The last thing that has to be said about the openers and closers of the systems – inputs and outputs is that the outputs of one system should be the inputs of others. Likewise the outputs of one system should be used as inputs to another (see above!). This is how systems connect and systems become part of the larger system.

Perpetuity

Many people do not believe in perpetuity of system. They believe a system is started, rises and then falls. I do not believe this and experience tells me I am correct.

Sure the system can fail and we have to be aware of this. A smaller system can fail and systems failures can cascade into total system failure of the whole system. That's why we put safeguards in place to prevent total failure. If the greens we grew for rabbit feed do not come to fruition we will have another food source available.

However, the proponents of a climax-failure system will never explain how rabbits live in the wild without going extinct in one generation. If we make peace with the fact that some inputs are one-off inputs and that consumable inputs can be provided from the land we can maintain perpetuity. In other words, we bring our system into equilibrium.

Equilibrium requires more than just a good system. It requires balance. It requires knowledge of capacity and other subjects. For instance, if we dedicate half of our arable cropland to rabbit cages we should understand and be prepared to allocate an adequate amount to raising the food for the rabbits. In addition, if we do not return the rabbit output of waste as an input of soil amendments into the crop field we will not maintain equilibrium.

Planning

The first step in realizing a successful food system is considering the plan and making adjustments. Let's get something out of the way quickly though. Humans do not design natural systems. If we did, they wouldn't be called natural systems, they'd be called artificial systems. So this begs the question: What can we plan?

There are a few things that need to be planned. First, we have to identify the systems we want to propagate. As humans we have the choice to nurture certain systems. We'll talk later in the book about nurturing your soil – something that should be important to everyone. "The soil" is really "the soil system".

Next we have to plan our role in the system. There are some methods that preach human non-involvement I tend to favor human non-intervention. We should be involved in the system, but we should not intervene in natural things when it serves no purpose for ourselves.

I'm going to talk about building things in this book as well. Some of the things I talk about building like chicken coops and cowsheds might not seem natural or may seem interventionist, but these are things that aid what the animal needs without disturbing their naturalness. They can still eat, breed, defecate and just in general live. The shelter is a nurturing method that can, but in most cases does not interfere with the natural way.

Lastly, we can plan interactions, roles and allocations. I liken some of our roles in the food system to the game of chess. Though we cannot change the colors of our pieces, or move squares around we can interact with our pieces and reap the rewards of the success.

Small and Simple

The role humans play in planning our roles in these natural systems and which systems we want to encourage is a stewardship and labor role. We should consider ourselves another life form in the labor pool to help move the natural system and the components into a position that makes sense. However we should ensure we don't add unnecessary elements to the systems that contribute to complexity and allow potential for breakdown in the system.

To use the chess analogy further, we don't add new rules that constrain our pieces' movements. We also don't add additional pieces to the board. In fact, many chess players (me included) play a little better after we lose a few pawns and can concentrate on the fewer pieces we have.

In a system there is quite a bit of complexity already present. The point is to not add additional steps that don't need to be there. Furthermore anywhere we can actually keep the natural system in mind while taking the least steps, involving the least inputs, the better.

In a smaller, more real sense I posit that reliance upon complex machines, tools, equipment is just as bad as relying upon complex systems. I will use things in my systems that use electricity and fuel, but I think at the very least it is worthwhile to know how to do without these things. There's nothing wrong with living a little like the Amish. There is certainly something to be said about their ability to forgo the use of complex machines.

Maintainable

A system that is allowed to work within natural laws and constraints should require very little maintenance, but since we include ourselves as part of the natural system we have to keep in mind that our tasks are sometimes that of maintaining things that don't maintain themselves.

For instance, we might move a resource around; that's one form of maintenance, but if we don't consider this when we arrange our pieces to constitute the system we could be moving heavy things long distances. If we build something we also need to keep its maintenance in mind. Every time I build a structure I wonder how hard it would be if I had to replace the roof, the floor. How often do I need to clean it?

The truth is that this isn't some consideration that makes me feel all zen about my natural surroundings and gives me a sense of oneness. The simple fact is that hard to maintain systems can fail just from laziness. All of us have our level at which we will quit bothering with something. The level is different in everyone, but believe me, it exists!

Consideration

I hate to say it, but humans are poor observers. I don't think we were always this way, but we certainly are that way now. It's not that we are inferior in any way, we've simply not needed to be good observers. Seatbelts, airbags, and good medical care have made sure that the bad observers in us live on to breed and make new bad observers.

It's not a problem if you have the right tools to combat poor observation.

I prefer consideration to observation anyway. Observation is simply looking. Consideration is looking with a purpose. When you look at the forest surrounding your house you see trees. If you are a good observer you might see pines and oaks, but if you consider the forest surrounding your house you consider it as a source for food. Or you might see a windbreak, but also a fire hazard. Observation implies disconnectedness and ambivalence. Consideration implies involvement and action.

Nature

Many people would have you believe that a human can perfectly recreate a natural system. This would be similar to the chess player I mentioned earlier brushing in squares where they see fit or adding new pieces and setting up new rules for them.

Other people would have you believe that a human has no business being any part of nature. That we've ruined what we've been given and our touch is poison. And in this case, we not only should not be changing the colors of the squares on the chess board, but that we should not even be near the chess board.

I tend to believe somewhere between, but make no mistake, we are the chess player. Being at the top of the food chain, we move our pieces around and as long as we play inside the rules (of nature this time) we can effectively be involved without being obtrusive.

On the same hand, the notion that we can replicate nature is overplayed. Replicating nature by default makes something unnatural – and that is just fine! Rather than replicating nature we should recognize nature where we see it, nurture it when we can and live with it and the consequences when we cannot.

Section 1A - Hunting

Introduction

Why Hunt?

It's a simple question. Why – in our modern age – would someone need to hunt? We have all the food we'll ever need at the grocery store, right? Perhaps you even live in the city and don't really spend any time in the woods. Maybe the thought of going out and harvesting game scares you a bit or makes you feel guilty.

Mankind started out as hunter-gatherers and as much as I preach growing your own food I think it's equally important to connect with your roots by hunting your food.

Eating supermarket meat is nothing to be ashamed of. If you hope to cede your responsibility of killing an animal and feeding your family you are still killing by proxy and instead of walking the woods de-stressing and connecting to your roots you potentially spend 9-5 at a thankless job to earn the money to buy your meat.

There's never been a better time to learn to hunt!

The author (at 19) with a Kentucky 8-point

Is Hunting Compatible with Permaculture?

This is a question I often get. There is some expectation that a permaculturist is a hand's off steward of the land. There is the tendency to think that the system should be set and we should observe and interact, but by fulfilling our role in the food chain we are somehow upsetting this balance. I find that way of thinking to be completely wrong.

Hunting, as a topic, is almost completely ignored in permaculture circles and the current literature on the topic.

The truth is that my stance hasn't changed much since I was a younger man pondering the question of whether hunting has a place in my life or not. As a steward of the land it is our responsibility (not a right or privilege) to take on the role we were meant to play at the top of the food chain.

Joel Salatin often talks about treating livestock well by letting them express what they are meant to be. Humans are not livestock, but hundreds of thousands of years hunting has made us into hunters and consumers of meat. It seems wrong to deny that role.

Done in a responsible manner that follows and is even stricter than the laws and regulations where we live, hunting follows the permaculture ethics.

1. It takes care of the **earth** by helping regulate populations of wild animals and preventing sickness and starvation. In fact, due to human encroachment into wild areas the permaculturist who hunts is more humane to the wild animal than the typical yuppie city or suburb dweller that looks down upon the hunter.
2. It takes care of **people** by providing food as well as keeping down animal to human transmittable diseases.
3. If we comply with the laws and regulations and only kill what is legal and we can reasonably consume we are taking only our **fairshare**.

Furthermore, the permaculture principles can be applied to help us be more thoughtful hunters and stewards of the land.

1. Observe and interact - We become part of the natural system only when we fulfill the role evolution has designed for us.
2. Catch and store energy –Harvesting meat from the wild is a form of capturing sun energy and preserving it for later use.
3. Obtain a yield – A successful harvested animal is a great yield in calories and experience.
4. Apply self-regulation and accept feedback – When we see population changes and experience less activity we know to lessen hunting pressure and let the natural populations rebound. Regulations help with this, but are simply a guide. We can often do better.
5. Use and value renewable resources and services – We can look at wild game as a self-replenishing resource that we don't have to put much work into.

6. Produce no waste – We utilize every part of the animal and by doing this we respect the life it lived.
7. Design from patterns to details – We can see the patterns in the food chain and take only what can be sustained.
8. Integrate rather than segregate – We are integrating ourselves into nature instead of segregating ourselves from it.
9. Use small and slow solutions – We harvest in small amounts at first to see the changes we have.
10. Use and value diversity – Hunting is another way to use the diversity of the land.
11. Use edges and value the marginal – Wild land is sometimes thought of as marginal so many people struggle with what to keep wild. By making use of it, wild land becomes very valuable in more ways.
12. Creatively use and respond to change – We adapt what we harvest based on changes to the situation and changes in nature.

Goals

After reading this chapter I hope that with my help you have reached a few goals.

1. You are safe, ethical and conscientious and realize that hunting must be taken seriously.
2. You are confident in your abilities and skills and ready to take a game animal.
3. You realize all animals deserve your respect. When you kill you don't take it lightly and utilize the animal.

Safety

Safety is first and foremost when hunting. Every decision and thought and action must reflect a willingness and commitment to safety. Some of the things I recommend in this book may seem a little "off", but the reason I suggest them is that they elevate safety to a new level.

Gun Safety

Safety can be divided into two sections when hunting. Those sections are Gun Safety and General Safety. Because they are inherently more dangerous when used improperly, gun safety comes first.

The NRA Safety Rules follow:

1. **ALWAYS keep the gun pointed in a safe direction.**
   This is the primary rule of gun safety. A safe direction means that the gun is pointed so that even if it were to go off it would not cause injury or damage. The key to this rule is to control where the muzzle or front end of the barrel is pointed at all times. Common sense dictates the safest direction, depending on different circumstances.

2. **ALWAYS keep your finger off the trigger until ready to shoot.**
   When holding a gun, rest your finger on the trigger guard or along the side of the gun. Until you are actually ready to fire, do not touch the trigger.

3. **ALWAYS keep the gun unloaded until ready to use.**
   Whenever you pick up a gun, immediately engage the safety device if possible, and, if the gun has a magazine, remove it before opening the action and looking into the chamber(s) which should be clear of ammunition. If you do not know how to open the action or inspect the chamber(s), leave the gun alone and get help from someone who does.

4. **Know your target and what is beyond.**
   Be absolutely sure you have identified your target beyond any doubt. Equally important, be aware of the area beyond your target. This means observing your prospective area of fire before you shoot. Never fire in a direction in which there are people or any other potential for mishap. Think first. Shoot second.

5. **Know how to use the gun safely.**
   Before handling a gun, learn how it operates. Know its basic parts, how to safely open and close the action and remove any ammunition from the gun or magazine. Remember, a gun's mechanical safety device is never foolproof. Nothing can ever replace safe gun handling.

6. **Be sure the gun is safe to operate.**
   Just like other tools, guns need regular maintenance to remain operable. Regular cleaning and proper storage are a part of the gun's general upkeep. If there is any question concerning a gun's ability to function, a knowledgeable gunsmith should look at it.

7. **Use only the correct ammunition for your gun.**
   Only BBs, pellets, cartridges or shells designed for a particular gun can be fired safely in that gun. Most guns have the ammunition type stamped on the barrel. Ammunition can be identified by information printed on the box and sometimes stamped on the cartridge. Do not shoot the gun unless you know you have the proper ammunition.

8. **Wear eye and ear protection as appropriate.**
   Guns are loud and the noise can cause hearing damage. They can also emit debris and hot gas that could cause eye injury. For these reasons, shooting glasses and hearing protectors should be worn by shooters and spectators.

9. **Never use alcohol or over-the-counter, prescription or other drugs before or while shooting.**
   Alcohol, as well as any other substance likely to impair normal mental or physical bodily functions, must not be used before or while handling or shooting guns.

10. **Store guns so they are not accessible to unauthorized persons.**
    Many factors must be considered when deciding where and how to store guns. A person's particular situation will be a major part of the consideration. Dozens of gun storage devices, as well as locking devices that attach directly to the gun, are available. However, mechanical locking devices, like the mechanical safeties built into guns, can fail and should not be used as a substitute for safe gun handling and the observance of all gun safety rules.

These rules are immutable. If you can't follow them then you have no business owning a gun or having one in your hand at any time. These rules are there for everyone's safety. A day in the woods is not worth knowing your actions caused someone else harm. A bullet can never be recalled once fired.

Besides these rules a good general rule is to always be more safe than you think is even appropriate. If there's a chance the bullet might not be stopped by an appropriate backstop – don't take the shot. If there's even a slight chance that the gun is loaded – check the chamber.

General Safety

Even if you are safe with a gun, accidents can still happen in the woods.

One thing to consider is safety at elevation. If your hunting area has hazards such as sudden drops or tree stands you should exercise extreme caution in these areas. Aside from shooting accidents the most common type of accident while hunting is probably a trip/fall. One of my hunting mentors fell from a tree stand and lives everyday in significant pain from a resulting back injury. Needless to say he taught me with an extra level of safety built in.

Another thing to consider are the other hunters in the area. I suggest that even while small game hunting, especially if you are moving, wear hunter orange. Some states require it. Even if your state does not you should consider it. Keep in mind that even though you might practice an elevated form of gun safety not all hunters do. The orange may be the deciding factor between walking out of the woods and rotting in them.

You also have to take care not to get lost and stranded in the woods. For the purposes of starting out I highly recommend that if you go to the woods without a mentor you keep a road, creek or other easily tracked landmark in view to find your bearing at all times.

That being said it's a good idea to keep a basic kit in case you are lost. The kit should include:

- A good knife (yes, in addition to the one you carry anyway).
- Compass/map
- Waterproof matches/fire steel
- Small Tarp
- Water

If you can you should always carry your cell phone with you in the woods. It might not be in the "spirit" of being in the wild, but it's better to be alive with a cell phone than dead without one. A GPS is also a good idea, but don't rely on it. Learn other methods of extraction.

Make sure you "file" a plan with at least two people. I generally let my wife and my father know where I'm going. If I can't get in touch with one of them I leave a note with a map and paths I'll take. Once you file the plan you cannot change it without filing a revision. Searches are conducted into the wild every year for lost people who are eventually found (their body anyway) outside the area they were supposed to be occupying. File the time of expected return as well.

Know the weather before you go. You should look at **www.weather.com** and know exactly what the conditions will be for up to 4 hours after your hunt is supposed to conclude. **If there is any chance things can turn bad – STAY AT HOME!**

I can't name all of the hazards in your particular area. It's your job to research and know these things. It could be anything from venomous reptiles to grizzlies to forest fires. Know the hazards and keep an ear to the ground (and an eye on the internet).

The final and best piece of advice about safety that I can give anyone is to complete your state hunter's safety course REGARDLESS of whether your state requires it legally OR NOT.

My disclaimer: This writing is by no means a catchall and I take no responsibility for anyone's actions – it's your responsibility to learn how to do this right – this is just one resource to get you started

Laws and Regulations

Having members of my family working for my state's Fish and Wildlife Department I am a keen observe, follower and preacher of all game regulations. Failure to follow regulations can lead to fines or seizure of property (gun, vehicle, etc.). Playing by the rules is good sense and shows consideration to other hunters.

I highly suggest well before hunting that you pick up a copy of your state's regulation handbook. Most are generally free at any place that sells hunting licenses (which you will need as well) or on the organization's website. Read the handbook cover to cover. There are so many intricacies about each state that I couldn't begin to list what to look for.

In general though you will need the following things/information:

- License and permits (you may need more than one or two!)
- Possession and daily limits (possession means what you have in total everywhere (including at home) and daily limit refers to how many you carry out of the woods).
- Season (day) and legal shooting times (hour)
- Hunter's safety card/permit (where required – see above though!)
- Capacity limits on firearms (some guns hold more shells than you are allowed!)
- MORE – Your responsibility to find additional requirements.

Ethics

It's true that the game wardens can't be everywhere at once. Hunting works by laws, but also on the honor system. Kill only what you can use. Obey the laws and limits and pretend you are being watched at all times. You know what is right.

Tools of the Trade

Besides the kit I mentioned there are really few other basics you need to get started hunting.

Knife

The first is a good knife to be used for skinning and dressing. A medium sized (3-4" blade) knife is pretty good for a beginner. A larger knife is better for deer and a smaller knife is better for small game. This knife is a good compromise. There are relatively few other requirements for the knife. It should be fairly sharp; with a sharp point (drop point is good). I like fixed blades and stainless steel whenever possible. I do not like serrations. They are not conducive for use in hunting situations.

Clothing

Buy and wear clothing appropriate to the area and climate. If you plan on hunting mostly during the fall then buy clothes for your weather in fall. You should pick up some decent camouflage. If you don't know what is appropriate then buy something multi-purpose. I always lean to the side of too warm rather than too cool (meaning long sleeves). A simple pair of pants and a button up shirt is a great first outfit. A good pair of boots with some insulation is also warranted. Buy things a little large because you might want to wear layers beneath them.

The camo pattern should be a good all purpose pattern. Don't buy something overly green or grey or brown. Buy something with a combination of these colors. That way you'll fit in no matter what the season.

Also pick up a hunter orange vest and hat. You'll need these for deer season eventually, but I highly recommend them for even small game hunting, especially while moving. Most state DNR or FWD agencies will specify certain coverage of orange.

Firearm

The other item is of course the firearm.

When choosing a hunting weapon (excluding bows – which I won't get into here) you have three choices.

1. High-powered rifle - .223 size and up to .45-70 caliber rifles are great for hunting large game. However you are limited generally in the types of game you can take with a rifle. This makes it a good choice long term, but a poor choice for a beginner unless you have a specific type of hunting in mind and a rifle fits as the correct tool.
2. Rimfire rifle - .22 caliber rimfire. This rifle is great for small game, but requires some practice to get right. Plus it has a decent range that I want to limit for beginning hunters. An errant shot could put others in danger.
3. Shotgun - .410, 20, 12, 16, 10 gauge. This is the optimal firearm for the beginner. For one, it makes missing harder. For another, its range is limited so a mistake from a beginner is less deadly (but still deadly SO EXERCISE EXTREME CAUTION – my advice for this gun is not so you can be reckless, rather it provides a margin of safety). Finally, a shotgun is so versatile. You can hunt everything from a quail (small bird) up to a whitetail deer (large game).

Shotgun

I listed it last, but the shotgun should be your first purchase. The reason being is that you can hunt nearly everything with it. Now you might need to change out chokes or barrels, but we will talk about that further.

It may sound contrary, but for shotguns the larger the gauge the smaller the barrel diameter and the less the recoil (in general), but also the less shot and power out the barrel (in general).

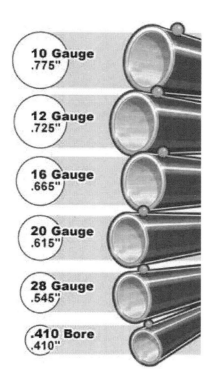

For a child aged 7 to 12 I recommend a .410. For a child aged 13 and up I recommend a 20 gauge. For the adult beginner I recommend a 12 or 20 gauge shotgun. I hate to sound sexist, but if you are a lady with a smaller frame I'd really recommend the 20 gauge. If you are a guy with a smaller frame or a fear of guns I suggest a 20 gauge. A 20 gauge will kill with nearly the same effectiveness of the 12 gauge. I started with a 20 gauge when I was a young man.

The shotgun does add a level of complexity. With any gun you have to get the right ammunition, but with shotguns you have more complex choices. For a 20 gauge you buy 20 gauge shotshells and so on. Make sure you get the right ammunition and that your gun is rated for that ammunition. You also need to know the shot size you need. Shot size is rated in numbers. The lower the number, the larger the shot will be. 2 shot is larger than 4, 4 is larger than 6 and on and on. There are also buckshot sizes that are rated in B's, but let's ignore those for now.

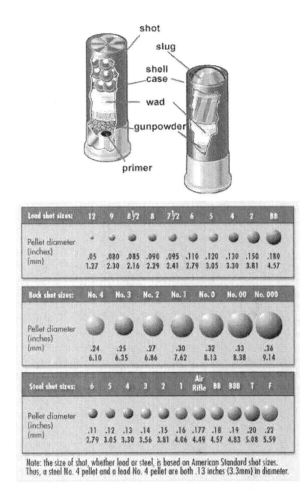

shot
slug
shell
case
wad
gunpowder
primer

Lead shot sizes:	12	9	8½	8	7½	6	5	4	2	BB
Pellet diameter (inches) (mm)	.05 1.27	.080 2.30	.085 2.16	.090 2.29	.095 2.41	.110 2.79	.120 3.05	.130 3.30	.150 3.81	.180 4.57

Buck shot sizes:	No. 4	No. 3	No. 2	No. 1	No. 0	No. 00	No. 000
Pellet diameter (inches) (mm)	.24 6.10	.25 6.35	.27 6.86	.30 7.62	.32 8.13	.33 8.38	.36 9.14

Steel shot sizes:	6	5	4	3	2	1	Air Rifle	BB	BBB	T	F
Pellet diameter (inches) (mm)	.11 2.79	.12 3.05	.13 3.30	.14 3.56	.15 3.81	.16 4.06	.177 4.49	.18 4.57	.19 4.83	.20 5.08	.22 5.59

Note: the size of shot, whether lead or steel, is based on American Standard shot sizes. Thus, a steel No. 4 pellet and a lead No. 4 pellet are both .13 inches (3.3mm) in diameter.

A good general shot is 6 or 7 ½. These sizes work for a wide variety of small game. Here is a list for future reference:

Upland Game (lead or tungsten alloy shot)

- Turkey - 4, 5
- Pheasant – 5, 6, 7 ½

- Chukkar, Grouse, and Partridge - 6, 7-1/2
- Quail - 7-1/2, 8
- Dove - 7-1/2
- Rail, Snipe and Woodcock - 7-1/2, 8
- Rabbit - 6, 7-1/2
- Squirrel – 6

When you get ready to hunt whitetail deer you will need to buy slugs. I prefer sabot slugs as they are much more accurate and produce less recoil. Buckshot is illegal for deer across much if not all of the US.

You may also need to know about barrel choke. The choke is the restriction at the end of the barrel that controls the shot pattern. Too much restriction and the pattern is too small. Too little and it scatters. Because it's the most versatile, I recommend that beginners buy a shotgun in a modified choke.

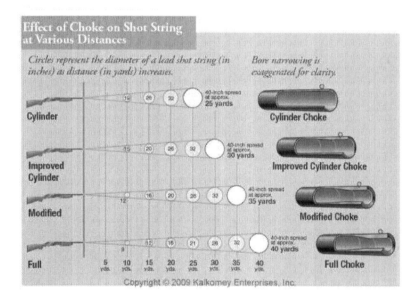

Slugs should only be shot through a barrel with cylinder bore. Shooting a slug through a barrel that is choked in any way can reduce the effectiveness of the choke or damage the weapon.

In many instances, for hunting with slugs you are much better off buying a barrel suited to the purpose. These will only run about $80 and also include front and rear sights which you will need for shooting accurately anyway.

Unless you borrow a gun, you will need to buy one. If you have a range that will let you try guns out then you should try a 20 and a 12 to see which you like best. Purchase a gun that fits you well. Assuming the gun is loaded pull it safely to your shoulder a few times to check the fit. The gun should feel like another appendage.

What gun do I recommend? Well it's hard to say which will fit you best. I suggest trying a Remington 870 first, then a Mossberg 500 series. Winchester also makes a fine gun. All of these guns I recommend are pump actions. If you have limited funds you could also consider a New England Arms single shot – it will run less than $100, but in my experience it is not super reliable or versatile.

The way the shotgun works is called the action. There are several different types of actions available.

The cheapest is the single shot. A lever opens the barrel and you insert shell. Pull the hammer back and fire. Double barrels work in a similar manner (but with two barrels), but are much more expensive in many cases.

The next cheapest is generally the pump action. The pump action has a tube magazine. You load one or more shells in the magazine. Push a button and rack the foreend (pump). Release the safety and fire. Cycle the action (by pumping) and then fire again.

The least cheap is the semi-automatic. You load the shells into the magazine and cock a lever, release the safety and every trigger pull results in a shot fired until the shells run out.

There are also older bolt action and lever action shotguns. These are uncommon, but not difficult to learn.

On most modern shotguns (except single shots and some double barrels) usually the choke is interchangeable meaning you can remove it and put another size choke in. If you have a gunsmith add a set of sights or find removable ones (or a scope mount) you can also easily and cheaply turn the gun into a deer gun.

Rifles

Rifles are generally easy to learn, but dangerous in unsafe hands. The danger with rifles lies in the fact that the bullet may travel up to a mile with deadly force. You have to be sure of your backstop in an elevated manner.

Rifles are simple guns that fire a single projectile with great force and speed from a barrel that has inner grooves that are twisted. The twist puts spin on the projectile and makes it more accurate at greater distances.

Rifles come in many many calibers. A caliber is the measurement of the bullet in inches. A .30 caliber bullet is $3/10^{th}$ of an inch in diameter (across the round bullet). The larger the caliber the larger the bullet and usually the subsequent recoil. There is a long and ongoing debate about the best rifle caliber. Everyone has a favorite and you can be sure that they will tell you when you pick the wrong one. It's not necessary to conform to what everyone expects. Pick what is effective for you.

Popular calibers for deer are .243, .270, .280, .30-06, .308 and .30-30. Usually regulations will set a minimum caliber. There are usually no maximums (except on number of rounds the gun will hold). I have personally hunted with a .270, a .308, a 7.62x39, a .44 Magnum and a .45-70. All did the job just fine. I hunt now with my .308. It is light in recoil and it works every time.

The conditions will sometimes dictate the best caliber. In heavy brush where short shots are the norm you can step up to

44

a .30-30 or .45-70. In long range shooting such as prairie situations you can go with a .243 or .270. If you might hunt larger game then the .308 and .30-06 make sense.

The other important decision is ammunition. The weight in grains of the bullet you choose as well as the bullet configuration will affect the weapon's ability to kill effectively and humanely. The heavier the bullet the more force it packs, but also the less the range it has. Lighter bullets travel faster and farther, but with less force – it could go right through and the animal could run very far. So it becomes a tradeoff. That is why for beginners I recommend a middle of the road weight. If you access to ammunition for your gun between 100 and 200 grains I recommend 150 grains – no contest.

You must also choose the bullet type.

You do not want to hunt with full metal-jacketed bullets. These bullets are made to penetrate. All of the others work well for hunting. Partition bullets are used on large game where bullet fragmentation is a problem. Hollow points, round nose, soft tips, and spire points are all made to penetrate well, but expand creating a larger wound path. These all work well.

Buying a Gun

Check the gun for basic function. If it's a single shot or double barrel it should open and swing freely and lock securely when closed. If it's a pump the action should slide and not be too sloppy. If it is a bolt action then the bolt should cycle easily and lock closed. **The safety MUST be checked. Ask permission to dry fire. If you can dry fire with the safety in the safe position DON'T BUY.**

Shooting

It's always a good idea to shoot your gun a few times with the ammunition you intend to use before taking it into the field. You will get a feel for the gun and be able to aim better.

Aiming a shotgun is nearly a point and shoot exercise. You need to put the bead on the target. There are no sights to line up or things to remember. Backstop ok? Stock pulled to shoulder. Bead on target. Pull trigger swiftly and smoothly.

Aiming a rifle is more complex. If it has a scope you will look through the scope (keep your eye OFF and away from the eyepiece) and put the crosshairs on the target. For open sights you will have to align the sights (see below). Take a deep breath and as you exhale, squeeze the trigger slowly and gently until the gun essentially surprises you as it fires.

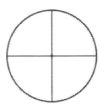

For open sights I always remember "to put the pumpkin on top of the fence post!"

Game

Before you wander into the woods you need to know what game you will be pursuing. The information above makes that clear. You will need to know what gun and ammunition to carry. It's not uncommon for game seasons to overlap. That being the case you may want to hunt two things. A common combo is rabbit and quail because they live in essentially the same place and can be shot with the same shells.

For the purposes of this book I highly recommend that you start hunting by pursuing either rabbits or squirrels. Now that won't be happy news for most people reading this and probably a good deal of people will completely disregard my advice and that's okay. There's not much glamour in hunting a squirrel or rabbit. I'm just saying that you can spend three years hunting deer and trying to learn on that long curve or you can spend one year learning the basics with squirrels and rabbits and then hunt deer the second year better than a newbie who is three years into just deer.

The truth is squirrels are easier. Going into the woods new and trying to be safe you need the easy score. Of course what you decide to hunt first is entirely your decision and you might take to this hunting thing quite easily. Of course a good mentor can get you started on the right path quicker than anything else.

Squirrel

The optimal choice for your first hunt is squirrel. Squirrels are plentiful, noisy, and easy to find and fun to hunt.

There are two basic ways to squirrel hunt.

1. Moving – You simply walk the woods slowly. You kind of just meander through the woods. You stop about every 10 steps and just observe. You will likely hear a squirrel before you see it. If you hear something, stop and observe.
2. Sitting – This is much easier, but you are kind of locked into you spot once you pick it. You can get up, but it ruins the stillness. If you pick a spot near acorns (oak trees) or walnut trees you can be assured you will see something if squirrels are in your area.

I mostly hunt moving for squirrels. You'll find that you might prefer one to the other. Don't fight it. The purpose is to have fun and be successful.

When the squirrel appears, the next task is to harvest it by shooting it. Make no mistake; your task is to kill it dead. Positively identify the animal. Check your backstop. If there is a house, road or other human habitation or possibility of humans beyond the target, pass on the shot and wait until the animal is in a safe position. Put the bead on the animal in a way that directs the maximum amount of shot into the vital organs. I make an effort to aim for the head, but because it is such a small target to focus on, I recommend new hunters make a body shot. Wait until the animal stops moving and pull the trigger.

This is what proper aim on a stationary squirrel will look like!

If the animal doesn't stop moving you can shoot it while it's moving. That's one of the advantages to using a shotgun. You aren't projecting a single bullet. You are creating a dust cloud of deadly shot, but you will need to "lead" the squirrel. Shot moves a little slower because it's light and you also have to keep time with the movement of the animal. So when you aim you put the bead just in front of the animal or at the front. This is a good time to aim right at the squirrel's nose. You don't have to get exact and you won't be able to. Eventually it will become an instinctual movement.

This is what proper aim on a moving squirrel will look like!

If you miss, cycle your gun in the manner that you should have learned when becoming familiar with it and make a follow up shot if it is safe to do.

Then the question of what to do with the carcass. I like to field dress all animals as soon as possible. For mammals, simply make a slit from throat to tail and pull out as many entrails as you can. Put the squirrel in a game bag or vest and continue your hunt. The squirrel should stay good for up to an hour in warm weather 60 or above, up to two hours in 45-60 degree weather and longer in weather close to or below freezing. My times are pretty conservative. You might find that the meat keeps longer.

Rabbits

With rabbits you are limited to one way of hunting (unless you have a good rabbit dog) and it's quite fun.

Basically you walk around a field with high grass and kick at clumps. If there are brush piles there kick them and see what happens. In some cases a rabbit will break out and run. Sometimes you will flush more rabbits by walking up on a clump or pile and just stopping and watching. The rabbit will get nervous and make a run for it.

You will have a limited time to shoot and the rabbit is moving. Use the advice I gave above on "leading" a squirrel.

Deer

For most hunters in the US the holy grail of all beginner hunting achievements is taking a deer. For most of the country this means a whitetail deer, but if you are further west it might mean a mule deer or an elk. I will only talk about whitetails here, but a lot of the same methods apply.

Male deer are obviously called bucks and females are does, but not all bucks are antlered according to most state agency definitions. What I mean by that is that button bucks (bucks with furry nubs for antlers) and some spike bucks (exposed horns, but shorter than a set length) qualify as actually antlerless. Regulations usually allow you so many deer per day and so many deer in either configuration. Usually the antlered deer are regulated to a lower kill rate.

One of the reasons I recommend you start with squirrels and not rabbits or birds is because the methods of hunting squirrels and hunting deer can be almost interchangeable except for the type of weapon/ammunition and the size. So with a few exceptions I talk about below you very nearly can think of a deer as a large squirrel.

I will tell you this though – for the beginner I recommend a seated hunt, preferably from a tree stand. It adds a level of danger for you, but it makes you safer to other hunters. What is different is that it puts a lot of your shots against a very solid backstop – the earth itself. You still need to check, but when shooting directly down you will get a good backstop in a good deal of instances.

Stand hunting requires certain additional skills and precautions. For one you should never climb a stand with a loaded weapon. The stand must be sturdy and durable and on a tree that is not rotten (don't laugh – it happens!). Additionally when climbing the stand you should do so with both hands unimpeded. In most cases this means tieing a rope to your unloaded weapon and pulling it up after you get seated. I highly recommend a safety harness. It is another added layer of protection against falls.

The real challenge for the deer hunter is where to sit. When you sit down for squirrels as long as you are in the forest you are likely to find them. If not you can get up and move, but when hunting for deer that could mean moving a tree stand. It's not easy.

There are a few nearly sure ways for the beginner. I could spend another book talking about the advanced stuff. Look for trails. Usually wildlife trails mean deer. Squirrel and other smaller animals rarely make trails (though they may use them).

In the absence of trails look for tracks – can you find the one below?

A rub indicates a buck presence and as a result - does.

If you set up near any of these areas you are increasing your odds of seeing deer activity.

Deer are also more wary of hunters than squirrels. I've never been successful with a walking hunt unless it consisted of a drive (where hunters actually scare deer toward a waiting hunter (who is seated), but that's a technique that isn't for beginners. It can be dangerous and unpredictable.

That being said, you'll have to be extremely quiet and still. When hunting a deer it's best to anticipate its path and have the gun ready and aimed there waiting for it to step in.

You may encounter something called "buck fever". This is not a deadly disease carried by a deer, but rather a rush of adrenaline and hormones into your bloodstream. I like to think of it as border between the modern untested human side and the primal instinct side. You might start shaking uncontrollably – to the point where you can't aim right and you scare the deer off. The best thing you can do at that point is hang on and try to steady the gun, but don't take a shot you aren't certain will kill the animal.

That takes us to the shot itself. Ostensibly you will be using either open sights or a scope. Regardless you will need to know ranges to a degree. Your gun is sighted in at zero to a certain range. Meaning at that range the point of impact should be exactly how the sights or scope show it. At closer or further ranges it may be higher or lower. It is useful to shoot your weapon beforehand and know these ranges. You don't have to be precise to $1/10^{th}$ of an inch because the vital area on a deer is so large.

If you are using a scope you have the benefit of having the crosshair be the aiming point. If you have open sights you will need to align them. Place the aiming point at the point just behind the deer's front shoulder muscle and about ¼ the way up from the belly. This is the heart/lung area. A good shot will get the heart, an ok shot the lungs. Either shot is a kill shot.

Here are some illustrations of deer vital organ areas. You can see that as the deer changes position so do the relative positions of the organs.

Once you pull the trigger the deer will jump, hunch down, leap or maybe even just look around obliviously. None of these situations really indicate anything about the shot. If the deer was keyed up prior to you shooting it may rush away. The important thing for you to remember is to shoot, blend back in and observe. Watch the deer's reaction - it will be important later. Note what direction the deer goes toward. Make a note also of landmarks. DO NOT RUSH AFTER THE DEER.

Even if you made a perfect shot the deer may run for 25 to 50 yards before it collapses. If you've been still and waited you will hear this "crash". Wait a few more minutes and savor the moment, the deer may not be totally dead and you don't want to have to chase it another 25 yards.

When you haven't heard movement for about 10 minutes climb down or get up and walk toward where you saw or heard the deer last. You will also want to check the area for blood where the deer was standing when you shot. Don't worry, not all shots cause immediate bleeding. If you find the deer quickly, great, if not you will have to track it.

Use the blood trail (if any) and the trail of upended leaves to follow the deer's path. This is a particular art that is not teachable via text. This is another good reason for a mentor, but with some practice you can find a deer if the deer is nearby and dead.

When you find the deer it will look very much alive in many cases. Take extreme caution and poke the deer with a stick to see if it reacts. If it does not you can rest easy and the fun part is over. Now you have to field dress the deer.

Some recent publications have advocated the quarter in the field method. For a new hunter this is just not a good suggestion. It will be hard enough to do everything that has to be done next. Quartering in the field is another added level of complexity.

The illustration below shows where to make the incision to begin field dressing. Essentially you want to cut the skin and the gut sack lining, but not the guts. Run the knife all the way to the line at the deer's sternum. At the rear end of the deer you will have to cut through the cartilage holding the two hams together. Cut carefully and around the colon so you can remove the entire waste system in one shot.

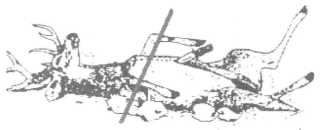

When you've released the guts at that end you will need to reach up into the deer's neck and cut the esophagus. You will hear gurgling sounds. Once this is done flip the deer over and allow the guts and blood to drain out for a few minutes. Flip the deer back on its back and make sure everything is out. You may have to pull some things out with your bare hands.

The next step is dragging. This is the real benefit of quartering in the woods. Dragging a deer is tough, but if you drag it out you get more time to work on the carcass and remove all meat. Those who quarter in the field only take the choice cuts. If the deer has antlers that is the handle for dragging, if not then use the rear legs.

Butchering is not terribly hard, but it is challenging for the first timer. You'll need to skin the deer, separate the front loins and rear hams from the body and then find the inner and outer tenderloins. Many first timers choose to take the deer to a professional butcher. There's nothing wrong with that. If you do choose to butcher the deer yourself make sure to get the meat cool as soon as possible (down to at least 32 degrees F) and then frozen or otherwise preserved. You will inevitably mess up on certain cuts. Don't get discouraged – it will still be edible.

Birds

Hunting birds can be a complex operation. I don't recommend a beginner start with birds unless there are no other options, but with the right mentor and a good spot to hunt birds can be enjoyable prey.

There are two main types of small birds that are widely hunted in North America. Waterfowl are the ducks, geese, swan and cranes. Upland birds are the quail, doves, grouse and pheasant.

Upland Birds

The easiest birds to start with are upland birds. You need little more than the equipment you squirrel hunt with. A shotgun, some decent clothing and your licenses and tags. You then find the appropriate habitat and go about kicking brush and to try and flush out a few birds. When they flush you lead the bird (I talk about "leading" in the chapter on squirrel) and fire. If you chose the correct lead – or aimed sufficiently in front of the bird – your bird will tumble to the ground. It's that easy!

The proper shotgun and shot size for upland hunting depends on the prey. A 12 or 20 gauge is the most versatile. The shot size should increase with the size of the prey.

Waterfowl

Waterfowl are harder to hunt properly. Generally waterfowl are hunted during the colder times of the year. This is because they are migrating during these times and looking for water in liquid form to feed and rest. In the case of geese though this may just be an open field near water (preferably after a harvest!).

When hunting upland birds no camouflage is needed – when waterfowl hunting it is a necessity. Instead of flushing the birds you are trying to lure them to you. Therefore you will need to blend in with the landscape. So in addition to being properly hidden you will also need to be extremely still.

There are two tools to lure waterfowl to your position. This is assuming you chose a decent hunting spot to begin with. The first tool is decoys. Decoys are set up to give the impression to the birds that the spot is safe and worthy of habitation. Calls that duplicate the sounds of birds are also great tools to have and use. If the birds believe there are birds there already they are more likely to come down into shooting range. It's never ethical to shoot a sitting duck.

Another thing that makes waterfowl hunting more difficult is that the birds have to be properly identified. Some similar looking fowl are not only undesirable to hunt, but they may not be legal to take. It's important that you take the time to learn proper identification through both sight and sound (different birds make different calls).

Another difficult aspect is judging range and again – lead.
Lead is extremely tough on a bird that is coming to you
instead of flying away (such as the case with upland birds).
You simply can't know how far away. You learn little tricks
over time and use instinct to lead, but this is an acquired skill.

**The author (RH), family friend and brother with a limit of Canadian
Geese**

In the case of waterfowl the best shotgun is almost always a
12 gauge due to its added power, range and load. Again, shot
size is totally dependent upon the size of the birds being
hunted. However, it is a legal requirement in most if not all
states that steel shot is used (not lead). A good general shot
size is #2, but goose hunters may upsize and teal and wood
duck hunters may downsize.

Where to Hunt

At one time (when I was young – a long time ago) it was
relatively easy to find a hunting spot. You simply asked about
five landowners and chances are one would say yes. Today
it's not that simple. You can still try this tact. Don't mention
deer hunting though – you will immediately put them off.
Most landowners today understand that people will pay money
to deer hunt so they are not likely to let you for free, but a
good deal of landowners will be glad to let you take care of
squirrel or rabbits. Don't count entirely on it though. Do not

hunt land without permission – preferably written.

Many states bless hunters through the availability of Wildlife Management Areas (WMA). These are areas available to the public to hunt for no fee (other than license and permit fees). You can rest assured though that there will be other hunters there during deer season and duck season. Rabbit and squirrel season – not so much. Your DNR or DFW will likely have maps and information available online. The WMA may have additional rules – follow them religiously and learn them well.

Basic How To

Many people are decent hunters, but don't know how to blend into the woods. They aren't able to track or determine where game is and they are lousy at being quiet. Here are some tips to help with the basics.

- If you are moving, step forward and place the ball of your heel down then roll forward on your foot.
- If you are sitting still, move your eyes first then your head second. In other words, small slow movements only. The smaller the better.
- Look for signs such as chewed acorns for squirrels or bent over grasses for rabbits.
- In cold weather breathe in through your nose and out your mouth. Gulping air will cause you to cough.
- Pop your ears (hold your nose and blow through it) to gain a better sense of hearing.
- In keeping with safe firearm practices, make your gun as ready to shoot as possible. Keep the safety on, but keep the gun at what is called half-ready (stock to shoulder, but barrel pointed in a safe direction) as much as is safely possible.
- Learn to identify animal sounds. Squirrels make certain sounds when "cutting" (cracking a nut) or when sounding an alarm. Sometimes you learn the most from a squirrel you don't shoot.
- If you are trying to harvest a buck be aware that bucks follow does. The doe comes through then the buck

follows about 75 yards behind.

The Mock Hunt

If you've never been hunting before I highly recommend two things for your first hunt.

1. You go with a mentor
2. You take no ammunition.

That is going to run counter to much advice, but I say it for simple reasons.

First you go with a mentor so you can watch someone do it successfully. You will learn a lot about unwritten techniques. They can also watch you.

Second you go with no ammunition because you can always reflect on a shot you didn't take. Aim and pull the trigger as if you were hunting. Treat the gun as if were loaded at all times. Let your mentor watch. He/she should point out any errors, especially in safety. Make sure you give them permission to tell you the truth.

If you can't find a mentor I still recommend going into the woods without ammunition. In fact it is even more important. I occasionally will do something or take a shot and think: "That was probably not the best thing I could have done." I'd rather you go back to your home and say "if the gun had been loaded I would have been in real trouble" than to actually be in real trouble.

You can always recall the shot you don't take. Once the trigger clicks though you cannot take back a shot. Once you are complete with your initial mock hunt you should reflect. What did I do right? What did I do wrong? Do I need to improve? Should I seek more training? Am I safe?

There is nothing requiring you to follow my advice for your first hunt. If you are already proficient with firearms you might choose to skip taking a mentor or going out without ammo the first time.

About that I will say this: Most smart people test things out in a safe manner beforehand. The purpose of this writing is to get as many people that have never hunted to do so in as easy of a manner as possible. Safety cannot be overruled by expediency.

Your First Hunt

Your first hunt alone will be different. Your heart will beat fast and you'll hear it in your ears. You'll be keyed up and super alert. You have to make your instinct follow your brain.

Let's use squirrel as an example because they require some more skill than hunting rabbits in regards to the actually hunt (rabbits are harder to shoot). Also they are more plentiful than deer and a little less of a challenge.

You purchase a good set of camouflage, a gun that fits you well and your licenses and permits. You shoot your gun at a local range and get some instruction. You take a hunter's safety course and pass easily.

At home, you plan your hunt by researching the game animal. You find maps to a good WMA on your DNR website. You print two copies – one for you. You file the other one as a plan. Using a pen you circle the area you'll hunt and write the time down you'll be home. You give the plan to your spouse.

After a drive you arrive at your destination. You park in an area out of the way and where you won't block entrances or other users.

You remove your unloaded weapon from your vehicle. You walk a short distance away and load it, but keep the safety on. You walk a safe distance from your vehicle and all roads and areas that might be hazardous to shoot in to begin your hunt. You remember the safety rules taught earlier in this book. You are familiar with your gun because you took time to learn it and shoot it beforehand as I advised.

If you are going to sit and hunt look for a good area with visibility. Any obstructions will limit shots. Find a spot near nut trees. Squirrels will be sure to congregate there. Sit with your back to a nearby tree and wait.

You won't see or hear much for about the first 10 minutes. You've scared everything away. Then you start hearing and seeing birds. The forest comes back to life. Then you hear a *shhhh shhh shhh shhhh* sound in the leaves. Remembering the basic how to tips I taught, you slowly turn your head to that area and wait. The squirrel may be on the ground hunting for a nut or it may be in a tree bounding from limb to limb.

When a squirrel gets within shooting range, check your backstop, aim as I've taught you and fire. Make note of where you shot. Do not pop up and run. Be calm. Make a follow up shot if necessary.

When all has settled you will either hear the squirrel bounding away or nothing. Then you will slowly rise and walk toward the squirrel's last position. You look on the ground and you should find a dead squirrel. If the squirrel is not dead you step on its head/neck and pull its body. The neck should break.

Congratulations you've made a clean ethical kill and once you skin and quarter the squirrel you will have secured your own meat. You will find that most people say squirrel tastes quite a bit like tender chicken, but to you it will probably taste a lot like success and self-sufficiency.

Pass It On

You are likely reading this because someone neglected to take you hunting. It's no one's fault probably. Maybe they didn't know or maybe you showed no interest. You are here now and willing to learn. What will you do once you become proficient? You must pass your skills on to the next generation. Without hunters keeping game population in check, conservation becomes difficult. We want to teach our children to be self-sufficient and there is no better way than by passing on hunting skills.

The author and son Jackson (3)

Other Choices

Frog Gigging

The water was pushing against my belly button. I was standing with one foot firmly planted in mud and the other hovering over deeper water. I was trying to balance a light in one hand and a 10-foot spear in the other while keeping an eye out for snakes. I've never had more fun.

For the uninitiated a frog gigger's paradise may seem like lunacy, but once you've set foot in the warm summer water something primitive takes hold. Maybe it's the fact that you can't get much closer to nature. Or maybe it's that your hunting weapon is a spear. Either way it can't be fought and shouldn't.

The best I can tell from my research, frog gigging originated right here in the American Midwest/South probably soon as viable alternative light sources were invented and mass manufactured. It certainly hasn't changed much except for maybe the equipment.

Equipment

One does not need a great deal of equipment to frog gig. The essentials are the gig and a light. Many people do this from a boat. I hate to be rude, but we considered those people to be sissies. I'm sure they considered us crazy. Of course the waters we waded were pretty shallow and devoid of any dangerous predators other than snapping turtles.

Gigs are easy to come by in this part of the country and can be bought at just about any country store or even at the local mega mart. The gig is simply a long pole tipped with small tines. The tines are pointed and barbed. The number of tines varies from gig to gig, but four or five is the generally accepted "right" number. Anything more is ok, anything less is not. I've only really seen gigs in two configurations. One is made of two pieces of cane/bamboo that fit at a ferrule and the other is an aluminum-knurled pole that extends and locks into position. Either will do the job. The aluminum one is a little more expensive.

Just know that when you buy them, the spear tip is common at the tines and is a poor design of which there is no good solution. The tines are attached in a manner that allows them to loosen and separate over time. You can weld them if you can work with the very thin sheet metal. You can also pour in lead to keep them in place, but be aware it may make your end heavy.

You must keep the tines sharp and the barbs sticking out.

Frogs are soft creatures, but spearing one is like cutting very soft bread. Without a firm surface, it's sometimes a little tough to get good penetration.

For lighting we've used lights as complex as a coon-hunting light with the belt battery pack. I prefer just a Maglight or other sufficiently powerful flashlight. It is important to keep the batteries fresh. The light lets you see the frog, but also helps to blind it to the travel of the spear.

Waders are optional equipment. Hypothermia is generally not a concern with air temperatures approaching the 90's at night. Jeans and a pair of tennis shoes that drained easily were sufficient attire for our gigging ventures.

Disclaimers

In some states you will need a license. In my home state either a hunting or fishing license will suffice. Be aware of your creel limits as well.

There are dangers that are unique to the area you may be hunting. Know what venomous snakes inhabit your particular region. Cottonmouths will be the big threat here, but water sources will also draw rattlesnakes and copperheads to nearby banks. We humans aren't the only frog hunters in the night.

If you are way south, you are undoubtedly aware of the larger reptiles, which are also nocturnal. As I alluded to above, a boat will not only be nice to have in such situations, but for safety's sake, a necessity. Just be aware that alligators and snakes can find ways into boats as well.

How To

The technique itself is quite simple to describe, but tough to master.

We generally spend a few minutes off the banks of the pond and listen for a quiet place to enter. Depending on how the pond lays you may be able to walk the bank or you may need to get a little wet. You'll learn which as you gain experience.

If you hunt with a partner you can alternate light holding and gigging chores (read: fun). If you are particularly experienced you can hold the light with one hand and gig with the other.

When you find a frog—and it's quite easy, as their eyes grow bright yellow when hit by light—you will want to approach carefully of course. It is important that the light does not bounce. You will want to keep the light squarely in the frog's eyes until it's on the end of the gig. If the light wanders the frog will do the same. If the frog's eyes aren't glowing then you aren't providing enough light. You will also have to make sure the approach angle of the gigger is wide of the light holder. Shadows will send the frog into the water quickly.

Ninety nine percent of the time the frog will be facing out into the water. I like to approach from the frog's 4 or 8 o'clock position. Once you are within striking distance, which will be just a little shorter than the length of your gig, glide to a smooth stop. I like to wait a moment for everything to settle.

Hold the gig like a javelin (but don't throw it!) over your shoulder and resting on your palm. The tines should form a line that is perpendicular to the ground. Ease the gig forward toward the frog, aiming right behind the eyes. I bring the gig to within 6 inches to a foot and then swiftly lung forward.

Don't withdraw the gig immediately. The frog will likely be buried in the mud. Even if the gig didn't penetrate you have him trapped. Pull the gig back slowly. If you can feel the vibrations of the struggling prey you can rest easy. If you don't, you may want to have your partner move forward to see what happened. Or you can run your hand down the gig and hope the frog is at the other end.

The best frog containers for us were feed sacks. Just open it wide and stick the frog, gig and all into the bag. Grab the frog

68

through the bag and pull the gig out. Onion bags or burlap sacks work just as well.

Always be aware of the other frogs. Too much commotion or a light show will send more of them into the water. This will ruin a night, as the next frog is always bigger for some reason. It's also inevitable that the largest frog that you see will most certainly be spooked because you slid down the bank or you screeched at the sight of a small water snake. You have to have a sense of humor when you do things like this.

Afterward

Frogs are pretty easy to clean. Some people will simply use a pair of shears and cut the legs off at the hip joint. You can also use a knife. Once the legs are off it is quite easy to peel the skin away.

Let the meat soak overnight in salted water in the coolest part of your refrigerator. If they aren't going to be cooked right away freeze them. The tried and true cooking method is dredging them in cornmeal and deep-frying in an iron skillet. Despite folk tales, frog legs do not hop in the skillet when cooked (not that I've seen anyway). Were we disappointed young men when mom put the legs in the skillet the first time and nothing happened!

Frog legs have a taste that is difficult to describe. It almost seems like a cross between fish and pork. It's hardly ever tough or chewy and rarely does it taste fishy. Of course, the older, larger frogs will be tougher than the younger, smaller ones.

Snapping Turtles

When the first of the snapping turtles roamed the lands during the Oligocene epoch in the Tertiary period of the Cenozoic era some 40 million years ago they emerged onto a changing earth. Grass was sweeping across the continents and giant tropical forests were shrinking to the equatorial belts. By most accounts mankind was less than human and still relegated to the trees. It makes one wonder how many species the lowly snapping turtle did watch rise and fall.

In some parts of the US it's easy to take the snapping turtle for granted because they are so common. Many people in my neck of the woods consider them a nuisance as they can play havoc with waterfowl. I know from personal experience, but we'd often catch them as they crossed a road from one wetland to another. Holding one it's hard not to feel like you are holding onto an ancient wizened being even if they do seem slow and dumb.

The aptly named common snapping turtle has a wide range and can be found in Southern Canada, Northern Mexico and west out to the Rocky Mountains. It's thought that the snapping turtles survived the eruption of at least one supervolcano so its ability to adapt to changing conditions is not without precedent.

Here in Kentucky and throughout much of the south there's a saying: "Meaner than a snapping turtle", but in actuality each individual specimen seems to have its own personality. I've picked some up that couldn't be bothered to even open its mouth or hiss and others snapped and squirmed and fought with reckless abandon. So the saying, like most snapping turtle folk wisdom, is just false.

One piece of snapping turtle wisdom is correct though; once their head is severed they can and will still snap for quite a while afterward. When I was about eight years old I experienced this firsthand. Our favorite fishing hole kept getting worse by the day one summer to a point where it was difficult to catch even a single bluegill (and we weren't keeping any). In addition we would occasionally get hung up where there were no sunken limbs.

One day dad got hung in this spot and pulled and pulled hoping to dislodge the hangup. The line broke soon after, but not before a massive moss-covered head emerged and seemed

70

to part the water. Later dad set a trot-line with heavy tarred line and a large hook. He baited the hook with one of the few bluegills we were able to catch.

Only a day or so passed before we went back and dad realized he had caught the snapping turtle, but could not muster enough strength to pull it from the mud. This is a common tactic of snapping turtles. They will essentially use the mud to anchor themselves into place.

We enlisted the help (and .357 Magnum firepower) of a neighbor and soon they made slow progress in getting the turtle to shore. My dad is a stubborn man. I watched him fight a devil ray in Florida one time for at least an hour before the line snapped. So with much effort they were finally able to get the turtle up and get a shot off. The revolver barked and the turtle gave no additional resistance.

That turtle was large enough that eight year old me could have easily ridden on its back, but back to my point, which is, I still remember that with a lead slug in its head and being separated from the body it was still snapping. The maxim that a snapping turtle would not release its bite until lightning strikes is most certainly false though.

What makes snapping turtles so ubiquitous is their ability to live in just about nearly any hole that holds water, mud and something to eat. It may be difficult to tell if a pond or lake in your area has snapping turtles. It's a safe assumption that if that piece of water is within their range they are either in the water or just haven't found it yet. Occassionally you may see the turtles sitting on a floating or partially submerged log. Being cold-blooded reptiles they like to sun themselves just as much as a snake or alligator would.

Their highly adaptive nature has made the snapping turtle a very opportunistic feeder. Though it will ambush hunt prey – snapping quickly at any passing fish or small animal – they can and will eat other things living or dead. This includes just about anything that moves. Fish, turtles, snakes, frogs, salamanders, lizards, birds, rodents, etc. are all fair game.

Capturing

Catching a snapping turtle is not difficult except for the actual "catching" part. They will take most baits and hook themselves pretty easily. As long as you have a strong back or a few friends and a good dose a hardheadedness it can be done. As always, with harvesting wild game be sure to check local laws and regulations and follow them!

Lately, the method of noodling for snapping turtles has gained a bit of fame with the introduction of the show "Wild Man" on NatGeo where one of my fellow Kentuckians demonstrates his ability to capture snapping turtles simply by feeling for them and then lifting them from the mud. This is inherently dangerous and most people of sound mind would not attempt this.

The best method is to use the same type of bank line that my dad used all those years ago. You simply tie a five to six foot length of tarred line to a tree limb, stump or other imovable object on the bank, tie a hook on the opposite end, bait it, throw it out into the water and check it every day.

The same juglines and trotlines I mention in the section on "Lining" are also viable techniques as long as the lines and the location allow the bait to reach the bottom of the body of water. The jugline probably being the superior method since it will help prevent the turtle from burrowing into the mud to a large degree.

I've found the best bait to be a very small live bluegill, but chicken gizards, pieces of beef, goldfish and any number of different baits work well. The best bait for turtles has a tough consistency. Otherwise it will be easy to bite off the hook. The goal is for the turtle to essentially swallow the bait and hook whole. Hooking a turtle in the hard mouth would be an exceedingly difficult proposition.

Once you check the line and it's clear that you've snagged a turtle the process of pulling it up is simple, but not easy. Slow steady pressure will eventually dislodge the turtle and once it is beyond the reach of mud or a solid foothold it will come up quite easily. Ocassionally one will become lodged in hangups or vegetation and you have to make the decision to go after it (hopefully with some type of tool) or cut the line and your losses, but it's best to make all efforts to harvest the animal as it will surely suffer and die with a hook lodged in its throat.

The best times to set your lines are almost always in the hottest parts of the year – mid to late summer and on nights with no moon. Snapping turtles are mostly nocturnal and hunt very well in the dark.

Trapping

Another method of catching snapping turtles is by trapping them. I mentioned previously that snapping turtles, like most reptiles, like to sun by climbing onto a floating log. One could reasonably construct a trap that is nothing more than a welded wire (like used for fencing) cage closed in on four sides and the bottom. Around the open top put floats, logs or any other bouyant surface that turtles can climb onto. Attach the floats securely to the cage. Either bend the wire inward into the cage or place some type of object that keeps the turtles from climbing back out. When the snappers go up to sun and then back into the water about half of the time they will dive off the wrong side and into your cage.

I used to shoot turtles as a young man with my .22 Hornet. First of all this is not a great idea anywhere close to civilization (I was not) as richochets are a real problem with shooting toward water. Secondly it's not a good idea because of the ancient reflex mechanisms in turtles. Even the one my dad's friend shot with a .357 had quite active reflexes. Chances are even a mortal shot will result in the turtle burrowing into the mud and dieing there.

Afterward

Once you've captured your turtle the next step is processing the meat. The first step is removing the head. Place a broomhandle or other hard object in front of the turtle and if it is still alive (or even recently dead) it will snap onto the object and hang on. Pull the neck out as far as it will extend and then sever it as close to the shell as possible. Allow the blood to drain out for an hour or so.

The next step is to cut off the claws and dip the whole turtle into boiling water. At this point you can attempt to remove the bottom shell and cut the meat away from the top shell, but in many cases it will be easier to just make filet-like cuts to remove the tail and four legs. This keeps the guts intact as well. The bottom shell can be removed and then the meat can be scraped and cut away from the top shell.

Then the cuts (neck, four legs and tail) must be skinned. Debone the meat and cook as desired. The meat tastes quite a bit like chicken, but the best use of the meat is by far in a turtle stew. There's a reason why eating turtle meat is associated with turtle stew.

They may be somewhat less than loveable creatures, but snapping turtles have a lot going for them. They are prolific in numbers, they are easy and fun to catch and they are delicious. In other words, a great component to a homesteader's bag of tricks when it comes to self-sufficient food.

Section 1B – Fishing

Introduction

The most obvious form of food from the water comes from one of my personal favorite activities – fishing. Fishing is a great way to have fun while gathering enough food to fill a freezer. The fight of the fish, the mystery of type and size and the capture all provide extra levels of excitement.

Equipment

To make a good showing of fishing you at least need a rod/reel, line and hook. I myself have spent countless hours as a young man and also in more recent times with just a cane pole or fiberglass pole with hook, line and live bait pulling panfish after panfish out of the water. It's literally so simple that my four year old Jackson can do it successfully.

I've watched this scenario play out many times: Man in forty thousand dollar bass boat and $300 rod and reel setups juxtaposed by a kid fishing nearby. The man is zipping a ten-dollar lure out repeatedly and catching nothing. Meanwhile, the kid with laughably simple equipment is slaughtering the fish, pulling them in with reckless abandon.

The scene is instructive, but the instruction is rarely heeded. Catching fish need not require a lot of equipment.

Stuck in the wild by choice or chance we could find ourselves in a situation less prepared than the barefoot kid with the basic equipment. Yet there are small bodies of water virtually everywhere in the US that isn't desert. It's shocking how few people pack basic fishing gear in their kits.

There can literally be fish swimming at your feet. However, without a small bit of equipment or the knowledge and ability to improvise the gear, the fish might as well be on the moon!

Fishing gear need not take a lot of space or consume a lot of thought. When we cut through the luxuries of gear we find that for fishing we need very few things. We need line, a hook and bait. Certain situations may call for extras, but with these three basic items, almost 90% of fishing can successfully be handled.

Disclaimer: Check all regulations in your area and follow all game laws.

Rods

The first step is the rod. In many parts of the country you can find rivercane, the only native bamboo in the US. Cutting a cane of the appropriate size will yield a quite capable rod. Just tie a line to the end and you're in business. Cane is pretty hard to cut so a machete or large knife helps here.

Luckily we don't have to rely on an insecure source of cane for our fishing rods. Modern advances in fishing rod technology have left us with an endless assortment of fishing rods made of various materials. One of my favorites in recent years is the invention of cellulose plant based fiber rods. The first one was called the Carrot Stick and was fittingly orange.

The old standbys are still great for everyday use as well. Fiberglass and graphite are great. Fiberglass is durable and flexible and graphite is sensitive and light. If you are fishing for sport, graphite is the obvious choice, but for putting food on the table I usually choose fiberglass when I have a choice. One of the best rods on the market for just sheer food fishing is called the Ugly Stik. It is very ugly, but it's extremely durable and it works and it's cheap!

Rods are chosen based on length, action and type. Type is obviously related to the type of reel that the rod is made for. Casting rods with triggers and short or long handles are made for spincast and baitcasting reels. Spinning rods with long straight handles and no triggers are made for spinning reels (but other reels could also be used on these).

Reels

As I noted above, the reel must be matched to the rod type. As a general rule I've found that the more complex the reel, the more prone to failure it is.

The simplest reel is a spincasting reel. This is the typical reel that we would give a young child. The most common brand is Zebco. These reels have a spool and retrieval mechanism hidden behind a cover. The line feeds through a small hole in the cover. These are easy to use, easy to set up and quite reliable. However they are less durable than other types and over prolonged use may break and never work again.

To cast one you simply push and hold the button. Swing the rod in a cast and at the apex of the swing release the button. The baited end will fly out.

The next complex type of reel is a perfect choice for novices and pros alike. It is the spinning reel. It operates somewhat similar to the spincast reel except the spool is exposed and the retrieval device is a bail. To cast these you put a finger on the line just above the reel and push it to the rod. Then you flip the bail and cast. At the apex of the cast you release the line. These reels are extremely durable and simple to use.

The most complex type of reel is the baitcast reel. This reel uses a complex spool system that is slowed by magnets, but is otherwise free to spin once the button is pushed. The retrieval device is actually the spool itself, which spins. A small guide helps put the line on in the appropriate spots.

To cast this reel you push the button and place a thumb on the spool. When you cast you release your thumb, but keep it nearby. As the baited end approaches the water you will need to feather your thumb down to slow and finally stop the spool. If you fail to do this correctly the reel will backlash. Essentially the spool moves faster than the line can leave the reel. This results in a rat's nest of line that can be impossible to untangle without cutting it out.

Line

Of the three essential components of fishing gear, this is the most essential. Modern fishing line comes in three varieties these days. Monofilament is just like it sounds, one continuous synthetic filament of extruded polymers. It's commonly called "mono" for short. Braided line made a comeback a few years ago when materials advanced sufficiently. Braid is simply man-made fibers joined in way to make them stronger. A newer type of line to emerge in the last few years is called fluorocarbon. It is simply composed of one extruded fiber from a fluoropolymer. Then, of course, some of these line types are mixed to form hybrid lines.

So with so many choices, what does one pick and why? I immediately rule out fluorocarbons. Fluorocarbons are great for fishermen because they are very difficult for the fish to see, more so than the other lines. However they are very brittle and it seems to me that the quality from batch to batch can produce widely varying results. Fluoro snaps very easily and it not very flexible.

That leaves mono and braid. Mono has the clearness of fluoro, but is more flexible, easier to use and less prone to snapping. Its disadvantages are susceptibility to light degradation and lack of abrasion resistance. However, it's very good for hand lining. I typically recommend that monofilament be used by all but the most experienced fisherman.

Braid is stronger by diameter than either of the other two lines. It is abrasion resistant, has medium stretch and is flexible. It's almost perfect except for the fact that braid is quite easy for finicky fish to spot. However, for makeshift trot lines it is just about perfect. For rod and reel fishing, unless you are fishing for larger or toothier fish or you are fishing in heavy weeds braid is not a superior choice despite its strength.

The next step is choosing the strength – and by proxy thickness – of your line. Six pounds is just about right for mono. This will allow you to catch fish as small as bait sized bluegill up to fairly large bass and catfish. For large fish I choose test weights around 20 to 25 pounds or larger. You should adjust the line test to the weight of the fish you intend to pursue.

Hooks

There are tons of types of hooks and styles and colors and brands. I won't summarize all of the types. Instead I'll give you a basic approach to what works for kits and what I use. I use 3-4 hooks in a few different sizes. The first type and size of hook I keep is a number 6 or number 8 Aberdeen long shank wire hook. This is a thin, small hook for bluegill, crappie, etc. It holds bait well, but is also tough for the fish to see. The next hooks I use are larger 3/0 or 4/0 circle hooks for catfish and trotlines. These are brawny hooks designed for fish that eat by smell and taste rather than sight.

The hook brand matters; do not buy cheap hooks. Hooks are not pricey anyway. Buy the best brand with the best finish. The Aberdeen style is usually not finished well in any brand, but buy ones that look shiny. Shiny is a good indication of the metal's ability to resist rust. For the larger circle hooks I try to find those with a stainless steel finish. It's important to check the hooks in your kit often. Smaller hooks are made from thin wire that can quickly turn into small brittle pieces of frustration.

As with essentially everything when it comes to fishing use the size appropriate for the size of fish you intend to pursue.

Bait/Lure

The equipment aforementioned make it possible to catch a fish, but you have to get them to the line in the first place. You have two choices – live bait or artificial lures.

When I begin to look for bait I have a priority list in my head of what I'd like to find first. The bait I like first requires little energy and is most effective. The list works down from there, decreasing in effectiveness and increasing in energy expenditure.

The top bait in my book is a worm. I speak broadly of worms to include larval insects as well. For my time, a night crawler, redworm, small grub, maggot or waxworm are equally reliable and require the least amount of energy. The best places to find them are anywhere wood is rotting. You can simply lift the chunk of rotting wood and usually find a few grubs. Dig deeper into the soil and the moisture held by the wood will usually make prime earthworm habitat. Lacking rotten wood look for deep leaf cover or moist areas on the ground where anything natural or manmade has covered the soil for some time.

Second on my list are any above ground insect such as crickets, grasshoppers and other insects. I never pass any insect up if they are in abundance, but if they prove to be ineffective I have no problem moving on. Crickets and grasshoppers just about always work well. I've used Japanese beetles to good effect as well.

Last on my list is any water dwelling creature. The time and energy is just not worth it. Minnows are tough to catch. However, in a worst case scenario a small minnow trap can be made of a plastic pop bottle. Simple remove the cap, cut off the upper "funnel" portion. Reverse it and pop it into the body of the bottle. Poke some holes in the body; secure the funnel with ties, wire or string. Tie a piece of cord to it and put a chunk of bacon in the bottle for bait and toss it a few feet out. This trap will also catch crayfish, which make good bait (or good eats!).

Four Essential Panfish Lures

When I was a younger man I'd sometimes find myself doing crazy things to save a snagged lure. One time I shimmied to the end of an unfinished wooden dock in the hopes of freeing my last white Roostertail.

I don't know if it was the fact that I was fifteen and reckless. It might have been the result of already having caught at least a dozen crappie of eating size. Certainly not wanting to hike the two miles back home to get my spare Roostertail played some part in my decision. All I can recollect is that the little two-dollar lure held magic that was inescapable by fish…or young man.

So maybe I'm remembering the day in melodramatic tones that have gotten richer with time, but I am confident that these ordinary little panfish lures have drawn countless others in with their mystical ability to catch fish and provide countless hours of enjoyment as well as food for the table.

Favorite lures for game fish such as bass and walleye vary by region and come in such an assortment of sizes, colors and variations that almost every section of a lake warrants a different approach. Thankfully panfish fishing is a much simpler venture. In fact, I've found four lures to be essential panfish lures; old standbys that hardly ever fail.

Roostertail

There is no better lure to talk about first than the one who got me into the predicament I described at the beginning. Roostertail is a brand name of a lure made by Wordens, but it's become synonymous with any inline spinner lure. As early as a decade ago, Mepps was the brand that held that title. That fact alone should make it pretty apparent at how popular Roostertails have become.

The Roostertail is a complex lure for such a simple type of fishing. It is essentially a straight thin wire, looped at both ends. At one end is a treble hook, at the other an empty loop to tie your line. In the middle is a clevis that spins around the wire. On the clevis a small metal "blade" is attached. The particular blade type is called "Indiana Style". It is oval shaped and elongated. The blade is embossed with the company name and a scale pattern. Below the blade, moving toward the hook is a small cylindrical shaped lead weight, painted in any number of patterns. Below the weight and just above the hook, the wire is tied with a small tuft of dyed fibers.

As I mentioned, the Roostertail comes in many different colors and sizes. I've used sizes from 1/32 ounce (very light!) up to ¼ ounce with success, but I have to say that only one very specific color has worked for me with any degree of satisfaction. Normally I'd be hesitant to let such a secret out, but I'm reinforced by the fact that almost every fisherman I've ever met disagrees with my color choice and has his/her own favorite. My color is simple white.

The Roostertail creates attracting action as it is pulled through the water. The blade spins and the fibers at the "tail" undulate. It imitates best, a small baitfish. Because the lure simulates the action and look of a baitfish it appeals to almost any fish in the water that eats other baitfish. It is not a shock for me to catch four different fish species on one outing with a Roostertail.

Use is quite simple. You cast as far as you can and reel the line back it. The lead weight gives the lure bulk to aid in casting, but is balanced so the lure doesn't fall through the water column too quickly. In fact, it is balanced so well that as it falls, the blade spins all the way down. The retrieve can be varied to bring the lure to the proper depth as well as imparting more or less vibrations and flash. The vibration can be felt by the angler and serves as an indication that the lure is "working". Occasionally, waterborne weeds will cause the blade to foul and the spinner to stop. Cleaning will remedy the situation quickly.

The lure is effective in all bodies of water from huge lakes to small streams. As long as the blade will spin, fish will come.

As for the Roostertail I mentioned at the beginning of this article, I was able to free that lure and finish out my limit of crappie. I savored every bite!

Curly Tailed Grub

When fishing with my wife for the first time I realized she was getting frustrated with the Roostertail's tendency to foul and she couldn't keep the blade going. Though I'd been having luck with mine I switched her to a curly tailed grub in chartreuse so I could go back to fishing in peace. Needless to say I soon switched as well after she started pulling in yellow bass one after the other.

There are a few manufacturers of curly tailed grubs today. Mister Twister and Riverside seem to be the most prominent and are brands in which I have and still do place my trust.

These lures are soft plastic and with all lures come in a variety of colors, sizes and variations. My favorites are the simply white and chartreuse colors and small enough for a panfish to chew on. These lures are almost always used in conjunction with a small lead jig that is nothing more than a hook with a ball of lead at the forward end where you tie the line. Without the jig, the lures have very little weight and would neither cast nor sink very well.

These lures could imitate a range of prey. Moving fast through the water they look like baitfish. Jigged (pulled up and dropped repeatedly) they look like crayfish or a terrestrial creature.

I place the grub onto the jig head tail facing away from the hook (prevents fouling) and cast and retrieve at a consistent rate. This seems to produce the most bites. I'm not averse to jigging when all else fails. Jigging is the action of dropping your rod tip, reeling in all slack, raising the rod tip and repeating.

Like the Roostertail, a curly tailed grub and jig is effective in different bodies of water and on different species.

Tube Jig

The next lure I'm going to talk about is one that I had not had any luck on throughout my life despite numerous uses. Only until my parents moved to Kentucky Lake and were taught this technique for the lake's numerous crappies was I able to effectively learn how to use this lure.

The tube jig is similar to the curly tailed grub in the regard that the material is the same soft plastic. The tail is different however, being filaments of the same soft plastic that "feathers out". The body is also hollow instead of being solid. Also, like the grub a jig head is used to provide weight and balance. With this setup, the lure can be jigged through the water.

84

However, the effectiveness I found was through the use of a small float 8-24 inches up the line. The float allows the tube jig to "hang" in the water column where fish are feeding. Small jerks on the line cause the float to move and the lure dances underneath and can be worked repeatedly. This, no doubt, simulates a dying baitfish.

Unlike the other lures I mentioned there seems to be no one sure-fire color that works. Varying the jig head color as well as the body and tail colors of the tube jig can produce wildly different results even on the same day.

As I mentioned, this lure is most effective on crappie, but will work on other panfish as well.

Marabou Jig

This last lure is another one from my childhood and definitely holds some magic for me. Unfortunately, the marabou jig has fallen out of favor in the past few decades. Advances in soft plastics have no doubt taken the toll on this old favorite.

The marabou jig is really a pretty lure. It is a jig head wrapped with marabou feathers. Marabou feathers at least at some point were obtained from a bird called a marabou stork. These feathers are famous for being used in the past for adorning women's headgear. The feathers are wrapped tight to form a "body" on the lure then they are allowed to fluff out at the hook side. When the lure is jigged through the water the feathers take on a life of their own.

My favorite technique was to use the jig around boat docks and other standing structures near deep water. I'd let out some line and then "dance" the lure by twitching the end of the rod. Once you see the motion of the lure in the water and experiment you begin to understand the capabilities of the marabou. This lure can also be cast out and retrieved by jigging.

Again, I found the most effective use of this lure to be on crappie, but I caught bluegill and bass as well using it. The lure also seemed able to coax fish lulled by a tough bite. Whenever I had difficulty or seemed to have fished an area out, I found that by switching to the lowly marabou jig, I could turn the bite back on. Therefore I have always found a place for it in my tackle box.

Why is white a good color for lures? In the water they look like minnows or other baitfish. Despite what luremakers tell you, fish eat other fish the majority of the time simply because terrestrial creatures seldom make it into the water. It helps to know what lures work for which fish in your areas of frequent occupation. Pick accordingly.

In the rare occasion that bait cannot be found and lures are unavailable, simple items can be fashioned into effective lures. Examples include, but are not limited to, small clothing threads, tufts of cotton, bubble gum, small bits of plastic and much more. Anything brightly colored and/or able to create movement in the water can be considered.

Accessories and Setup

As I said before, I consider hook, line and bait to be the three essentials. Sometimes you may need to keep bait from sinking or help promote sinking in order to get the bait into the feeding zone of the fish (strike zone). You may want to keep an assortment of sinkers and floats to help get your bait or lure at the proper depth to catch the fish. Be sure to keep sinkers and floats at least a few inches away from the bait as fish can sometimes spot them.

For a knot I always use a palomar knot, which is simply a loop passed through the hook or lure eye, formed into another loop and passed through and then the lure is passed through the original loop. When tying line to a branch rod or somewhere I can't tie a Palomar I always use an improved clinch knot. Diagrams on how to tie these knots can be found easily on the web.

Application

It's usually not reasonable to start fishing and catch fish. Even the best indicators of behavior can sometimes be unreliable. The first step in application is to determine what fish you will target. I really break this up into a few categories. Panfish will generally all bite much the same things with the same applications. Sportfish are picky and must be individually targeted. Catfish and rough fish are not picky, but are pursued differently from the other two types. For people in different climates and locations it helps to familiarize yourself with what fish can be found in your area or areas of travel.

How – The Technique

Your technique will vary depending on your own individual conditions, but some things always remain the same. In order to maximize fish you need to minimize movement. Eyes of most fish are on the top of their head because they commonly feed upward. Therefore they have great peripheral vision in that direction. They can contrast a man standing on the bank quickly against the sky. Therefore you either need a long line or a small profile. If you find yourself with a short line it will help to lay prostrate upon the ground and fish by feel. As I mentioned, a rod extends the line and helps hide your profile.

Once you've found a spot (I will cover that in a moment) and your equipment is ready, simply cast the bait or lure out. With bait you want to the leave the line still for a few minutes and then you can jiggle it a bit or move it closer. You may find that sinking through the strike zone will produce a hit.

Lures each require unique movements, but the two I choose to talk about here generally work best with constant retrieves. Of course you should vary your retrieve until you find a pace that produces bites.

If you find yourself with an abundance of hooks, line, bait and lures you can always tie off a baited hook to a limb and make a limb line or simply to a cane or green branch stuck into the ground. Then you can also cast a lure and double your results with little extra effort.

When the fish take the bait it's important to resist the urge to jerk the line as hard as you can. Just pull up sharply and smoothly, but not too hard. Bluegills have small mouths and you can pull the bait out of their mouth. Crappies have paper-thin mouths. You can rip a lure right through them. Catfish have hard bony mouths you have to jerk hard. If you are using a lure and retrieving at a decent rate then you don't really need to set the hook at all. Different fish sometimes require different hook sets so experiment if the standard approach doesn't work.

Getting hung up is just part of fishing. Chances are likely that the curved part of the hook caught an underwater branch or the point snagged a rock. Slowly pull the line taut and release it suddenly. Occasionally the lure will backpedal free. If that fails after a few attempts pull directly back, slowly and keep increasing pull. Pull the line directly or with a stick. It is sometimes possible to bend the hook free (this is another place where light wire hooks come in handy). In that case, once the lure is retrieved the hook can be bent back into reasonable shape.

Where to Fish

Fish do not commonly frequent open water. They only use it to get from one feeding spot or breeding spot to another. Most fish stick close to transition points. From the bank, with no sonar it will be difficult to find all the transition points, but it can be done. The first step is to make use of the transition points you can see. These include bank edges (especially cut-ins), half submerged logs, man-made semi-submerged structures and more. Your ability to take risks may be lessened by the equipment you have, but it's best to throw as close to these transition points as possible. The important point is to not throw in open water if you can avoid it.

That being said, there are instances when panfish such as bluegill will come to shallow open flats to spawn (breed and lay eggs). These "beds" are generally recognizable as light colored circles on the muddy bottom. You should always cast to these as the fish will strike to protect the eggs or young fry.

There may simply be times where you can't locate the fish. In those instances you have to conduct a methodical search. This is accomplished by "fan" casting. Fan casting is simply cutting the arc of water in front of you into a pie and casting in 10-degree increments. So the first cast is just off the bank then 10 degrees to the right and so on until you have covered the complete arc. Then move down well past your first arc and repeat.

You may need to also vary your retrieve or use a sinker or float depending on where the fish are in the water column. This can be tricky, but it is mostly a function of temperature. During the warmer and cooler times of the year the fish will go deep where the temperature is more constant. During spawn, the fish will go to shallow water to breed and lay eggs. During the lead-up to the spawn and during the fall, the fish will go shallow to feed.

It also helps to know where fish like to feed. As I mentioned above, I set up completely different for catfish than all other fish. This is because catfish use their whiskers and olfactory senses to feed along the bottom even though their eyes are on top of their head. Other fish generally feed upward as I mentioned above. Therefore if you are fishing for catfish it makes sense to use a sinker and get the bait down quick. For other fish you might want to use a small float to keep the bait just off the bottom.

When to Fish

A general rule of thumb for when to fish is this: weather that people don't like, fish will. A bright, sunny day is what fisherman call a "bluebird" day, but don't let the name fool you; it will be dang tough to catch fish during those times. The best times for fishing are before and after a storm or during heavy cloud cover. It is not easy to hunt in the bright light of day. Fish instinctively know this and they rarely try to feed when it is bright out. The hours right before and after dusk and dawn (even on bluebird days) are usually superb.

Quarry

Panfish

The term "panfish" does not refer to a specific fish species. Instead it refers to any smaller type fish that is commonly caught for the purpose of putting into a pan! Species that are applicable here include, but are not limited to bluegill, redear, pumpkinseed, crappie, perch, white bass and yellow bass.

There are many advantages to fishing for panfish for food or for fun. They fight hard, but are generally easy to catch and fool. All of the species I listed above are great eating and easy to prepare with no small bones or hard scales.

As a general rule, panfish are much easier to catch with live bait than with artificial lures. They are, however fooled by fast moving and shiny or vibratory lures such as roostertails, curlytailed grubs, hair flies and small poppers.

Sportfish

While larger fish such as bass, walleye, pike, muskellunge and striper are generally pursued for sport, they can also provide food for the table as well. These fish are generally harder fighters and weigh more and therefore your equipment should reflect these facts.

While the fish are larger with more meat they are usually more wary, more difficult to catch and of course more difficult to land.

Catfish

While they are large and hard fighting, catfish are worth the extra effort. They are easy to catch and will eat a wide range of baits (but rarely a lure). They provide a lot of meat for even smaller fish and are easy to clean and cook. Catfish generally hang out near the bottom so you need to be able to reach these areas with weighted lines.

Saltwater

Fishing in saltwater for me was always an adventure. I never knew quite what I would catch. One day it might be mackerel and the next it was a bonnet head shark. There were general baits to be used when fishing from the beach or canal side. These were commonly shallow baitfish such as mullet or just simply shrimp.

The important consideration for saltwater fishing is knowing what you catch and if it's edible or not. A good guidebook will make a huge difference. You can also pull up some pretty undesirable stuff so you may even need to know what is safe to handle. Get a guidebook and study it.

Lining

Fishing with a single line is not the most effective or efficient use of one's time when the goal is to harvest fish for food. At the best, I have seen fishermen attend to four or five lines with limited success. Any more than that will cost the fisherman bait and bites. The purpose of this writing is to describe the several methods that will produce large catches with little or no attention needed.

The techniques have varied names depending on where you are from and some work in different ways, but the goal is the same: to present lines to the fish with a means to work against the fish, thus hooking it, fighting it and/or notifying the fisherman of a bite. Thus, many of the techniques act essentially as water bound traps.

The primary prey pursued with these techniques is catfish. Catfish are one few fish with a very wide range. Different types can be found on every continent save Antarctica. [1] However, they may not all be edible (I know of several saltwater species that are not). Catfish are very nutritious as well. One three ounce serving (of freshwater catfish) contains about 146 calories, 17 grams of protein and 8.7 grams of fat. Not to mention essential vitamins and minerals.

Smaller variants of the methods described and different baits can be used with other species of fish however. It must be said, also, that when fishing for catfish, turtles are likely. However turtles are usually not an unwelcome catch as they are as tasty as catfish (though they are more difficult to pull up).

In my home state of Kentucky most, if not all, fishing techniques have clear and strict regulations to ensure fair harvest and safety. For instance, here in Kentucky sport lines (like those described in this writing) must be certain distances from dams and are restricted in bodies of water of certain sizes. In Kentucky, each sport fishing trotline, jug line or set line must be: 1) permanently labeled with the name and address of the user; 2) baited, checked and all fish removed at least once every 24 hours; 3) removed from water, bank or tree when fishing ceases.

Check local regulations before embarking upon any fishing venture.

Jug Lines

I begin this writing with the subject of jug lines because of all of the techniques in this article, there are none more productive or entertaining.

As with most fishing techniques there are several variations so experimentation cannot be discounted. Anything that fits the purpose is sufficient. That purpose is nothing more than to present a baited hook to your prey and attach it to something (a jug) that pulls back sufficiently to hook the fish and notify the angler. The jug line advantage is that the line depth can present the bait at multiple depths if the feeding zone is not known. This allows the angler to set multiple jugs at varying depths until a successful depth is discovered.

The simplest and most recognizable setup involves nothing more than a jug, a line, a hook and a sinker. The jug could be almost anything that floats. Two-liter or 16-ounce soda bottles are fine. Empty and cleaned detergent or bleach bottles are superb as they are thick and float well. As of late, more and more anglers are determined to refine the technique by "building" jugs. The most effective ones are nothing more than a length of PVC pipe threaded through a "pool noodle". The pipe should be longer than the noodle and the noodle should be pushed on and secured to one end. The line and accompaniments are tied to the pipe at the exposed end. Thus, when the fish pulls down, the noodle stands up as notification of a "fish on". The jug can float on the current or it can be anchored by tying on another line or by placing the hook line off the main line by using a swivel.

Kentucky laws restrict the quantity of jug lines to no more than 50 per boat. Jug lines may contain only one hook per jug. Check local regulations.

Limb Lines (Set Lines)

Limb lines are simply lengths of line with the end opposite the hook secured to an overhanging limb. This technique is probably better suited for rivers because limbs overhanging lakes will more than likely be located in shallow water.

One variation of limb lines is cane poling, where the limb is provided by the angler. Basically the longest and most sturdy (while flexible) length of cane is equipped with a hook, line, sinker (optional) and bait. The opposite end of the cane is driven deep into the ground of the nearby bank. The arc of the cane is the indication of the bite.

Kentucky laws restrict the quantity of limb lines to no more than 25 per person. Set lines may contain only one hook per line.

Trotlines

Trotlines are simply limb lines with more than one hook. The additional hooks are attached to shorter lengths of line which are attached to the main line via swivels. Knots keep the swivels from moving the shorter lines where they are unwanted. One end of the line is attached to a stationary object on shore such as a tree (limb or trunk) or a fence post. The other end should be anchored in some way. A coffee can filled with dry cement and an eye bolt is fine or a brick works equally as well. Do not do as most old timers do and bait up your hooks from shore and toss the brick. It is a good way to get an arm (or head) full of hooks.

There are variations to the standard trotline. Both ends can be tied to stationary shore objects and the line can be strung across the water with a weight in the center. As with the other techniques, improvisation is an art and can yield better results.

Kentucky laws restrict the quantity of trot lines to no more than 2 per person. There are also strict regulations on the quantity of hooks per line as well as the spacing of said hooks.

The line must also be set three feet or more below the water's surface.

Hooks

Hooks must be chosen based on the application. As a general rule, for these techniques, the stronger the hook the better the performance. Stronger is relative not only to the material of the hook (which should be steel) or the thickness (thicker the better), but also the coating. The hooks should be zinc-coated at the very least. Stainless steel is best. Remember that these hooks are going to spend a great deal of time submerged. In fact, the best trotline hooks are probably saltwater hooks.

The style of hook to be used is mostly personal preference. Some will argue that certain styles work better. Choose the appropriate hook for the prey and bait. I personally prefer a circle hook as I think it does a better job of hooking the fish and keeping it hooked. I don't have any data to back up this claim. The engineer in me tells me this is correct and that also the deep circular bend would also prove stronger. Maybe one day I'll test that theory.

The size of the hook, again, must be chosen to fit the application. Most sizes from size 3/0 to 6/0 are used commonly. The middle ground is the most common.

Line

The line used should be strong and most synthetic materials can be used. Cotton should not be used, however. Surveyor's twine is strong when dry, but is absolutely the worst line to use. The line must be like the hook, impervious to the effects of being submerged for extended amounts of time. Some suppliers in New England offer a line that is tarred for water resistance. Heavy braided fishing lines can also be used. The diameter is not very important. The fish will not see the lines or hooks; they will come to the lines by smelling and feeling the bait.

Bait

The bait placed on the line will, in most cases, determine the catch.

Flathead catfish are notoriously picky and most times will only take live bait such as shiners, chubs or bluegill. Most times, these baits can be lip-hooked. I feel, however, that hooking them through the eye or toward the tail improves the bite. It may seem cruel, but the more injured the bait appears, the more likely the predator will strike.

Blue catfish and channel catfish will bite live bait and almost anything else including, but not limited to, shrimp, leeches, worms, chicken liver or gizzards, catalpa worms, doughbait, stinkbait, and cutbait.

It is important not to overlook anything as bait. It should also be noted that certain baits work better on certain days or seasons. The good news is that you can set enough lines to experiment and see what works.

Location

The best places to set jug lines are along large, long flats where large catfish roam, hunting their prey. On lakes, creek arms or shallow bays are prime locations.

Timing

Most fishermen prefer to try their luck during the hours just before and after dusk and well into the night. Full moon nights seem to produce the best. Catfish are great hunters in any light due to their amazing senses however. Catfish can taste with many different parts of their body. They are sometimes called "swimming tongues". Combine that with the electroreceptors in their head and they become the perfect killing machine—a virtual freshwater shark—in low light conditions.

While blues and channels will eat anything, including junk, the flathead prefers live bait and thus is more vulnerable at night when hunting is easy.

After the Catch

Once you've caught your fish you will obviously want to eat your catch.

There are a few ways to prepare the fish for cooking. The simplest way with 99% of panfish and bass is to make an insertion on the belly below the gills and run it just under the skin all the way to the tail. Pull the guts out and wash out the cavity.

Next you will need to scale the fish (if the variety you caught has scales). Take the dull side of a knife and while holding it perpendicular to the fish, run it from the tail to the eyes. The scales should loosen easily. Leaving a few on won't matter much, but scales are made of the same stuff as fingernails and you wouldn't want to burn fingernails next to your food.

A fish in this shape is pretty easy to cook just by simply putting it on a roasting pan and placing it in the oven with some accoutrements.

Alternatively, you could filet the fish of course, but that method wastes a lot of meat and is not a good idea if the fish is small. It's also hard to do with any knife that isn't made for that job. The filet method also leaves the meat exposed and unless you have a pan and some oil it's going to make it tough to cook and less tasty. If you are going to freeze the fish this may be the best method since you only freeze the meat and not everything else as well.

Fileting a fish is pretty easy though. You simple make a cut behind the pectoral fin (the one right behind the gill. Make the cut from back to belly and bone deep. Then rotate the knife so the sharp edge faces the tail. Holding the knife against the bones, run it toward the tail and remove the filet. Then you can run the knife between the skin and the meat or if you've scaled the fish you can leave the skin on.

Despite what many people say, a catfish can be fileted as any normal fish might. Skinning is not necessary, but can decrease the amount of meat that is wasted. The knife used for fileting must be very sharp.

Start with a cut that runs parallel to the fish's gills, but is rear of the pectoral fin. Make that cut, also parallel to the cutting surface or ground, until the knife hits bone. Remove the knife. Reinsert the knife, with the flat of the blade parallel to the bone you just hit, starting with the tip at the fish's back. While slicing, insert the tip further and work the cuts toward the rear of the fish. If you are contacting the rib bones you are making the cuts deep enough. Once you move the knife rear of the ribs you can insert it straight down and out the other side at the bottom of the fish. Continue rearward, keeping the knife as close to the bone as possible. When you have reached the tail, flip the meat over and severe any additional attachment points. After the filet and skin combination has been removed from the fish, lay it on a flat surface with the skin down. Lay the knife blade parallel to the cutting surface and remove the meat from the skin. Place the first filet in cool clean water with a dash of salt added. The salt will prevent bacteria growth and will season the meat a bit. Repeat for the opposite side.

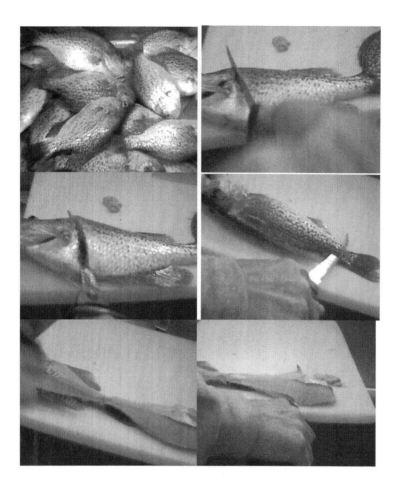

Once your fish have been fileted, wash your hands and proceed with steps to cook your catch.

Pat the fish dry and dredge in cornmeal, fry in a cast iron skillet full of hot cooking oil. Enjoy!

Other Methods

Though it's relatively new as a sport, bowfishing has been around a long time. Many indigenous cultures around the world practice this art of securing food with a bow and line. Regardless of its sport status, it's a great way to put food on the table and relatively cheap too.

Getting started bowfishing can be costly. You will need the right equipment in order to do it safely and effectively. This includes a bow, fishing arrows, special rest, slides, line and reel. The reel is spooled with line, which is attached to a special arrow via safety slides.

The quarry pursued is quite different from other fishing methods. The fish as a group are called "rough fish" and include gar, buffalo, carp, bowfin, paddlefish, catfish, bighead carp (asian). Other prey can include tilapia and alligator.

All of these fish can be eaten. The best are the bighead carp, catfish, paddlefish and gar. Buffalo and most other forms of carp (except for bighead) are usually not as tasty as the others and they have tons of bones.

The technique is pretty basic - find a spot where the fish congregate. Here on my lake, it's near the dams. You just have the find the best spot on your water. In many lakes carp and gar go into flooded marshes and are easy to spot and shoot.

Bowfishing can be accomplished from boat or from shore and at day or night. When you see the fish, aim below them and shoot. Aim low, aim low, aim low is the motto of the bowfisher. The reason you aim low is to overcome the refraction of light, which causes the fish to look higher in the water column. A great tip is to know the visibility. Hold something under the water and gage the depth. You adjust your aim 6" lower every foot under the surface the fish is.

When you make a successful hit it's as simple as pulling in the fish.

There is a safety factor involved. Not only do you have to take care being near the water's edge, but you also have to be aware of snapback. This is when the arrow is shot, but the string attached to it catches on something. The arrow can't continue forward and will snap back, potentially hitting the shooter. For this reason it's important to use safety slides and line that will break rather than stretch.

A technique that requires even less equipment, but perhaps more knowledge is poisoning fish. This technique is illegal just about everywhere there are game laws, but in certain situations you may find yourself with little choice. Disclaimer: I provide this information as just that, information. Use at your own risk and only as a last resort.

The most common plants (but not the only ones) that I know of as fish poisons are black walnuts and pokeweed, also commonly called polk sallet. Black walnut trees contain a concentration of a toxin called juglone in the bark and green nut husks. Pokeweed contains phytotoxins in the leaves and berries.

Either or both of these ingredients crushed and placed in still water where fish are should stun fish long enough for you to harvest them. In concentrations low enough to not hurt humans you will only yield smaller fish. If larger fish start to surface, you've used too much.

Again, it's hard to say how much you should use and this technique is extremely risky so use only as a last resort and with great caution. It can also taint your water supply.

Section 1C – Trapping

Introduction

When I introduce the subject of trapping I almost always tell the story about my mom and the fox. Growing up in the outdoors my family pursued just about any backwoods adventure you could think of from raising animals to trapping them. My dad was, and still is, a pretty skilled trapper and he taught me what I know about the subject.

My parents had a simple arrangement on our first homestead. Dad would set the traps every evening and check them and after he left for work, mom would go out in the late mornings to check them again. As a five year old I was lucky enough to get to go along and watch. I was enthralled with the life and death game.

Now trapping is not an easy task for most things. We caught quite a few raccoons and possums. Raccoon hides sold for a little bit at market in Louisville, but possums were essentially worthless. My dad coveted the rarer and more valuable game such as minks, weasels and foxes, but they were difficult to catch.

Then one day my mom and my brother and I were out in the field checking traps and from far off we could see something unusual. Due to the color we knew the trap had captured a red fox. We were excited, but approached cautiously.

I'm not sure if it was because dad was afraid mom would put a bunch of holes in a hide or if he thought she might actually be dangerous, but mom never carried a gun on these little excursions. And though it may sound cruel or harsh, a wooden baseball bat to the skull is also a quick and painless (most of the time) way to dispatch a caught animal.

So with a solid "thunk" my mom swung on the fox and it went limp. She then loosened the trap picked up my little brother in one arm and with her free hand she grabbed the fox and we all went home. Mom tossed the fox into an old empty chicken coop at the house and we all anxiously waited for dad to get home from work.

When dad got home I remember the pride and excitement my mom exuded when she told him about what she'd brought home. He nearly ran to the pen where mom had put the fox. I also remember the look on his face when he returned to the house with the news. The fox was still alive!

Apparently mom's swing had been just enough to render the fox unconscious. We still talk about that story to this day and wonder just exactly what would have happened had the fox came to life in mom's hand!

The Fox and I

With a backstory like that it should come as no surprise that I've been trapping since an early age. And though trapping is a dieing art I hope to one day pass my skills on to my son, who at 4 already knows a little about trapping.

The Basics

Trapping is different from snaring in that a mechanical device is used. This might include a livecatch trap, which is made from welded metal mesh, but for the purposes of this article I will only discuss the holding type traps.

A trap in its set mode and in position with potential to catch an animal is called a "set". The set doesn't include just the trap, but rather the whole elaborate ruse you've designed to trick the animal into stepping into said trap. A lot of "educated" people who believe trapping is cruel and barbaric do not understand the time, effort and skill needed to fool even a single animal.

The two traps that I've worked with differ in design and application. The first is the common leghold/foothold trap. These come in many different variations and sizes, but they essentially work the same way. They are made of steel entirely and have two semi-circular jaws that meet completely under spring pressure. A pan in the middle holds a trigger bar. When the pan is depressed the trigger bar releases and the force of the spring or springs push the jaws closed and hold under the spring force.

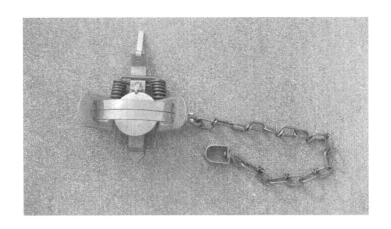

The second type of trap is called a Conibear. Named after its inventor – Fred Conibear -this trap is also made of steel, but instead of stamped flat steel it is made of bent rod stock and consists of two open squares connected at the sides. Two spring handles slide up the sides of the squares, adding the force. The squares are pulled apart and the trigger bar is placed against the trigger whiskers. When the whiskers are disturbed the two squares "scissor" and lock down on the object in the trap.

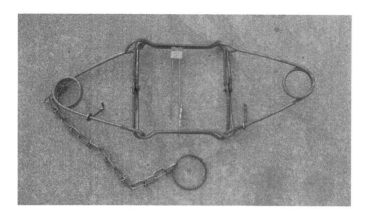

Rules and Regulations

Check your local state and area for rules and regulations.
Most specify what types of traps you can use, how many you
can set and how they must be identified. You may also need a
license and as always you need permission when trapping on
land that you do not own. There is generally also a season
when you can trap, limiting such activity to a set time period.

Preparing the Traps

Besides the traps you may also require setting devices and
stakes. The stakes are there to keep the animal from running
off with the trap.

Before you use the traps it is advisable to dye and wax them.
Dyeing them prevents them from rusting, thus making them
last longer. Waxing them allows the working parts to slide
smoothly, helping them work better. All that's needed to
apply either is heat and a vessel.

Setting a Leghold Trap

The act of setting the trap itself is pretty straight forward. I
carry a small board into the woods with me. Lay the trap onto
the board in its upright position. Then step down on the two
"ears" on either side. This releases the spring pressure and
allows the jaws to move freely. Use caution because your feet
can slip off of the ears quite easily. Move both jaws to full

open – forming a circle. Move the trigger bar to the notch in the pan. While lifting up on the pan with a stick slowly release the ears with your feet. The spring force should hold the trigger bar against the pan.

Now that the trap is set you will have to make the fine adjustments. This is accomplished by tapping on the pan with an object (I use a hammer or a stake). When the pan is hanging by only a small ledge, the trap is ready to be placed. This takes some practice. Don't worry if the trap springs, just reset it and repeat.

Before you do the work to set the trap, you should pick a spot and prepare it. Legholds are good for terrestrial mammals such as foxes, raccoons, bobcats, possums, etc., but can also be used for water dwelling mammals as well.

A land set is quite easy to arrange, but difficult to locate. What I mean by that is the actual step of preparing the site is easy, but finding a site is much tougher. I look for animal sign and place it near a source of water such as a small creek or pond. The traditional set is dug into a hillside, but they can easily be placed on flat land as well.

Dig out a small depression and retain the dirt. It's best to do this when the dirt is dry. You will not be able to cover your trap with mud. Place the set trap into the depression and sift the retained dirt to cover the trap. According to the teachings of my dad, the trap should be covered up to the pan and the ideal amount of dirt over the pan is equivalent to a layer of dust.

Next comes the act of baiting the trap. You should have evaluated the site and understand what direction the animal will approach and how it will approach the trap. When you find the position of approach you can go just beyond the trap and with a stick, jab a hole into the ground. Dip another stick into your bait and place the stick into the hole. You never actually put bait on the trap. All you will do is scare the animal when they stick their nose to the pan.

You should check the trap every day. In some states this is regulation, but beyond that it is a good ethical practice that gives trappers a good reputation. Leaving an animal to die on the trapline is just cruel.

Setting a Conibear Trap

With some of the larger Conibear traps you will need a device to open the jaws. With the smaller ones you can simply compress the handles. Once you have the handles compressed set the trigger bar onto the whiskers and release the safeties. No additional action is required.

The site preparation and placement of a conibear trap is usually easier in both cases. There usually is no site preparation needed. The placement is generally in the direct path of an animal. The path of the animal is generally obvious in these cases. That is what makes the conibear trap so appealing for aquatic mammals. The path for a muskrat is down a mud slide they create. So simply put the trap in the path. For a beaver it's the entrance to the beaver mound. Nearly every aquatic mammal has a similar giveaway.

Sticks, limbs and rocks can be used to hold the trap in an upright position.

The positive thing about conibear traps is that they almost always kill immediately. Rarely will an animal escape a conibear trap and almost never will they suffer.

Special Sets

There are two special sets that I will describe that flip the wisdom I gave you on the applications.

Muskrat/Beaver Float

The first trapping device my father taught us was the raft. The raft consists of two cedar (ideally, but other wood works too) logs about 3 feet long lashed or nailed together. A stick is placed in the middle of the raft and half an apple is speared onto it. A rope is tied to one end of the raft. A leghold trap's chain is nailed to the bottom side (opposite the stick and apple) at both ends and it is set and placed on the deck. Then the raft contraption is pushed into a body of water. The rope is tied to a shore-bound tree.

It works very simply. The muskrat comes onto the raft to eat the apple. Pop – the trap springs and he dives off. The trap drowns it.

Raccoon Cubby Set

Cut two notches about 1 inch wide and 4 inches deep into a five-gallon bucket rim. Place the bucket on its side in a ditch or culvert. Place a fish or a can of tuna with two holes punched in it inside the bucket. Then put a set conibear trap into the notches so the trap covers the entrance. A raccoon will enter into bucket and will immediately be trapped.

Conclusion

Like most outdoor activities, trapping requires caution. Use your good judgment and good ethics. Set the trap in areas away from pets and people. Learn the regulations in your area. Aim for the clean kill.

Because of the bane of political correctness, trapping is a skill that is dieing and for that reason it is all the more important to try and learn how to trap. We talk about connections with our past, but we read books and watch television to do it. Why not take an hour or so and do what the mountain men did?

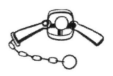

Section 3 – Gathering

Introduction

Of all the ways to secure food sources, the one that is truly lost
to the modern world is gathering. Gathering is the oldest form
of feeding one's self other than hunting, which evolved right
along beside it. In a certain way, gathering led eventually to
an intensive type of gathering (actually cultivating wild plants)
and then eventually to farming whereas hunting eventually led
to domestication and animal husbandry.

Before this divergence, hunting and gathering was the perfect
combination. Hunting requires intense concentration on
surroundings and a natural byproduct was that hunters would
commonly return with a combination of game and gathered
food as well. It is for this reason that it advisable to undertake
these activities together in your own ventures as well.

Gathering in ages past consisted of finding and eating just
about any edible and nutrient rich food source. This might
have included insects and other things that are repulsive to
Westerners today. These are all viable sources of food, but
unless you are simply stranded in the woods you want to eat
something that is tasty and nutritious and prevalent.

For the purposes of this book I've listed some of the most
common edible foods that can be gathered in the wilds of the
US. I have purposely not listed foods that are easily confused
with others for the purpose of safety. No one should be doing
any foraging based only upon book reading, but should enlist
the help of a mentor. In the case of one or two foods that have
dangerous look-alikes I have taken the time to list the

differences, but as always you are responsible for what you put in your mouth. It's your job to ensure proper identification.

However, I would be remiss if I did not offer at least some basic way to help you identify the plants around us. And although my ID method is not 100% foolproof it may help you be more in touch with those plants – edible or not.

Plant Identification Made Easy

The only thing more frustrating for me than coming across a plant on my land that I absolutely cannot identify is getting rid of the plant and then later finding out it was useful. As a young man I could walk the woods and have a pretty good idea of what plants were around me, but time away from the woods and learning new things pushed out those useful skills.

It took me a while to gain back the skills I'd lost, but even beyond that I wanted to be able to identify any plant I came across. It became very clear, very quickly, that not only do many plants look alike either through chance or evolutionary circumstances, but also the shear abundance of life in the forest makes it mostly impossible to know it all.

Luckily we live in a time where we have the internet, but search engines and computers are machines that are only as good as the information the operator (you) puts in them. You put in junk, you get junk right back out. So it's important to merge naturalist thinking with technological know-how.

After some successes and more failures I had an epiphany. I don't need to know how to identify every plant, but rather every plant feature and some basic information as well as geography and plant type and I'd have my answer in no time!

The Basics

Plant Type

The first important step may seem simple, but some people have trouble with it or leave it out of the equation. That step is just identifying what type of plant is in front of you on the most basic level. Is the plant a tree, shrub, bush, vine, bramble, evergreen, deciduous?

Sometimes simply knowing the plant type is a bit of a challenge. For instance, a woody shrub or bush can look very similar to a tree sapling. In addition, more than once I've looked up in a tree to find a leaf only to be fooled by the leaf of a vine growing within the tree. Therefore, it's important to conduct a good observation of the area and the plant you are looking it.

Observation is about more than just seeing the obvious, but rather inferring some things. Due to the simple physics of plant reproduction, it's likely that the subject plant will not be alone. Look around. Do you see any larger siblings? Working with a larger subject will sometimes answer the question of bush or tree. As well, many other questions can be immediately answered.

Evergreen

Knowing if the plant you are dealing with is an evergreen is important as well. Of course, answering that question with a coniferous (plant with needles for leaves) is easy (most are). With non-coniferous evergreens many amateur naturalists might tell you to simply wait until winter comes and if the plant still has its leaves, it is evergreen. This is always a surefire way to tell, but you can also tell in the heat of summer. In general, the leaves on an evergreen plant will be dark vivid green and the leaf will be thicker and very glossy. If you see these characteristics keep an open mind about the nature of your plant.

Key Identifiers

Some other key identifiers are features that stand out. For instance, not every tree has thorns so if you find thorns using that as a search term will help. If the plant is unusually tall or unusually spread, then noting that is a good idea. Berries and/or flowers are, of course, good things to note. It's rare that you'd find both at the same time on the same plant though. I will also sometimes note not just color, but specific berry or flower features. Berries can be ripe, unripe, glossy, matte, round, oblong, etc. For flowers, the number and configuration of petals might be important.

Geographic Location

This identifier doesn't require a lot of clarification. Some plants are very specific to certain regions so noting at least a region, if not a state, is a good idea.

Advanced

Some of the more advanced characteristics require new vocabularies or at least specialized vocabularies with words possessing specificity.

SHAPE & ARRANGEMENT

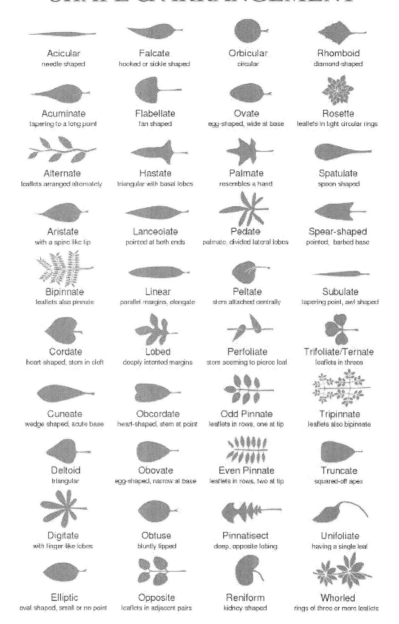

Acicular needle shaped	**Falcate** hooked or sickle shaped	**Orbicular** circular	**Rhomboid** diamond-shaped
Acuminate tapering to a long point	**Flabellate** fan shaped	**Ovate** egg-shaped, wide at base	**Rosette** leaflets in tight circular rings
Alternate leaflets arranged alternately	**Hastate** triangular with basal lobes	**Palmate** resembles a hand	**Spatulate** spoon shaped
Aristate with a spine like tip	**Lanceolate** pointed at both ends	**Pedate** palmate, divided lateral lobes	**Spear-shaped** pointed, barbed base
Bipinnate leaflets also pinnate	**Linear** parallel margins, elongate	**Peltate** stem attached centrally	**Subulate** tapering point, awl-shaped
Cordate heart shaped, stem in cleft	**Lobed** deeply indented margins	**Perfoliate** stem seeming to pierce leaf	**Trifoliate/Ternate** leaflets in threes
Cuneate wedge shaped, acute base	**Obcordate** heart-shaped, stem at point	**Odd Pinnate** leaflets in rows, one at tip	**Tripinnate** leaflets also bipinnate
Deltoid triangular	**Obovate** egg-shaped, narrow at base	**Even Pinnate** leaflets in rows, two at tip	**Truncate** squared-off apex
Digitate with finger-like lobes	**Obtuse** bluntly tipped	**Pinnatisect** deep, opposite lobing	**Unifoliate** having a single leaf
Elliptic oval shaped, small or no point	**Opposite** leaflets in adjacent pairs	**Reniform** kidney shaped	**Whorled** rings of three or more leaflets

Leaf Shape

Properly identifying the shape of a leaf is, for me, one of the more difficult tasks. Adding to the trouble, insect pests and irregular growth can lead you down the wrong path. As with all of the key features in this article, if you don't know you, can leave it out or simply use general terms like elongated, short, or lobed.

For those who do go to the trouble of proper leaf shape identification, the task of the search can become much easier. In many cases, such as with young trees, leaf shape is the best clue. In my woods it is exceedingly difficult to tell a pawpaw sapling from a hickory of certain types. The best clue is simply looking at the difference between the shapes of the leaves.

It would be hard to list all of the leaf shapes here or to adequately describe them in writing. However some of the easier to describe shapes are:

- Lobed – deeply indented with fingers (like oak)
- Rhomboid – shaped like a diamond (like grapes)
- Cuneate – wedge shaped with a narrow stem area (like pawpaws)

Leaf Arrangement

The pattern of the leaves along the stem is called leaf arrangement and can make more of a difference in positively differentiating two like plants than just about anything else. The more positive aspect of this feature is that it's almost always easy to tell right away the subject plant's leaf arrangement.

One of the more troubling identifications I had to make for a listener to my podcast was that of a leaf where the stem seemed to penetrate through the center. I later found out that this type of leaf was called perfoliate (*perf* – penetrate, *foliate* – foliage). This turned out to be a mile-a-minute weed, which needed to be controlled. The plant also had a very small specific range in the Northeast (see Geographic Location above).

The two most common leaf arrangements are opposite and alternate. Opposite arrangements will find the leaves simply opposite from each other and adjacent across the stem where they originate. Alternate arrangements are such that the leaves alternate along either side.

Here are some other examples:

- Rosette – originating from one center point (like a plantain)
- Trifoliate – leaflets in threes (like a clover)

Leaf Margin

Leaf type can seem fairly easy at first glance, but there are a great number of different leaf types and all kinds of subcategories. The best example is for leaves with jagged edges. The edges can be straight points, curved forward, small, large, etc. Punching one of these words into a search engine will sometimes work, but many of the things you'll find on the web are likely to use words that are more specific. Take just these few examples for instance.

- Large symmetrically straight teeth – dentate
- Small symmetrically straight teeth – denticulate
- Large curved forward teeth – serrate
- Large curved forward teeth with smaller teeth – doubly serrate
- Rounded teeth – crenate
- Smooth (no teeth) – entire

This is just a sample of the unique language that is leaf identification.

Bark

As with most of the features I've listed, properly typing the bark can be a tie-breaker for proper identification. The color is also sometimes important. Here are some examples:

- Scaled – bark in large chunks attached at one point (like sycamore trees)
- Furrowed – large, long ridges (like walnut trees)
- Paper – thin and easily removed (like birch trees)
- Plated – large scales (like shagbark hickories)

The color can be tough sometimes so if you can't tell the difference between light brown and light gray, then skip it.

Conduct the Search

At this point you should formulate your search phrase. It is important to note that if you aren't sure about a characteristic leave it out. If you know for sure that the plant is a tree then add it. If you are not sure don't worry about it. A wrong term is more harmful though than leaving the term out completely.

A search formula I use commonly is this: Plant type – leaf type – leaf configuration – berry/flower and color – geography (order isn't important).

One of my recent searches went like this: vine dentate opposite leaves glossy purple berry Arkansas.

The results – peppervine. Of course, you won't usually get the word "peppervine" or any other word; you will get a bunch of links to websites/articles/blogs. At this point, it's your responsibility to search through and find the ones with descriptions that sound right. The positive thing is that on most occasions you will also have access to photos so you can do a side-by-side comparison. Once I get a result I think is correct I will search for that specific plant again to cross-reference my answer.

Not every feature you've identified should or need go into the search box, but it is at least a good idea to note them or jot them down to narrow the results of the search. Don't use unspecific words in a search. The word "and" and "the" is unnecessary, as is the word "green" or "plant".

Disclaimer

My method is by no means a catchall. It's very possible that relying only upon your information and the Internet that you will improperly identify a plant on occasion. That is why I find it important to put out this disclaimer.

Many of the plants you find may at least look similar to plants that are at least thought to be edible. There is no substitute for firsthand experience and a solid mentor. I assume no liability for any plant you intend to eat. The content of this book is to help get you one step closer to identification and relying on it solely is not advised.

As I've stated this isn't a surefire method, but it certainly has made my plant identification process about ninety percent more accurate. Many people don't like to rely on the Internet and technology for their naturalist skills, but even the best naturalists had to learn through some means and the Internet is a teacher that never sleeps. Before long, with this method you can become a pseudo-expert on your little piece of the plant world.

Tree Fruit

The paramount gathered food is tree fruit. The advantages are many. First of all, hunting under a fruit tree is a good way to guarantee success. Deer, squirrel and many other animals seek out and find these fruit trees and frequent them. Secondly, the fruit is nearly always nutritious, tasty and able to be transported. It doesn't ruin quickly and usually comes with some sort of skin to keep the goodness inside.

If trees grow where you are, it's very likely that you will find tree fruit in some manner, shape or form. On the North American continent there are several that are worth seeking out and many more that provide adequate sources of food.

Pawpaw

During my formative years, my brother and I knew where a small grove of pawpaw trees grew on the family farm and we checked them often for fruit between September and October. Some years they produced and others they didn't. There was a reason for that which I will explain in a moment.

Pawpaws are a unique plant—distinctly American. They produce the largest native edible fruit (actually a berry!) on the continent and a delicious fruit at that. With a creamy texture, no two fruits seem to taste alike. One may invoke a banana flavor while others are tinged with mango and tropical flavors. The taste never disappoints though.

The trees are usually quite easy to find and identify once one is aware of what they seek. Small in height (rarely over 25 feet), the trees appear tropical with huge ovate (oval shaped) leaves, which are actually fatter on the end away from the branch. The leaves alternate, which means on each side of the branch, the leaves will not form directly in line with each other, instead stepping up the branch. The bark is thin and gray with small bumps all over.

Pawpaws usually grow in groves. They propagate poorly from seed (but it is possible) and instead reproduce through root suckering. This means that a mother plant's roots form buds or suckers, which grow up and to the surface forming a new and identical child plant. It's nature's way of cloning. Therefore, where you find one pawpaw tree you will likely find many.

Finding the trees is not a difficult task. I usually look in low-lying shaded areas near a water source. Young pawpaws will not survive in the open due to sunscald and wind. If you find an accessible grove you may need to open up the canopy a bit to let them get some light. Otherwise they may not produce well.

The flowers are unusually beautiful. The color I heard best described as flesh-colored. They are quite large and emit a rotten odor. Insects that are lured by the rotten smell are the only natural pollinators and they don't seem particularly attracted to the flowers so they are sporadic at best, thus the reason for intermittent fruit set. In addition, most colonies are root suckered off of the same parent, making the flowers incompatible. Some old-timers I know will hang rotten meat from a limb to help ensure pollination.

The fruits start out green, alone or in clusters and ripen to a dark yellow and then later to brown and may even ripen with darker splotches. The fruit ruins quickly and must be eaten or preserved. Common in the south is pawpaw pudding and I've even read about a pawpaw ice cream.

Lewis and Clark subsisted on the pawpaw when rations ran low during their return trip. If it nourished them, it can nourish you.

Persimmons

It is almost tradition to start any writing about persimmon with mentioning the extreme bitterness of one in an unripe state that it would be pretentious of me not to do the same. However, most everyone by now should know that persimmons in a ripe state are one of the most delicious fruits available for forage.

Like pawpaws, persimmons are unique and present special challenges which I believe help attribute to their status as lower class foraging material. One challenge is the ripeness itself. I'm not going to talk again about the chalky bitterness except to say that in the bitter unripe state, the fruit is only slightly firm. Once it reaches full flavor and ripeness though, the small pumpkin looking fruits are delicate to handle at best. The slightest pressure squashes them and falling from a tree will downright leave them in a puddle, but there is a secret that I will divulge in a moment.

The persimmon tree is also easy to identify. Some may grow very large. One I foraged from on the edge of a cow pasture (complete with embedded barbed wire) was huge, probably over 60 feet tall with a trunk so large I could not wrap my arms around completely. The leaves are ovate, alternate and small and pointed at the end. The brownish to grayish bark is characterized by large scales that look like pieces of charcoal glued over an orange base. The orange fissures are very visible from even several paces away.

The small off-white flowers never seem to have a problem finding pollinators.

The fruits start off green and then ripen to a pumpkin orange. The best ripest persimmons I've ever eaten though had started to take on a purple hue. They are very difficult to harvest and gather. I went through several methods before I decided on the best method, which is a ladder. I spent time shaking branches with a rope. I shook the trunks of the trees, but always the same thing happened. The ripest, best fruits would land with a splat. Best case, the skin would be breached with the fruit mostly intact. I'd harvest those fruits, but they were always just short of full flavor and ripeness. If the shaking method is to be used though, the best time is during the morning of a heavy frost. The frost will add another layer of protection to the skin and help keep some intact on the way down.

Persimmons can be made into a pudding or jelly or just simply dried and eaten as snacks. They do have seeds that will need to be dealt with prior to consuming.

Speaking of dried persimmons. It is commonly thought that the word persimmon originates from the Powhatan Native American word for dried fruit. Persimmons also kept civil war soldiers fed.

"We marched northward into Tennessee over frozen ground and how cold it was! Our shoes were worn out and our feet were torn and bleeding...the snow was on the ground and there was no food. Our rations were a few grains of parched corn. When we reached the vicinity of Nashville we were very hungry and we began to search for food. Over in a valley stood a tree, which seemed to be loaded with fruit. It was a frost bitten persimmon tree, but as I look back over my whole life, never have I tasted any food which would compare with these persimmons." - **Memories of Milton B. Cox told by his son John T. Cox**

And then of course, the folk song:

> *"Possum up a 'simmon tree*
> *Raccoon on the ground*
> *Possum says you son of a gun*
> *Lay my 'simmons down."*

In addition, folk stories suggest that by splitting the persimmon seed and analyzing the shapes inside you can predict the coming winter.

A fork means mild weather.
A spoon means plenty of snow.
A knife means cold winter winds.

Nuts

Of all of the wild edible foods in North America, the most beneficial has to be a nut. They are easy to find, nutritious and prevalent. There are too many varieties to talk about independently so I've broken them down into a few categories.

Common

Some nuts are so common that it's hard to not find them when walking in the woods just about anywhere in the US.

Hickory nuts are very common and easy to find. However the squirrel oftentimes will beat you to them. This nut is very tasty. The shell usually peels right off leaving the inner nut. This part must then be cracked. There is a bit of an art to cracking a hickory nut. The best way to crack it is by standing it on its head and hitting the end with the little tail on it. If you crack it wrong it will splinter into a million pieces. Once open you'll find that there isn't a lot there, but if you work for it, it's quite a treat.

Hickory's cousin, the pecan tree, is a little harder to find unless you are in the Deep South, but I find it is very much worth it. It is superior to many of the native nuts in the US. It is easy to crack. It tastes delicious. And best yet, it's easy to work with.

Oak trees are also very common. And while its nut – the acorn is not edible in its raw state it can be processed to make it so. White oaks have the most edible acorns. Red oak acorns should be avoided due to the high amount of toxic tannins. Acorns are easy to crack and once cracked the nut meat (which is abundant) should be ground or pounded into a paste or powder (depending on the moisture content). This mixture is then steeped in water for several hours. The water is filtered off and then the process is repeated. It's hard to say how many times it will take. If you taste of the paste and it's bitter at all you must repeat until all astringency is gone. Filter the water off and let the paste dry into powder.

Less Common

One of the best eating nuts out there is of course the walnut. Once you find a walnut tree of any size you'll find that it will produce copious amounts of nuts and that the nuts are delicious. The only two problems are that they are a little tougher to find and they are difficult to work with. Walnuts have a soft, but fibrous outer covering that is green and has no seams by which to open it. The covering turns black as the nut matures and then it more or less degrades and rots off of the inner nut shell. And THEN once you get to it you find that the inner shell is less than cooperative.

Rare

These other nuts are worth mentioning only to illustrate that there are so many edible nuts in the US. Beechnuts and butternuts are edible and delicious not to mention easy to work with. They are just hard to find.

Chestnuts and hazelnuts are extremely delicious and extremely easy to work with as well, but these are rare due to blights that have rendered them very nearly extinct on this continent.

Berries

Elderberries

For some reason a lot of people think of elderberries as a tame plant grown in the backyard garden. These people might be surprised to find that the Common Elderberry grows wild in many places in the US. This small shrub grows well in marginal areas, commonly popping up on the edge of a forest or along railroad tracks.

Elderberry shrubs are usually about as tall as a person and are characterized by ovate, alternate leaves that are long and lance-like. The white flowers form on large umbrella shaped structures and then turn to purple berries, the stems of which usually turn a maroon color around harvest time.

The very small berries turn from green to a dark purple/blue color. They are not edible in their unripe form and actually said to be slightly toxic as is every other part of the plant (except the flowers). ONLY BLACK OR BLUE BERRIES ARE EDIBLE! I've found the easiest way to harvest the berries is to remove the entire umbrella and sort out the good berries from a nice seated position later.

There are three edible things that elderberries are noted for. One is in a nice elderberry pie. Another is a delicious jelly. Finally, my favorite is a great red wine that can be made from the berries.

Native Americans not only used the hollow stems for musical instruments, but they also used straight branches for arrows.

Blackberries

In the south blackberries are celebrated as an essential crop for the homestead. It wasn't until I was an adult that I realized in certain countries and areas in the US they are thought of as a weed. That may be so, but there are few weeds that produce so delicious a berry!

Blackberries are unmistakable as a plant. They grow in large thickets, taking over fencerows and edges of wooded areas. Wild plants have large hooked thorns, which make harvesting the berries, a difficult and bloody operation. In late spring/early summer they set loads of tiny white flowers, which draw in bees and other pollinating insects. Then they set pale red/pink berries, which eventually turn black.

Picking the berries is an art – which took me the better part of my childhood to learn. Berries that have turned black, but still have a tint of red are horribly bitter. So are any berries that are fully black, but still quite firm. The best berries have a glossy black look to them and are slightly squishy when squeezed.

Blueberries/Huckleberries

While the purist may disagree with me lumping these two delicious berries in one category, it's done to save confusion. While blueberries are more native to the Northeastern US and huckleberries are more native to the Pacific Northwest in areas where habitat or culture collide the terms may be used interchangeably.

It's not a surprise though. Both are from the genus Vaccinium and both taste somewhat similar and the plants themselves look alike.

The plants are somewhat compact and are best described as shrub-like. A normal mature plant may be about 5 feet tall. The flowers can vary in color, but are most commonly white. The leaves are very plain and round, but slightly elongated. The leaves can take on a red tinge as well on both types of plants.

Edible Herbaceous Plants

Once properly researched it is quite amazing the number of edible plants that exist in the wild with little or no cultivation from human hands. These untapped resources taste good and are nutritious as well.

Wintercress

I've never intentionally grown wintercress in my garden, but it always seems to find its way there. It's there because winter cress prefers disturbed soil like one might find in a garden. Even though I don't till my garden, the soil is still somewhat disturbed and even a few hoe strikes can give winter cress enough of a foothold to get in and germinate.

Winter cress is a member of the mustard family and is related to the brassica plants (cabbage, broccoli, etc.). It's typically classified as an "invasive weed" from Europe. I put quotes around both terms because I feel that neither is applicable to this plant. It is now a naturalized plant found in almost every state of the union except the very hot and dry places.

The plant is edible in two stages. The first is the tender young leaves when it's found very early in spring in what is called a "rosette" form. The rosette is a low growing cluster of leaves and stems radiating outward in a circle. The leaves are plucked from center rosette and stems and leaves can be added to a salad. I find their taste mild and pleasing with a bit of a bite.

Although it's completely edible, there have been warnings that exception consumption can lead to kidney disorders. I'm not sure where this comes from, but I found it in my research and felt it necessary to add that disclaimer. That is especially puzzling since the Native Americans (after arrival of the white man) used a tea from the leaves to actually aid kidney function. The leaves were also used in Europe as a wound dressing.

The form it's most often found in is after its formed a flower head. The act of forming a flower head is commonly referred to as "bolting". The act of bolting and the flower color has earned the plant the label of garden yellowrocket. The good news is that the flower buds at the tip can be consumed in exactly the same way as broccoli. The leaves at this stage are inedible.

In the rosette form the plant has almost next to no look-alikes that are dangerous that I'm aware of. A large heart shaped leaf tips the stems and smaller rounded leaves opposite each other on the stem closer to the root ensure proper identification.

Dandelions

To me there is no more delicious wild edible green than dandelions. Most everyone has seen a dandelion and can readily find some in their yard. The name dandelion comes from "dent-de-lion" referring to the dents in the leaves make it look toothed (like a lion). In early spring it sends forth a yellow flower (which is also edible and makes a fine wine) that later turns to a white puffball that sends seeds everywhere.

Basically the entire dandelion is said to be edible (but I've never tried the roots). In fact, it's not only edible, but thought to be medicinal as well. The bitter compound taraxacin, which forms the white sappy milk in older plants, will help remove warts and corns. I actually have used the sap on my son who had warts on his thumbs. Eaten, the greens have a cleansing effect on the liver and kidneys. Dandelion leaves contain tons of essential vitamins and minerals such as A, C, K, calcium, potassium, iron and manganese.

The best way to prepare dandelion greens is to boil them for about five minutes in sufficient water and then throw out the water. After that I like to sauté them in a pan with butter, garlic and bacon.

The only caution with dandelions is to be sure you harvest them someplace without the threat of herbicide or other sprays. Because people do not understand the benefits of dandelions they are common fodder for extermination.

Pokeweed

Pokeweed is an edible green that is best left for the experts. When eaten without processing it is full of alkaloids and can quickly sicken someone or even kill them. Furthermore it can only be harvested safely in the very early spring when it's

young and not yet full of dangerous alkaloid compounds.
Even beyond that, the only real safe parts to eat are the young
greens.

However it is still worth noting for the sheer fact that here in
the south this green is celebrated as an edible food via festival
and "poke sallet (salad)" days.

Harvesting pokeweed is done as I mentioned only in early
spring. If the stems have reddish purple streaks then the plant
is not considered edible. Any leaves less than 6-7 inches long
are harvested. The traditional method of processing for eating
is to boil in salted water once for at least 10 minutes. Then the
water is drained and thrown out. Then the leaves are boiled
again in new clean salted water for another 5 minutes. That
water is thrown out and the greens are served.

Still it's best to eat pokeweed in limited amounts at first at
least until you both know what you are doing and how your
body will react.

Purslane and Chickweed

These two plants are commonly found in disturbed areas such
as gardens. They are both edible and nutritious.

<u>Mushrooms</u>

The most fabled of all wild edible foods is of course the
mushroom. Why so fabled? Well for the simple fact that
there is a factor of risk involved in hunting mushrooms.
While eating the wrong edible green can be dangerous, eating
the wrong mushroom can be fatal.

However, most if not all cases where serious complications
occurred from mushroom hunting are found to be poor
identification. The truth is that there are many indicators that
the wrong mushroom is in hand and these indicators in certain
cases are simply ignored or scoffed at.

Mushroom hunting can be safe and incredibly rewarding if one takes the time to find a mentor, do the research and be careful. There's a saying that is appropriate. *There are old mushroom hunters. There are bold mushroom hunters. There are no old bold mushroom hunters.*

Mushrooms are commonly thought of as plants, but they are in fact part of their own separate group. The part that humans see and eat is actually the fruiting portion which comes to the surface to spread spores. The actual organism is composed of threadlike filaments called mycelium which may be many times larger than the fruit they produce.

Though there are quite a few edible varieties, we will cover only a few of the most common and popular mushrooms.

Morels

Certain areas of the country usually have a favorite fungus. In my part of the country that favorite is definitely morels. Commonly called landfish due to taste and method of cooking, morels are so prevalent across areas of the country that when one goes "mushroom hunting" it's assumed that morels are the "prey".

Morels have a unique look that makes them hard to find, but easy to identify. They can be yellow, pale white or grey/black and have pits and ridges that give it a honeycomb type look. They are most commonly found in early to mid spring during days when the temperature is around 60 degrees F or so and usually a day or two after a rain. The locations can vary wildly, but elm trees, ash trees, and sycamore trees are all good indicators of morel activity.

Be aware that there is a look-alike mushroom (well actually a whole group) that is quite poisonous called a false morel. If the name isn't indication enough note that this mushroom can look quite similar to a morel. Because there are multiple look-alikes, a successful hunter should not concentrate on using features to identify a false morel, but rather using the known characteristics to positively identify the real deal.

A bonafide morel mushroom will have a hollow stem when sliced lengthwise. The hollow part continues from base to tip (even inside the wrinkled part). True morels do not have wrinkles, but rather pits and ridges. Folds and wrinkles are not a good sign. In addition, most false morels are dark red/brown in color and are very brittle.

Chanterelles

Known across much of the country as "the other mushroom" chanterelles are not only more attractive than morels, but also arguably more delicious.

Chanterelles often grow in groups and I've found them growing in leaf litter next to trees I've felled recently. They are pale to bright yellow and almost orange in some cases. I've heard the color described as egg-yolk and that's a pretty good description. They are quite easy to find and most often appear in warmer times of the year than the morel – giving a mushroom season a little extension. They also give off the aroma of apricots.

As with other edible mushrooms, the chanterelle also has a hazardous look-alike. The Jack-O-Lantern mushroom is a similar color and can be found at similar times. There are differences however. First of all, the jack-o-lantern grows in decaying wood or dead trees while the chanterelle pops up out of the ground. The chanterelle's gills are wrinkled and folded and irregular, but the jack-o-lantern's are straight and knife-edged.

Section 3A – Gardening

Introduction

I can't remember a time that I didn't think of a garden as a way to produce food. Except for instances such as the occasional crisis, war or economic downturn (of which we currently find ourselves) most people look at gardening as a hobby or simply a habit. For myself and many other children of rural areas, my family relied as much on a garden for sustenance as they did the work off the farm that my father did to earn money. We planted a variety of foods and it wasn't until I combed my memories later that I came to realization that we never used a tiller or fertilizer.

The modern gardener has a bevy of tools and resources at his or her disposal. There are machines to till the soil, chemicals to boost yields or kill pests. The Internet provides all the information that a gardener would ever need to practice their art.

It doesn't need to be said again that it wasn't always the case, but it does need to be said that it might not always be the case going forward either. A lot of modern gardens work only because of the tools and information currently available. We take for granted that those tools will always be at hand or as close as the local mega-mart. Tillers run on gas and oil, which are finite resources and most are subject to frequent breakdowns that only experienced mechanics are capable of correcting. And most of us begin to pull our hair out when the Internet service lapses for even an hour.

I don't talk from a position of power or knowledge. I am subject to many of the same conditions, but I've set myself on a course to remedy that situation and I hope I can share some of my experiences.

I like to exorcise the complicated and embrace the simple. Gardening is a simple task that our ancestors practiced for many years and did so sometimes more successfully and intrusively than we—with our modern tools—could ever hope. The purpose of this book is to take out all of the extraneous steps and tools that we could not truly depend on if we were starving and relied on our garden for our next meal and did not have all the resources in the world to make that meal.

Occupy a Garden

I like protests as much as the next guy. There's no better way to say, "We're mad as hell and were not going to take it anymore" than by…literally saying, "We're mad as hell and were not going to take it anymore!" Protest without proper action to back up your claims and demands gives a protest very little meaning. Protesting not to protect what you have, but rather to get what you didn't work for is futile and unworthy.

In other words, how many of the ninety-nine percent have done anything to lessen their dependence upon the systems that they so abhor – government or corporations? How many are willing to shrug off the thought that the government could provide them everything they need? How many are aware that in a fascist oligarchy that no difference exists?

As an advocate of sustainable gardening, my point, in this roundabout way, is that one cannot claim corporate greed is robbing you of your future if you won't learn to dig in the soil. Saving the "what's wrong with this generation is…" talk, it's much easier to blame corporations or the government than to actually do what's hard – like taking a shovel to the ground.

Corporations

There's almost nothing that can't be cured by gardening. If you don't like corporations the solution is simple – you have to wean yourself off of them, but don't be fooled, chances are you will need something a corporation makes and you'll be happy to have it when the need exists.

Food doesn't have to come from a corporation and it doesn't have to come from a tin can, a box in the freezer or out of a plastic bag. It comes from the soil, but it takes work and you can't cede your responsibility any longer. If you want to eat, you are going to have to work for it. You can't spit in the faces of the people who make what you willingly give your money for.

Working for it also has its benefits. Instead of ceding your responsibilities you can do the work and become fit and able and learn. You will also save money in the long run. Take that - evil corporations (sarcasm intended)!

Government

For the other side, it's almost as tempting to claim helplessness due to excessive government intervention. I hate government and I'd be an anarchist if it weren't so anarchistic. Think about it, in the garden there is no government. Just try to lead, exert your influence. Have you ever tried to regulate a ladybug? Passed a law against squash bugs? Declared a war on weeds?

If you want to avoid government there's an easy way. Deprive them of the money that you rightfully owe them just for existing – taxes. The government can only steal from you because you allow it. We grin and bear a lot of these taxes. If you want to work and buy all those nice toys from corporations you have to earn money,

What if you could avoid hundreds of dollars in taxes per year by digging a hole and putting a seed in? By growing your own food you avoid paying a corporation and the double taxes (those from your purchase and those the corporation passed

141

on!). Or what do I know? Maybe holding a sign and chanting works just as well.

Something for Nothing

My problem with the occupy movement is that they want something for nothing. Well not all of them and I'm going to hear that not everyone there is a socialist shill. That may be true, but when three out of four news interviews involve someone griping that no one has stepped up and paid their student loan I get aggravated. Maybe it's because I paid my tuition as I went.

Just to humor those who want something for nothing. It isn't happening. The next best thing though is planting a garden. Where else can you do a little work (and work is a four letter word to some) and get so much in return? For the price of a seed (less than pennies) you can get pounds of produce (value measured in dollars). There's your something for nothing. I did the calculations one time and a pack of broccoli seeds that sold for a few bucks could produce hundreds of dollars worth of produce. And you don't have to sell your soul, or get on your knees and beg the government for it.

Like I said, protest has its place. I'd be glad to speak out and do what is necessary to defend my inalienable rights. However, when I can get what I need with a little work and not taking the easy way out I'm going to do it. I'll continue to take my son to the garden and I'll continue to teach him.

And one day he'll ask, "Daddy, where were you when the occupy movement was happening?"

I'll say, "Right here with you-occupying a garden."

Sustainable Methods

Most people do not want to be self-sufficient or use sustainable methods. In some ways it is hard. It is much easier to go to the store and buy a bag of fertilizer than to collect your compost scraps and dump them everyday and then turn the compost. It is much easier to hook a hose to the faucet and dump a few gallons of city water on our plant than to make a rain barrel and haul water by hand.

Is it any easier? After all, city water has to be bought and the fertilizer isn't free. Every dollar we spent had to be earned. And worse yet, every dollar we earned was taxed and then taxed again when we spent it on the fertilizer. The city water was taxed and the people that helped clean it were taxed. They bought gas that was taxed to put in their cars (more taxes) just to go to work. All this was done just so the government could work and figure out ways to tax us more.

People also resist becoming self-sufficient because they assume that the systems that they depend on will always be in place. So why worry about it?

What would have happened if the recent H1N1 flu pandemic had been something more than a convenient way for the government to sell vaccines? What if the death rate had been more akin to 25% rather than tenths of a percent? Would the trucks keep replenishing the shelves at the supermarket? Would the water and electricity keep flowing once the workers decided to play it safe and stay home? The answer to all of these questions should be quite apparent, but unfortunately, to the majority of Americans it is not.

In conclusion, true self-sufficiency will almost never be achieved completely. Self-sufficiency is an idea to be aspired to, but rarely achieved. However, completely relying upon systems of dependency that can fail and require money is never a good idea. That holds especially true when one is talking about the methods of growing food and sustaining life. A sustainable garden is a goal that can be achieved, and should.

Gimmicks

There is no panacea to the gardening problems that one can encounter. I have a particular disdain for gimmicks and trends in gardening. People tend to overcomplicate simple things. Gardening (at least in the context of this book) is about growing food. It's not about impressing your neighbors. It is certainly not a contest to spend the most money.

Yet there is a large contingent of gardeners eager for the next trick that's going to solve all ills. The fact of the matter is this: the newest trends won't change the necessary requirements or the balance of nature that must exist for a garden to be successful.

Gardening at its base is a balance of two things. The first thing is the constant balance in nature to keep the system going. The second is the constant balance between the numbers. A garden is capable of producing a certain amount of calories or energy. The gardener is the tender of this number game. Allow too much of your energy, nutrients and water to leave your property, the more capability you will lose. Lose too much and you will have to spend money (another form of energy) to regain the balance. There are plenty of people in the world that lose more calories working to make money than that money provides them in purchased food.

That's why we must think of gardening as a process – an inescapable loop from which nothing leaves and ultimately nothing must enter.

Beginning Gardeners

I believe strongly that all humans have the innate ability and instinct necessary to grow their own food. Some people just take longer to realize this drive. Doing so for the first time is a life changing experience.

As a newly awoken gardener you will be beset by opinions and recommendations. I attempt (emphasis on that word) not to talk in absolutes. There are things I do not recommend (including gimmicks-see above). However I make this caveat. Doing something I or anyone else is the world doesn't like is better than doing nothing at all. Some things I don't like because of my own specific experiences or personality. You should find what works for you and apply it with all of your skill.

Process

The goal of a process is to take a series of inputs and convert it into a series of outputs. The process of gardening is exactly the same. We hope to use certain inputs and a procedure to gain an output or harvest. All three must work together. We must get the right inputs and use the right procedure to achieve the best harvest possible.

A process can diverge in many places. In many cases, multiple inputs will work the same way. Such is the case with procedures. The hope is to use the easiest possible procedure to achieve the best possible output or harvest. The ease of the procedure must be weighed carefully against the output. A lot of time and energy and inputs can be thrown at a procedure, but the harvest that results may not be equivalent to the energy and materials invested. For this reason we have to break ourselves of the notion that a bigger harvest must be had at any cost. This is the same notion that has brought us to the brink with petrochemical fertilizers and slash and burn agriculture. This is the same notion that led to the dust bowl.

<u>Inputs</u>

A process begins with the inputs. Before any action can be taken that directly deals with the process, the inputs must be gathered. What do you need to plant and nourish a garden?

1. Seed/Stock/Bulbs/Tubers
2. Water
3. Sunlight and temperature
4. Growing medium (most commonly nutrient rich soil)
5. Carbon Dioxide

Given some preparation and forethought not one of these five essential ingredients cannot be gathered, created, harvested or captured on your own property.

Seeds/Stock

The garden starts with the selection of seeds, rootstock, bulbs or tubers for planting. Luckily for us, seed catalogs and manufacturers help us by providing plenty of information from which we can use to make an informed decision.

Picking Which Foods to Grow

The most obvious criteria in picking what to grow is what your family likes to eat. However, there are other factors involved that make a difference. If something simply won't grow in your area and you can't figure it out, it's best to move your concentration to what will actually grow for you.

Most failures in picking the right vegetable has to do with people not understanding the history of what they choose to grow. The origination, as well as evolution, help illustrate what the plant is "built" for.

Take the tomato's colorful history for example.

The tomato comes from south and Central America where it grew (and still does to my knowledge) as a perennial plant. For some reason, South America was great at growing many plants that have become part of our daily lives (potatoes for another example!). It made its way up from probably Peru and into Mexico and Central America due to travels of native peoples. In fact the word tomato comes from an Aztec word Tomatl. It is commonly believed that the Spaniard Hernardo Cortes brought it back to Europe from Montezuma's gardens probably sometime in the 1520's.

A highly controversial theory states that Columbus beat Cortez to the tomato and brought it to Italy. Needless to say, the origin stories depend a lot on a kind of unspoken fight between Italians and Spanish over who found and values the tomato more. It is very important to both modern cultures. Personally, I like what the Italians have done with it so it doesn't matter to me who got to it first.

The tomato's reception in Europe was not quite what one would imagine. I guess at the time there was such an influx of new plants that it was hard to find time to study them all. Cortez had apparently been bitten by the gold bug and got too busy plundering to ask what the plant was good for. Tomatoes were thought to be poisonous once they arrived in Europe and were grown as ornamentals. It was even trendy to pick the fruits and use them as table decorations at dinner.

It is thought that the first varieties were yellow not red and small. In 1544, the tomato made its way to the written page by the hand of an Italian botanist named Mattioli. He called it the Italian equivalent of "Golden apple" which indicates that the first varieties were probably yellow, not the more common red of today.

The old Europeans weren't stupid; there was good reason for them to be suspect of the tomato. The tomato is from the nightshade family and its leaves and stems were poisonous due to content of glycoakaloids. It even looks a bit like nightshade. It stands to reason that a little fruit growing in such conditions might be as well. To their defense also, the pewter eating utensils favored in Europe contained a good deal of lead so exposing them to acidic tomatoes would probably leach out some of this toxic heavy metal.

Also, it wasn't widely eaten in Europe because of a lot of bad press. A surgeon in Britain named Gerard even knew that the Spanish and Italians were eating the tomato, but he still believed it was poisonous and was not afraid to let people know how he felt. The French botanist Tournefort named the tomato Solanaceae *Lycopersicon (Family Genus)*. Later, in the 1700's, *esculentum* was added as the species, which means edible. Solanaceae means nightshade family. Lycopersicon means Wolfpeach. In Roman lore, a wolfpeach was a poison fruit used to poison wolves.

Finally by end of the 1700's, the tomato was accepted as edible (and probably delicious) fare across most if not all of Europe. The French even called tomatoes pommes d'amour or apples of love (love apples) due to some supposed qualities.

Tomatoes had made their way to the colonies that would later become the United States by the early 1700's where they were documented in South Carolina. It's likely that the wolfpeach had to once again be proven edible to all of the population. Supposedly, Colonel Robert Gibson Johnson of Salem, New Jersey accomplished this feat by eating a basket (or bushel) on the courthouse steps in Salem in September 1820. Needless to say, a great deal of people who showed up were disappointed that the spectacle ended with Colonel Johnson unharmed (except maybe for an upset stomach). Obviously they didn't have much entertainment back then.

Tomatoes are a fruit (truly a berry) not a true vegetable, but we do consider them a vegetable and not a fruit. Let's suffice to say that the arguments for and against it being a fruit are enough to induce insanity. Perhaps one reason why we consider tomatoes vegetables is mostly due to a Supreme Court ruling called Nix vs. Hedden in 1893. In 1887, a new 10 percent tariff was levied on vegetables and not fruit. Tomatoes, it was claimed, were wrongly brought into this tariff act. Nix sued the port of New York and its tax collector Hedden since tomatoes were botanically classified as fruit and should have been exempt from the tariff.

Because the common uses of a tomato were those of a vegetable, Nix lost his case and was forced to pay the tariff. The ruling applied only within the case itself, not to the much more clear science of botany.

Picking a Variety

148

Picking what types of food producing plants and which varieties of each is a very personal choice, but it must be practical as well.

When you choose a variety of tomato do you pick a variety…

*that is resistant to blight or one that bears larger fruit?
*that has a short growing season or a long growing season?
*based on taste or acid content for canning?

Every variety has certain characteristics. Even more confusing yet is that some varieties grow well in certain types of soils or certain weather conditions.

These obstacles can be overcome. First of all, know your conditions and pick the appropriate plant varieties for that area. If you live in a cold climate, pick cold climate varieties. If you live in drought stricken areas, then choose a variety that uses little water.

The choices we are given are amazing! I can choose to grow short and fat carrots to better work with the high clay content of my soil. I can choose bush beans to help me mulch and to work with my narrow garden. If I chose pole beans I'd have to concern myself with the shadows they cast.

Seeds should be procured locally if at all possible. If it is not possible to procure the seeds locally then at least find out what varieties are grown locally. Local grown varieties have the advantage of natural selection. You see, if the tomato grew well enough to ripen and produce fruitful seeds, then it grew well enough to eat. Therefore, you can assume to some degree that local conditions (along with whatever inputs the grower gave) nurtured the plant to the end of a life cycle, thus ensuring survival of the lineage. In other words, the seeds will grow where they originated, as they hold the best genetic traits to ensure survival in those unique conditions.

When I talk of procuring seeds, I talk of a one-time activity for most plants. Further in this book, I'll tell you how to save your own seeds with many varieties of plants. This will push natural selection one step further. Seeds saved from your plants will be adapted to your soil and your microclimates and more importantly, nurturing habits.

It is ok to be somewhat reliant on other people for seeds, but if you don't have to be, then why would you?

Logically Choosing What to Grow

Many people choose the actual plant type based on taste or what is traditionally done. The prepared person must be able to choose things that they and their family will like to eat (possibly for a long time) as well as things that provide a return on the investment of the work. If a person spend 2000 calories growing food that will provide them 1999 calories they will eventually succumb. It might take a while and that assumes no other food sources.

When we look deeper, it isn't the food that keeps us alive, but the calories within. It may be difficult to tell, but most garden vegetables contain more than 80% water and then a good deal of the remaining 20% is tied up in dietary fiber that is basically indigestible material. Water will certainly help keep you alive and dietary fiber will keep you feeling full, but water can be more easily gathered elsewhere and dietary fiber fullness is an illusion.

Whatever is left over is generally calories in the form of mostly carbohydrates as well as what vitamins may be present. I don't discount the need for vitamins, but without calories you probably won't make it to the point of vitamin deficiency.

The simple fact is that some garden vegetables are simply better calorie stores than others. I'm also not saying that variety isn't good when it comes to macronutrients such as carbs, fat and protein. I'm not saying to avoid the crops that aren't heavy on calories, but I'm certainly saying that if you plan on surviving on the ones that aren't you may be in for a rude awakening.

As I mentioned above, one major goal of gardening in good times (or whatever times we are in) is the fact that gardening can save money. In no crop is that better illustrated than with greens such as lettuce and spinach. Unfortunately, it would be quite tough to thrive or even survive on these crops if your life hung in the balance. Lettuce contains upward of 95% water (even higher than other veggies) and nearly the balance in dietary fiber. A hundred grams of lettuce will only yield you about 13 calories. Spinach fares only slightly better at 23 calories.

Another crop that's always popular is the tomato. While I love tomatoes, I do understand that at 93% water, the outlook isn't great. In fact, tomatoes contain only 18 calories per 100 grams. Even though the vines get large and produce a lot, we have to look at the time+work:rewards ratio. It's just not worth it unless you plan to live on lycopene alone.

The Cucurbit family (cucumbers, melons, gourds, squash and pumpkin) is also heavy on the water, not yielding higher than 20 calories per 100 grams.

The Brassicas (Broccoli, cabbage, cauliflower, brussel sprouts) are slightly higher at up to 40 calories per 100 grams.

The Root crops continue up the scale with turnips at 21 and parsnips at 60!

Now that I've ruined everyone's favorite crops, what's left?

These are what I call the big three of the food crops. There's a reason why people have subsisted on these crops since basically ancient times. They simply work and work well.

Beans

In most of the world beans refer to the kind that are grown and dried, not the green bean type, although some varieties of the green type are quite nutritious.

Simply put, beans are one component of a complete protein diet (I'll get to the other one in a moment). An incomplete protein is simply one is deficient in all of the necessary amino acids to heal tissue and promote growth.

Beans are also easy to store. Once dry they store almost indefinitely if kept from pests. Diatomaceous earth (edible type) is the best additive to prevent pest incursions.

In addition, beans are pretty easy to grow. In healthy soil they make their own nitrogen. Being a legume means that they form root nodules filled with symbiotic bacteria known as rhizobia. These bacterial take a small amount of oxygen and sugars from the plant and help make usable nitrogen. When the plant dies, the nodules fall off, leaving nitrogen in the soil.

Beans will grow during most of the year when frost isn't a threat and, except for bean beetles, they have few enemies.

Grains

The next part of the complete protein diet is a little harder to grow. All continents with substantial human populations have had grains growing over a large portion at one time or another.

It's true though; grains are hard to grow. The fortunate thing is that there is such a variety that finding one that grows in your particular conditions is possible. For instance, rice likes warm flooded land while wheat likes cooler drier land. In addition there are the more exotic types of grain such as quinoa and amaranth. Corn is a good grain to grow as well. Just be prepared to feed it tons of nitrogen rich matter and water.

Like beans, grains are generally easy to store as well although they might be a little more susceptible to pests.

Potatoes

Though they add little to the protein game, there is little doubt that, for carbohydrates, potatoes rule.

Except for the French who refused to eat the dirty common food, potatoes were a staple across much of Europe for a long while. Despite the Potato Famine in Ireland (due to monoculture) they continued and continue to be an important crop.

The benefit of potatoes is that they grow in conditions that grain isn't always fond of. Moist cold conditions are no real problem for potatoes because the bulk of their energy stores are below ground. Though they fare less well in storage than the other two foods, it's not impossible to keep a batch as long as they stay in a cool root cellar.

It's always a good idea to hedge your bets and grow a variety of things. Being informed about the calorie contents of our favorite vegetables is never a bad thing. We need to know which we can depend on in hard times and which might leave us wanting.

Open-Pollinated, Heirloom or Hybrid

Open-Pollinated

Open-pollination is a term that is often used incorrectly when one is attempting to describe what they want to accomplish. Open-pollination simply refers to the fact that the pollination process was untouched by the hands of man (or woman). So long as the plants that produced the seeds were kept isolated from other varieties the seeds were produced "true to type".

True to type means you can trust the seed to produce the variety indicated and that variety is not a hybrid type. When a seed supplier indicates that seeds are OP (open-pollinated) they simply mean that if you buy Roma tomato seeds, you will get Roma plants that are a non-hybrid variety. So long as you keep the Roma plants somewhat isolated from your other tomato varieties in the field (tomatoes make perfect flowers which actually pollinate themselves in *most* cases), the seeds produced from your plants will be Roma tomato seeds.

Hybrids

A hybrid is simply a crossing of two distinct individual organisms. The degree of difference can vary wildly. It can run the spectrum from crossing a tiger and lion and making a liger all the way to a brown-eyed man and a blue-eyed woman. That being said it might surprise you what plants are hybrids that we actually count   as open-pollinated (OP).

Simply put, when I cross a plant with one characteristic trait with another with a different trait for the same characteristic there is a chance that I will get a hybrid.

Hybrids can be bred true to the point where the traits stabilize and will no longer be unreliable from one generation to the next due to mutation or cross-dominance. However, this is not a task for amateurs and definitely frustrating.

OP San Marzano (LH) / Hybrid Super Marzano (RH)

Shadetree Genetics

Traits

A trait is any characteristic of an organism or in our case--a plant. Some traits are more important than others. For instance, we care about disease resistance, size, hardiness, etc., but, there are other characteristics that we don't give two shakes about. In fact there are so many traits controlled by genetics that knowing them all or having a plant or organism with every trait purebred is nearly impossible.

Why is there just a chance? Well that all depends on the Alleles that carry through to the next generation and if the plant is diploid or not.

Genetics has some weird sounding terms, but the functions they describe are sometimes even weirder and very important to know.

The first one is Ploidy. Ploidy describes the number of chromosomes in an organism's cells. Haploid is a term for half of the material needed for a chromosome. My biology teachers used the mnemonic device half-ploid just in case you wondered how I remember that. Humans are diploid which means they contain cells with two haploid sets. For those I have already confused that means they have two sets of paired chromosomes. Some plants (estimated at a vague 30-80%) are polyploid. I don't even pretend to discuss that subject— it's just too complex.

Alleles are instructions for traits within the genes. Being that humans and some plants give two haploids they give two pieces of information about each trait.

So if I cross a tomato that makes red fruit with one that makes green fruit what happens? You can't really know unless you know the lineage of each offspring.

The funny thing about genetics and something that Gregor Mendel found out is that you actually have to do the crossing and then observe to determine genetic coding. This is completely paradoxical.

Mendel

Gregor Mendel was an Augustinian Monk in Central Europe in the late 1800's. He worked with pea plants to determine the laws of inheritance that formed our basic understanding of modern genetics.

Mendel worked with peas because the traits are pretty simple and it was easy to control pollination and to observe. One trait that Mendel picked was the color of the pea seed itself. He noticed that some varieties made yellow seeds and others green. So he decided to cross them. To his surprise he found the F1 (or first crossed hybrid generation) had entirely yellow seeds. Where did the green trait go?

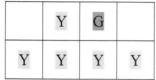

Table 1 – Y/G cross F1 Generation

He then forced self-pollination on the F1 generation. Lo and behold exactly 25% of the F2 offspring had green seeds.

Table 2 – Y/Y Self Pollination F2 Generation

The answer was clear, the green trait did not disappear it was merely masked.

Dominance

Dominance refers to the ability of certain genes to provide the visible apparent trait and masking of others. Mendel found that the yellow trait was dominant in the genes of the pea plant. All of the offspring in the F1 generation were in fact all hybrids in the same manner. They had a dominant yellow gene and a recessive green one. So in fact, superficially, Table 1 and 2 look correct, but in reality they look like this:

	YY	gg	
Yg	Yg	Yg	Yg

Table 1a – Y/G Cross F1 Generation w/Alleles

	Yg	Yg	
YY	Yg	Yg	gg

Table 2a – Y/Y Self Pollination F2 Generation

In the early 20th century, Reginald Punnett simplified this visibly by coming up with the concept of the Punnett square.

	Y	**Y**
g	Yg	Yg
g	Yg	Yg

Table 1b – Y/G Cross F1 Generation Punnett

Thus demonstrating the likelihood statistically of the potential outcome. The top and LH boxes represented the parents and each box inward (the combination of the top and LH boxes in that row and column) represented a 25% chance outcome. So, as you can see the F1 offspring had no possibility of being anything, but what I call "pure hybrids". This meaning that they are all alike, but all hybrids.

	Y	**g**
Y	YY	Yg
g	Yg	gg

Table 2b – Y/Y Self Pollination F2 Generation Punnett

So, as you can see from the F2 generation done the way that Mendel does, there is a 50% chance that the "pure hybrid" line will continue and another 25% chance each that the offspring will be purebred yellow or green.

This is why you cannot rely on hybrid plants that reproduce sexually—that is by passing on haploid chromosome pairs—to produce consistent results in the F2 generation. Or I should say you can rely on consistent results, but if you are looking for consistent traits you might as well forget it.

I mentioned that some Open-pollinated (OP) or Heirloom varieties of vegetables might be hybrids. This can be true only in the sense that the traits that are hybridized are not important or even recognizable in the offspring.

There is also the possibility of cross-dominance, which may occur when both allele traits are equally dominant. This could result in crossing a blue flowered parent and a red flowered parent and getting purple flowered offspring. Cross dominance hybrids can be bred out and bred true. The key is isolating the plants with the recessive gene if one is there and eliminating them from the genetic pool.

The only other way to use hybrids to get purebred stock eventually is to breed until mutations come about. This is tricky and could take thousands of offspring to accomplish if even possible.

Hybrid Vigor

This is a common term that is hard to actually quantify, but easy to observe. It is noted that in some hybrids, the F1 generation is particularly vigorous in growth, yield, and ability to resist disease, pests and other adverse conditions.

There are a few theories as to why this occurs, but nothing has been proven so far. The most likely one in my opinion is the dominance theory. The dominance theory essentially states that the F1 generation benefits from the effects of the dominant allele over the recessive one. To personify the genes, they get a confidence boost from winning out.

I'm not sure this theory has ever been documented, but another one I propose is what I call the Death Throe Theory. That is, the plants simply get a boost in the hopes that they live long enough to pass on some type of gene. Being superbly adapted to any condition in this stage in most cases, it makes sense for there to be some Darwinian mechanism that allows these superior traits to survive. Maybe it's a mechanism that promotes mutation in order for the plant to survive. It's sort of like a last gasp for survival.

Another theory of mine I coin the Nowhere Fast Theory. It states that since the hybrid population will decline in future generations it will never be able to out compete the plants vying for the same resources. Therefore, there is no real harm in the hybrid plant being the best for the generation or two it thrives. Essentially this is because the non-hybrids will always win out in the end.

Sterile Offspring

Unfortunately, the possibility of sterile offspring is often a myth that has been propagated wildly in the gardening community. There is a possibility that this could happen, but more likely you'd find that your hybrid offspring revert back to poor characteristics, which could lead to no produce, lack of growth, and other undesirable characteristics. It is all very dependent upon how the hybrid was constructed (the parents). The reason this myth comes up so frequently is because hybrids in the animal world such as mules (cross between donkey and horse) are most always sterile.

For most gardeners, having hybrid plants will pose no problem. They will enjoy the benefit of hybrid vigor for a time. However, for those intending to be more self-sufficient, hybrid plants are an unwanted diversion of resources that will never pan out in the long run. Simply put, they cost more and make seed saving a futile effort, thus increasing costs in both the short term and long term.

Regardless of your feelings toward hybrid plants it helps to know how they originate and why they function in the ways they do so you the gardener can make informed decisions regarding your garden inputs.

Heirloom

Heirloom simply refers to a plant type that has been passed down from generation to generation and can be expected to breed true to type. In other words, heirloom is a type of open-pollinated plant - one that has some history behind it. Personally I believe using subjective terms like this is detrimental to making informed decisions. What makes something heirloom? Does it take two generations or ten? I've even seen recently that some seed companies are calling hybrid seeds "Heirloom-style".

Seeds Conclusion

So, in summary, the self-sufficient gardener will avoid any seeds that are hybrid (F1). Despite all of the wonderful things that hybrids have been bred to accomplish, the seed stock from subsequent generations can be dubious in regard to production and desirability. Therefore, I can only recommend varieties of seeds that are clearly labeled as open-pollinated (OP).

In order to ensure the process cycle continues, when choosing seeds/stock/bulbs/tubers the process-oriented gardener:

- Chooses varieties that are known to grow well in the area and/or climate.
- Chooses OP seeds whenever possible to ensure production and ability to save seeds.
- Chooses varieties that fit the soil type of the garden location.
- Chooses varieties that match his/her nurturing habits.

- Doesn't reach by choosing varieties that may or may not thrive.

DON'T:

- Choose Hybrid seeds unless you are prepared to deal with the consequences of process interruption and input reliance.
- Choose varieties or stock that won't work with your conditions.
- Believe you can stabilize a hybrid easily.

Water

It would be easy for me to assume that all of my readers live in an area where water falls freely, exactly when needed and in the exactly appropriate amounts, but that would be unfair, irresponsible and just plain mean.

The good news is that water can be harvested, gathered, directed and captured.

Rainwater Harvesting

According to the New Mexico Office of the State Engineer, the elements of a successful rainwater harvesting system consist of **catchment, conveyance, storage, distribution and use** (or landscape). A filter can also be added if it is deemed necessary. What is most amazing is that these elements can be either natural or man-made.

A catchment is simply any area where rain concentrates or flows from easily. It is essentially a funnel area like rooftops, concrete walks or driveways. Soil areas can also be used as catchments, but the most successful catchments are ones that are as non-permeable as possible and preferably at a slope. That is a big reason why roofs make such good catchment areas.

The conveyance element is simply the way to move the water to the area for storage. The most common conveyance devices are the downspouts and gutters on roofs. Swales, which are shallow ditches dug into the landscape can also be used to convey, distribute and filter water directly for use, integrating several of the elements instead.

Storage devices that are commonly used are rain barrels, cisterns, tanks or holding ponds. Whenever possible, these storage devices should be covered to keep mosquitoes from taking up residence, laying eggs and harboring disease. Care must also be taken to keep children away from these as they sometimes present a drowning hazard. The conveyance device should hook up directly to the storage device. If the water flows directly into a berm, it can be used as a type of storage device as well, bypassing the distribution element completely.

Distribution can be as simple as hooking a faucet, valve and hose to a rain barrel and turning it on as needed. More complex systems such as drip irrigation hoses could be fabricated or bought and buried to provide a passive type of irrigation.

Lastly, the use or landscape area is the way the water is utilized by the plants and landscape. By creatively building berms and terraces you can slow down the outflow of water and allow it to be held by the soil so the plants can use it to their advantage.

Unconventional Water

It surprises people that there are ways to get water to plants without ever actually passively or actively dumping water onto the roots from either drip irrigation attached to a rain barrel, a soaker hose attached to a faucet or any other method which requires a reserve of water distributed in measured amounts.

In fact, the best water storage device is the soil itself. Good soil is like a giant sponge, able to retain water for amazing amounts of time. Thus, amending and feeding your soil will benefit you with water as well as nutrients.

Mulch

Mulch is absolutely the most overlooked garden accessory ever. If this was ever in doubt, just check the next five gardens you observe. The notion that gardens must be pretty places in complete order has done away with the functional elements of the garden. Form does not necessarily always follow function.

Mulch can take different forms and can be natural or man-made as well. The easiest, more reliant forms of mulch are natural however. The best two, in the opinion of the author, are leaf litter and lawn clippings.

Mulch acts as a shade cover directly over the roots of your plants and the surrounding soil—where they need water the most. The natural shade provided by the mulch blocks sunlight from entering and water vapors from leaving this vital area. Thus less water evaporates and fewer vapors escape, allowing the roots access to water longer than the surrounding bare ground.

Mulch also has other benefits beside water retention. I'll address those in subsequent chapters.

Water Summary

In summary, the process-oriented gardener does the following things to provide and retain water in the garden:

- Uses catchments and storage devices to concentrate, capture and hold rain to provide a steady source of water even through droughts.
- Uses existing or create new land features that divert and direct water to your garden.
- Uses existing or create new land features that hold water in your garden.
- Mulch your plants to slow the cycle of water evaporation.

Sunlight and Temperature

This necessity for growing seems to require little thought, but that is not entirely true. The gardener has a number of tools and methods to ensure the correct amount of sunlight and temperature reaches the garden to provide for optimal growth.

Orientation

The orientation of the garden must not be overlooked. Some of us count ourselves lucky to have a huge backyard with no obstructions to sunlight whatsoever. However, the author's suburban abode and country locale are both shaded in certain areas by manmade and natural objects (respectively).

Orientation can be as simple as just observing how the sun moves across the sky during the day. It isn't a daunting task. You could simply take a picture every hour or so and then compare. For instance, a long wall of my home faces a mostly southerly direction. This is a good thing. However, I have to be aware that the slight angle causes a shadow at the end of my garden. This isn't a problem really; more of an observation for which adjustments must be made. I will simply plant a shade happy crop in that little corner.

The funniest conversation I've had with my dear grandmother was regarding the sun.

"See the sun," she said. "I swear a few months ago, it sat lower in the sky. In fact, the shed blocked it out at this time of the day. I know, I've been watching it."

"That's right grandma," I said. "You aren't losing your mind."

That's my way of saying you don't need fancy equipment or even a compass to site your garden. My grandmother did it successfully for years by just simply observing.

The sun always follows an east to west path, but it does this across the southern sky (in the northern hemisphere). The sun never actually comes across directly overhead. Even at the sharpest angle in its travel (during summer solstice—June 21) it never reaches perpendicularity.

So, in summary, the self-sufficient gardener is aware of the path the sun travels in relation to obstacles on their property and the effect of that travel and plants accordingly. In some cases the shade may be a benefit and in some cases a burden.

Covers

The best artificial way to boost soil temperatures and concentrate sunlight in the garden setting is to use row covers. The three most common types of plant covers are row tunnels, cloches and floating row covers.

It's not terribly difficult to construct a row tunnel by bending sturdy material into half hoop shapes and inserting the ends in the ground on both sides of the row. Then the hoops are dressed with a clear or opaque plastic, which is pinned to the ground. The tunnel then is pierced in places to allow airflow. The tunnel acts as a small greenhouse, trapping heat and sunlight and preventing frost from falling on the plants.

Cloches are small bells made of different materials (sometimes glass) that protect individual plants and act as small, specific row tunnels.

Floating row covers are similar to row tunnels, but without support. These covers lay loosely over the plants in the row. While they do not trap a lot of heat and sunlight they do protect the plant

Crop researchers at WSU (Northwest Washington Research and Extension Center, Mt. Vernon) and OSU (Corvallis) have experimented with a number of crops under row covers in the Northwest. Their findings indicate that lettuce yields were increased up to 60% just by using the row covers. Earliness was also increased. And that was not an anomaly. They found that other crops benefitted in the same ways.

It may be hard to visualize, but more pounds of produce mean more food that is not bought through "the system". That's also less tax given to government. More importantly, it's fewer systems in which you'll find yourself dependent in an emergency. Thus, if methods of artificially warming the soil increase yields and result in earlier crops and prevent some types of pests then wouldn't it make sense to utilize them to their fullest?

Covers—Not Just for Raising Temps!

Covers can also be utilized in a different way. Some lettuce and leaf crops do better when the sun in some climates doesn't beat down so hard. A drop cloth raised above these plants could serve the purpose of dimming the sun down a bit to reduce scald. This will result in better produce.

Greenhouses and Coldframes

There is a little bit of confusion around about the difference between a coldframe and a greenhouse. Basically a greenhouse is larger and may be heated in some manner and may have mechanical controls. A coldframe is not heated; it's just meant to keep plants alive and growing in colder weather. A coldframe is a sort of intermediary step. Another big difference is that coldframes are usually used on existing ground, but greenhouses are used with plants in containers.

As a rule of self-sufficiency I can't endorse using an energy hungry greenhouse. They just aren't that sustainable or versatile. They require immense amounts of water and heat that just doesn't make sense. However, there are small models closer to a coldframe design that can be built cheaply that don't require a lot of outside energy and can help you get an early start on spring planting. There are several that can be built cheaply out of nothing more than pvc pipe and plastic. However, the big concern with these is the snow load during the winter so they will either have to be used in areas where there isn't much snow during winter or you might have problems.

When most people think of coldframes, they think of small boxes that are lifted over existing plants. These are usually more durable and made of wood frames with glass or plexiglass panels. Built at correct angles these are much more resistant to snowfall that a hoop type greenhouse.

The real challenges with greenhouses and cold frames are controlling the environment inside. This is really a closed space and disease can run rampant if you aren't careful. Also you have to get water to your crops and it may require running some type of irrigation system such as a drip hose if the space requires you to do so. It's also going to be hard to keep your hoses hooked up during freezing times when your faucets can crack. This may be a good time to hook things up to a rain collection barrel. That way you aren't paying expensive repair bills. Think about that before you make your final plans to set one of these up.

The closest I've come to solving most of these problems is by building my own greenhouse with these things in mind. I built it for very little money (about $250), out of treated lumber and greenhouse plastic that I purchased online. The size is 6 foot by 10 foot. The door is left open in varying degrees to control the temperature and I just simply bring water jugs in to keep the plants watered.

Building it was pretty straightforward. The first step was deciding on the site. For most people this might not be much of a question. You will have only a limited amount of room and the space simply IS the space. This might even have you questioning if a greenhouse is right for you. Well don't fret if you get only limited sun. Besides the sun you are also trying to keep the greenhouse warmer inside. Most people worry about getting a full 12 hours of sun. These people are too obsessive. Six hours is good, eight is best. Any more than that and you are just letting the sun evaporate your water away. Of course, the more sun in the winter gives you more heat, but also keep in mind that the more exposed your greenhouse is the less heat you lose to winds. You have to weigh these concerns.

If you live in the Northern Hemisphere (US) you will want to site the greenhouse with as much unobstructed southern sky view as possible. Again, I would not worry if you lose a few hours due to being blocked by a structure or tree. Once you pick a site though, it's a good idea to spend some time one day in the summer, and one in the winter, just hanging out there watching the path of the sun. In a wooded area take into account that any deciduous trees will be bare of leaves! Observe before you start buying stuff and cutting lumber. You'll be surprised by what you learn.

The next thing to take into account is level. The spot you picked must be accessible, but the more level it is the better. Otherwise be prepared to dig. You don't want your plants sliding off the shelves. If you can't find a level spot then don't fret, you will just have to dig a little. Is the ground easy to excavate? Most times you can dig it out with a shovel. If the ground is well packed or stony you may be renting equipment and that is not a good way to get started building a cheap greenhouse.

I mentioned access above, but it warrants more discussion. Keeping the greenhouse close to your dwelling is important because you are going to spend a lot of time there! Of course this is dictated by the other factors being met as well. The closest you can possibly put the greenhouse is directly adjacent to a dwelling or existing structure. This is GREAT for using the structure as a heat store and reflection of light, but be careful, if that wall isn't built well it may allow your heat to leak out. You also have to consider how you are going to seal the covering against this potentially uneven surface.

Once you have a spot picked you will need to layout the footprint. If your greenhouse is to be square then it's no big deal. If it is rectangular you will have to keep in mind that the long side should be the one facing south. That will give it the most sun exposure and thus the most light and heat.

The next step is gathering the materials. Here's the material list and costs:

All lumber is treated.

2 – 10 foot 4×4 ($16)

2 – 6 foot 4×4 ($12)

~31 – 8 foot 2×4 ($60)

7 – 10 foot 2×4 ($20)

4 – 3/8″ dia, 5″ long carriage bolts and washers ($5)

A roll of black plastic 6mil ($10)

Coated sinker nails ($10)

Green-tek plastic ($110)

Assorted firring strips (I ripped these from other lumber I had).

Stanley hinge package ($7)

3 – 8 foot 2×2 ($9)

I've found that the greenhouse is great and requires little control during the early spring to start seeds. It helps get them into the ground quicker and easier.

Sunlight and Temperature Summary

In summary, to properly manage the inputs of sunlight and temperature, the process-oriented gardener:

- Observes the way the sunlight and shadows move across the garden.
- Takes advantage of the ways sunlight and shadows move across the garden.
- Utilizes artificial means of capturing heat and light to increase yields and lengthen the growing season.

Growing Medium and Nutrients

Am I talking about soil? Yes and no. Soil is in my opinion the best at accomplishing this input because it takes care of both. However, any good hydroponic or aquaponic grower will tell you that you can grow a plant in a sterile medium such as lava rock and flush it with nutrient rich water.

I've tried the hydroponic approach and it either requires a lot of human input or a lot of reliance on systems. As such, I did not find it to be a good way to produce food. So for the purposes of this discussion, we'll leave the growing medium and the nutrient to the soil.

Soil Types

There are six characteristics to soil and these can actually be mixed in combinations. However, when talking about a soil, usually the major characteristics best describes it. The six characteristics are clay, peat, silt, sand, chalk and loam.

Clay soil is very heavy and clumps together easily. As a kid this soil used to stick to our shoes and stain anything we stepped on. It dries very hard and is difficult to cultivate. Clay retains water extremely well. The positive aspect of clay soil is that it will hold nutrients due to its tight structure and it will not let them go. Clay soil is dark, either in reds or browns. Plants from the Brassica family (such as cauliflower and broccoli) grow well in clay soil, but root crops absolutely do not due to difficulty in penetrating the hard and compact soil.

Peat soil is very absorbent, picking up water and holding it well. It also holds nutrients very well as it is mostly composed of decomposing matter. The color is usually dark brown or grey.

Silt is similar to sandy soil, but silt is actually finer than sand. Unlike sand however, silt will hold moisture and nutrients better. Silt is light colored like sand, but will be less "gritty".

Sandy soil is usually very dry and drains well—perhaps too well. It has the typical grainy feel and these grains are actually larger than they seem, causing gaps between each other. This is why the water drains so well. This is a difficult type of soil. The particles allow no moisture to be retained and all the nutrients wash away with the moisture. Sandy soil is normally very light colored tan or almost white. This soil is great for any vegetables that are harvested for their roots, such as carrots, turnips or radishes. These plants are able to work their way between the large sand particles as they grow deeper.

Chalky soil is very alkaline and also does not hold nutrients well. In fact the ingredient you add to soil to make it more alkaline is lime, which is chalky. Chalky soil is light in color—almost white.

Loamy soil is very nutrient rich soil. It is the perfect balance to hold moisture and nutrients, but not too much moisture. This is due to the fact that loam soil is actually a combination of equal amounts of sand and silt plus some clay. It is this combination that allows the soil to hold nutrients so well and to hold just enough water and drain the rest away.

What Plants Need

Plants don't always get what they want, but they do have ways of getting what they need. The innate intelligence in plants is quite remarkable. Plant roots actually exude many different substances. Sugars are exuded, for instance, to attract microbes, acids to dissolve minerals and inorganic ions to change the soil PH. They do all of this because of internal signals that tell the plant what it needs.

I talk a little bit below about legumes and their mutualistic relationship with soil bacteria used to create usable nitrogen, but there are other mutually beneficial plant-microbe relationships. Mycorhizal fungi are also attracted by plant root exudates and will form a net near and around the plant roots, effectively extending the roots range at a low cost of energy (simple sugar exudates). The extra range of the roots allows the plant to take up more nutrients and water.

Organic acids from plant roots help dissolve calcium, aluminum, iron, zinc and other inaccessible minerals. These minerals all play a vital role in plant health. For one, if your tomato plants don't get enough calcium they won't be able to close guard cells in the fruit against ethylene and therefore will get ripe too quickly and rot. This condition is commonly called blossom end rot.

Compost

Unequivocally, the best way to add nutrients and minerals to your soil is to add compost. Compost is easy to make, it works well and it will save you money on fertilizer. It also cuts down on the amount of landfill waste a family produces.

Compost is essentially broken down organic matter. The organic matter is provided by you and can be lawn clippings, food waste, leaf litter or even last season's plantings. The organic matter breaks down through heat and microbial activity. Eating the plant matter nourishes the microbes. The waste they produce is the compost. The heat of the compost breaks down and kills harmful fungi, bacteria and sometimes viruses. It will also kill the seeds from weeds or other "pest" vegetation.

Compost is simple to make for free, but buying a few simple tools can lead to dramatic improvements in the results.

Crop Rotation

Rotating the crops you grow in certain sections of your garden is a must. Some plants are nutrient hungry and will strip your soil bare of any nutrients and minerals. These minerals can be replaced somewhat through compost, but it's better if you rotate crops that are nutrient takers with nutrient makers ever so often. This is the reason why corn farmers rotate in soybeans at regular intervals.

Soybeans and more common garden legumes (from the family Fabaceae), such as peas and beans, actually help add nitrogen back to the soil through nitrogen fixation. This is but one

175

method (and a highly effective one) of getting the nitrogen cycle started within your soil.

The legume's roots release compounds called flavonoids. The rhizobia detect the flavonoids and release their own secretions called nod factors. The nod factors cause certain parts of the roots of the legume to slightly deform, crack or otherwise become susceptible to infection of the roots and subsequently the nodules by the rhizobia. Don't fret, this is a good infection. The plant gives the rhizobia adequate oxygen and food and in turn the rhizobia give the plant nitrogen which allows it to better compete against the other plants nearby.

Most nitrogen is in an unusable gaseous form, but these bacteria make nitrates from nitrogen.

After the legume dies, the nodules separate, spilling nitrogen into the soil.

The knowledgeable gardener can take advantage of this fact by rotating protein rich, nitrogen hungry plants into places where legumes have grown and died.

Cover Crops

Many gardeners have learned to take advantage of this cycle outside the normal course of vegetable gardening by using cover crops. Cover crops are very commonly legumes of the family I described previously, but these aren't grown for food. Common cover crops are clover, buckwheat, alfalfa and fava beans. There is such a variety of cover crops that they can be started during various seasons and can last different durations.

After a certain amount of time has elapsed they can be chopped and dropped. This use is called green manure because you are essentially planting a natural fertilizer in your garden.

Cover crops serve other purposes with the soil other than providing nutrients. They help retain topsoil which otherwise might blow away or wash away during the heavy winds and precipitation of the fall and winter. They also help suppress the growth of weeds.

Tilling

The first thing that many gardeners do is to bring the garden tiller out of the garage. Tilling your soil is such a harmful activity. If more gardeners were aware of this fact, the tiller industry would go belly-up in no time. If you will, think back to well before there were plows and tillers and metal tools on earth. Plants thrived for millions of years and even survived through the extinctions that killed out many other land dwelling things. Is tearing up the soil really going to help our ventures?

Even the big agricultural business farmers learned their lessons after the dust bowl and years of crop failure. It is a shame that some gardeners still have not caught on.

Tilling the soil disturbs the natural balance that plants rely upon. Soil stratifies. Certain minerals, chemicals and compounds move to certain layers. Plants know instinctively how to find those layers and utilize them. Done properly you can grow a blueberry bush (which likes acidic soil) a few rows down from a cabbage plant (which requires alkaline soil). The roots of the plant can find the layer it wants, and occupy that layer, taking advantage of the windfall. When these layers are tossed together like a salad, every inch has a little of everything, but nothing is concentrated. It would be like you going to grocery store and finding that soups, bread, deli, condiments, snack food and frozen foods all occupied the same aisle and were mixed within. You'd be there for days and still wouldn't get what you needed.

In addition, tilling also breaks the crust of the dirt and the root structure of weeds. While this doesn't sound like a bad thing, it really is. The next time a heavy rain comes, your valuable topsoil will wash away like a memory.

Chemical Fertilizers

I'd be a hypocrite if I didn't recognize the fact that many of us would not be here today were it not for chemical fertilizers. The three letters NPK represent three major plant requirements. Nitrogen (N), Phosphorus (P) and Potassium (K). Unfortunately, it also represents mankind's attempt to manipulate nature into doing what we want and not what it is designed to do.

The combination of endless tilling and chemical fertilizers is turning much of our farmland into deserts, not to mention effects on the oceans and the political repercussions of using petroleum to feed our population. That's right; every calorie eaten today by an American represents a net loss of over eight calories. Those eight lost calories were provided by cheap, but finite fossil fuels.

Chemical fertilizers have no place in the home garden. Dousing your plants with chemical fertilizers may have the effect of boosting plant growth for several seasons. However, I believe most people do it to feel "in control" and to exercise our "dominance over nature". However, chemical fertilizers will kill off soil microbes, fungi and give you the impression your garden is doing well when it fact the chemicals are slowing killing the soil-what the plants need to survive.

Square Foot Method/Raised Beds

Pioneered by Mel Bartholemew, the square foot method is brilliant – if you don't have any land to use for planting. By that, I mean if you live on a mountainside and your lawn is a giant piece of granite or if you live on Manhattan Island and you have a rooftop for a garden.

In other words, people who have no actual soil on their property could benefit from this method. However, there is a growing contingent that believes it is best to spend money on lumber to construct a large garden container. They then believe it best to buy a mix of ingredients to form their own "soil". Then, many people use an undue amount of space planting large plants like tomatoes.

First, this is a huge waste of money if you have soil that can be planted. You'd be better off amending the soil you have in the specific area rather than building a 4-foot square bed for one tomato plant. Essentially you are bringing inputs into the process that doesn't really need to be there.

Secondly, this garden is to an actual ecosystem what a zoo is to the African Savannah. The plants are extremely pampered and produce wimpy genetics for future seed stock.

In addition, I've found that the grid patterns induce people into thinking about individual plants and plantings rather than the relationships that work so much better within nature and consequently-the garden. For instance, carrots work so much better with tomatoes when planted closely. The carrots loosen the soil and the tomatoes take advantage of that. Plus the tomatoes keep away some carrot pests. By confining each of these plantings to their own specific grid, we limit the benefits they can convey. To use a bad analogy, there is a reason you and your spouse don't have separate beds (or maybe you do and there's a reason for that!).

However for those inclined to do this, I'll tell you a little about it. I'll also describe further in this book how to make beds from not only purchased material, but from salvaged material as well as material that may already be on your property.

With this method, you simply make beds that are dimensioned to foot increments (2'x 6', 1' x 8', 2'x 2' and so on) and rope each "square" off to create sections. Each section ideally grows a different crop. This method embraces polyculture and best use of space.

Making the Most of Space

Spacing of plantings (seeds and starts) can generally be deduced from the seed packets. It goes without saying that I don't completely trust them though, but don't worry, I won't leave you hanging without some solutions.

From reading seed packets, it is clear that the seed producers are not students of geometry and physics. Otherwise, we would not read about just seed and row spacing, but would instead read about heights, shading and succession as well. These people more often than not think in flat space-in two dimensions instead of four, and in a set moment in time.

For the gardener, the challenge frequently is how to break away from these accepted norms and develop our own ways of thinking. So we have to think about how to challenge ourselves. For many gardeners with enough of everything (including money and time) failure is ok and no extreme is too drastic to overlook. If a pound of lettuce costs fifteen bucks from the garden, it was still worth it right?

I found my challenge in the spring of 2009. I had lived on land holdings as large as 100 acres and down to less than one acre. Finally in 2009 I realized that in the process of upsizing houses we had downsized usable land. My previous gardens that were limited only by how much time and money I could spend had shrunk to a still very usable twenty by eighty foot patch of dirt. This has led me to be more creative in how I think about space and time in the garden setting.

Surface

These are the two basic dimensions when planning a garden, but as I've alluded, they are not the only ones. It is true that in order to plant a garden you have to lay out the general footprint for each plant or plantings, but this is the most basic way of thinking.

Like a typical man who can't follow directions I assume the words on a seed packet to be mere guidelines. I like to crowd my plants a bit and trial and error has taught me what varieties of what types of plants will allow for this and which will punish me overall for attempting such things. By crowding things a bit, however, you will find that the plants themselves begin to block out a lot of the weeds and as the roots intertwine ever so slightly, they support each other.

Generally I start out by reducing spacing requirements by about 10%. For example, corn that requires 9 inches of spacing I will usually knock down to 8 inches roughly. I have found that some varieties of corn can be spaced at 6 inches. It is important to read up on the varieties prior to purchasing the seeds. If one's garden is restrictive in size then one must also be equally restrictive when choosing plantings.

The most difficult plants for a gardener with little space are the vine type plants from mostly the cucurbit family of plants. These plants are highly productive, but are also very space hungry. They spread like wild, taking up valuable garden space. What must be understood though, is that the plant's root system doesn't spread equal to the vine. Therefore, the vine spread is not wasted space as long as you grow plants that the vines can't shade out.

That brings us to our next dimension.

Up

Here's where a gardener with little space has got to think in multiple dimensions first. Some plants utilize upward growing space very well while some stretch out like a greedy spouse who won't share the bed. By intermixing these plantings we can utilize both spaces very well.

The Native Americans utilized this characteristic to absolute perfection with "Three Sisters" gardens. In these gardens they planted corn to utilize the upward growing space. Three sisters gardening is so effective and widely known that it is a cliché at this point.

I divide plants that utilize upward growing space into two groups: those that do not need support such as corn and those that do need support such as pole beans. When these plants work together like corn and beans do in the Three Sisters Garden, it really is a beautiful thing. One must understand why it works though; that is the key. The beans get support from the corn, but the corn gets nitrogen from the bean roots. If the equation becomes too imbalanced, then the relationship will fall apart.

Some gardeners will grow "up" plants that require support such as cucumbers. In this gardener's opinion, that is a waste. Cucumbers grow such large leaves that they shade out the ground below quite well. Unless you need this shade, these type of plants are best left growing on the ground where they can do their work as a living much. I leave the upward supported growing spaces for plants with small leaves such as pole beans and peas. They shade less and leave more ground space available for planting. Sometimes this is simply not feasible. Fortunately, most of the plants we are told will not thrive under a small amount of shade do very well when managed properly (cucurbits mostly).

My favorite plant lately to lessen the shade effect is okra. Okra grows nearly straight up on a stalk that produces very few leaves and keeps the edible parts very close to the center of the stalk. If corn is a great upward growing plant that makes some shade, okra is the contrasting one as it makes very little shade with its leaves close to the stalk.

In order to produce a plant that rises above all others, the root systems of corn and okra have adapted to grow deep and fairly wide. The spread usually grows at a downward angle in an umbrella shape. Therefore, the ground a bit further out from the tall plant is mostly unoccupied by roots.

And that takes us to our next dimension.

Down

This one escapes many a gardener's notice because let's face it, we don't see downward growth.

Obviously the best way to utilize downward growth is to plant root crops. Root crops are great because most provide edible greens above ground and delicious roots below. They are also compact, making them perfect to utilize smaller spaces.

The best approach to radical thinking with down growing space is to know the depths of rooting of your plantings. Many plant recommended spacings are to allow roots to move freely and not to crowd the next root system and steal nutrients and water. If you know, for example, that corn roots grow down several feet and out at slight angles (I told you above), you can utilize the small space above the root growth between plants with a shorter root crop or lettuce, which root shallow and don't mind a bit of shade.

Lettuce and some of the root crops are quick growers that do best in cooler times (unless you plant some shade like corn first). That leads us to our next dimension.

Time

Planting within time constraints is commonly called succession planting, but thinking of it as simply succession planting is very limiting. For example, some plants don't do well when following others despite the fact that their growing seasons are separated.

By knowing the nature of certain plants and using this to our advantage we can harness their power for our own good and for that of our garden. It is helpful to know, for example, that root crops like radishes, carrots and parsnips help to loosen the garden soil. Legumes like peas and beans will bring atmospheric nitrogen into the soil. Contrastingly, it is helpful to know that corn is a nitrogen hog, which is why farmers rotate fields in a pattern of soy-corn-soy-corn. Therefore your sweet corn should follow and be followed by peas or beans.

Planting in the dimension of time takes a lot of practice and a lot of luck as well. My efforts this year caused a bit of nervousness on my part. I found a few small open spaces in and just outside my pea patch and I promptly placed a few pumpkin seeds in the dirt at these areas. My theory was that the nitrogen nodules created by the peas would greatly benefit the growth of the pumpkins and in June when the peas were done, I could break them off at the ground and let the pumpkins run wild.

Luckily I only lost one of my pumpkin plants. There were a few factors that caused my nervousness and that loss. First of all, I planted the pumpkin plants a little too early. They grew faster (due to the nitrogen) than my pea plants expired. A row of pea plants fell over on top of the one pumpkin plant, destroying it. One other pumpkin got a little leggy, but is thriving now that the peas are gone. The second problem is obvious; I planted the pumpkins a little too close. Luckily, failure in the garden leads to learning, not starvation (in my case).

The point is that this, more than any other aspect in this article, requires a lot of practice and first hand intimate knowledge of the plants you are using. The knowledge that the peas would help with the nitrogen was useful to me, but I overestimated the amount of nitrogen they would set and which direction they would flop when the wind blew.

Planting a Three Sisters Garden will give the gardener a general idea of how to plant in space and time, but it is only one way of doing so. By properly utilizing all of the space in our garden and planting at the appropriate times we can utilize the most important aspect many gardeners currently have— planting area.

Up	Up (Support)	Down	Surface
Corn	Pole Beans	Carrots	Cucumbers
Okra	Peas	Radishes	Melons
Tomato		Turnips	Pumpkins
		Onion	Squash

Very Early	Early	Mid	Late
Peas	Root Crops	Beans	Tomato
Lettuce/Greens		Corn	Pepper
Brassicas			Eggplant

Growing Medium and Nutrient Summary

In summary, to ensure what comes out of the soil goes back in, the process-oriented gardener's dirt:

- Is amended through natural and sustainable means such as cover crops and compost.
- Is never tilled, only slightly broken or mulched over and planted.
- Is protected from erosion by cover crops or mulch or simply letting it grow over a bit.
- Benefits through rotation of crops including fabaceae legumes that release nitrogen.
- Is a known quantity.
- Is utilized fully.

Equipment, Projects and Tools

There's a lot to be said for minimalism, but minimalism for no good reason is useless.

When I set about making my garden as self-sufficient as possible and podcasting about it on my show, The Self-Sufficient Gardener, I had dreams of needing nothing and doing everything for myself. I still follow that philosophy, but I've also found that a balance can be struck. In simpler terms, sometimes one step back gets me two steps ahead.

I've found that completing small building projects for the garden is the best example of that philosophy. Sure you will have to buy a bit of materials (not everyone can make everything), but in the long term you will find that the investment in materials will save you much more money in the long run. In addition, the result of such projects can last years and the lesson of building a project will stick with you forever. Who knows, over time you might find ways to do it even better.

Garden Beds

The embodiment of projects to gain self-sufficiency has to be the garden bed. Some people have plenty of space for a garden and with a little work can dig out a bed for plenty of plants. However, some people find that their suburban lot is mostly concrete or lawn. For some people, the best approach is to build garden beds. While I don't advocate hauling in dirt to fill the beds (and especially not to replenish the soil!) I can see where doing it one time wouldn't hurt self-sufficiency in the long run.

The garden bed is pretty simple; it's just a box with an open top and bottom. Because of this, it's a great place to begin honing one's carpentry skills. The dimensions can vary, but they should never be wider than four feet (for reaching purposes) and never any shallower than eight inches (to hold enough soil depth). The length can really vary depending on your space and other requirements.

The simplest solution is to go to the local hardware store and buy a couple of treated 2x8 planks. Many people have a problem with using treated lumber. Today's process is much less hazardous than it was in the past. However, I recognize that concern and if it is an overriding consideration then one can always purchase untreated boards. Just be aware that they will have to be replaced more frequently. This way will cost less than twenty dollars (depending on size and options) for materials.

The boards are then cut to length (you can have this done in most stores for a nominal fee). Pilot holes are drilled and the boards are screwed together with 2-3 screws per joint. Some people (myself included) like to put a corner board on the inside and screw that one in place as well. It makes the structure sturdier. That's all there really is to it. Fill it with soil and plant.

The less simple approach and one that I have taken in my suburban lot is to build the beds out of pallet wood. Pallets can be had for free and if you are even clever enough, you can salvage the nails making the beds virtually cost free. The bad part is that the pallets are rarely treated so they may need constant replacement (or sealing). In addition, the wood is usually not to the dimensions you need. However, once you find ways to work around these considerations you will find much pleasure from making these beds from pallet wood that would simply take up landfill space.

An even simpler approach is to harvest a few cedar trees, split long logs into two and use the halves for garden bed borders. These may have to be staked into place, but they make some fantastic looking beds and are cheap and very self-sufficient and sustainable.

Cold Frames

Cold Frames add to your self-sufficiency by letting you get a jump on the growing season and helping you harden off difficult plants in the spring. This jump can get you more food, quicker and curb failure to a great degree. I spoke about this earlier in regards to temperature, but it warrants mentioning again here as wise garden equipment.

I found that making a cold frame to be slightly more difficult than a raised bed, but with a little persistence and small adjustments I was able to have a working cold frame for a very small investment.

Of course the easiest route is to buy a cold frame, but just pretend I never wrote that. You'll find that the cost is so prohibitive you will pour blood sweat and tears into making one just to avoid the price.

A middle-ground method is to find the plans on the Internet, purchase lumber and fasteners and build one. However, because they are typically small, I found that using pallet wood again was a wise choice.

The method of construction is not tough. Again you are building a box with an open top and bottom. Mine is two feet by four feet and about 2 feet tall. I built mine with an angle to the top to capture the sun, but you could avoid that if you wanted to. It will just reduce the effectiveness a bit. I feel that the angle is important enough to add. The angle was the toughest part, but I wanted to track the angle of the sun, as it is lower in the spring.

After I built the box I simply built a small 2x4 (salvaged) lumber frame around the top perimeter. I stapled 3mil PVC plastic over the top, screwed on stops for the top around the perimeter and I was done.

Luckily I had all material on hand. If I had to purchase all of the materials, it would have set me back an estimated twenty five to thirty dollars.

The cheapest, easiest, and perhaps most sane method is to build a box out of straw or hay bales and place a salvaged piece of plexiglass, plastic film or glass over the top and secure it in place. This method is probably just as effective and cheaper. As a side benefit, the straw becomes mulch later on in the spring, once the coldframe is not needed. As a drawback, it's hard to replicate an angle.

Rain Barrel

If you have city water, it's hard to emphasize the importance of a self-sufficient water supply as city water is just so dang convenient. However, it is not cheap for most of us and it is definitely not foolproof. Before I made the choice to do things in a more self-sufficient manner, I could watch my water bill skyrocket June through September of the year. It was for these reasons that I decided to install a rain barrel.

The most expensive, but easiest method is to simply buy a kit. A few well-known companies sell complete kits at the big box home stores for less than one hundred dollars. These kits look nice and work well. They are, for the most part, easy to install and use.

However, I just can't make myself spend that much money. I made the decision to build my own and I was glad I did. It taught me a few things about the process and allowed me to customize the project to my needs.

I started off by purchasing a 55-gallon food grade barrel. These barrels have two screw-in plugs at the top. In each plug there is a separate knockout plug with another threaded portion. Some people choose to use the smaller threaded hole, but it is just as easy to remove one cap completely and use the large hole.

Once you have determined which route you want to use, you simply bring the cap to the hardware store and set about finding the right fittings. It might take a few trips and some trial and error, but with a little planning and luck you can build the setup you need depending on the flow rate, height, and water outputs you want. Simply add a diverter or direct pipe in your downspout and you are ready to go for anywhere between thirty and 50 dollars.

Composters

If you aren't going to purchase chemical fertilizers (and you shouldn't!) there are only a few choices to get nutrients back into your garden soil. The obvious choice is through adding soil amendments in the form of compost.

There are tons of expensive compost systems that you can purchase, but they are prohibitively expensive. I've tried the compost tumbler and even built one, but trust me, nothing composts as well as a stack that maintains direct contact with the ground and elements.

A good system can be built for less than thirty dollars; much less if you make good use of materials like pallets or other scrap wood sources.

The concept is simple. Build a small cage with mesh or wooden sides that can hold all of your green and brown matter. One panel or more should be easy to remove or open so you can both turn your compost periodically or get it out when it is done. More than one cage will allow you to rotate half done compost and start a new batch. This systematic approach will allow you to make multiple batches if you have the matter to add.

Another compost system that people rarely talk about is a vermicomposting setup. These are extremely easy to make and require a ten dollar or so investment in two 10-20 gallon plastic totes (the kind you can get at a big box store) and a dozen or so red wriggler redworms (found at most bait shops).

One tote you will leave unaltered. The other tote will require you to drill in plenty of holes in the bottom (for moisture drainage) as well as holes on the sides and in the lid. Stack the perforated tote into the non-perforated one. Make a bed of shredded newspapers, toss in a handful of garden soil (for microbes), the worms and then more shredded newspaper and some kitchen waste (no meats, cheeses or processed food).

The tote on the bottom will catch a rich liquid known as "worm tea". Dilute it and it is some of the best fertilizer known to man.

This project really is foolproof. If you notice too much moisture, simply punch more holes. Keep the bin somewhere between 55 and 75 degrees F and your worms will keep you supplied with as much fertilizer as they can make.

There are many projects that can make a gardener and his/her garden more self-sufficient. For the beginner, tackling a greenhouse or a drip irrigation system may seem a little overwhelming. Taking on these smaller projects will build confidence and lay the groundwork for a sustainable garden. The result is a sustainable gardener.

Tools

As far as tools go, I keep a very small selection of durable tools that I rely on to do almost all of my gardening tasks. I talk about a few below that I use for starting seeds both indoors and outdoors. Those are specialty tools.

As far as general tools, I use a cheap rake. It gets fair use, but generally I'm pretty easy on rakes. On the other hand, I can break a garden hoe in less than a season. The truth is that they are made so poorly now days that they are virtually disposable, but at $20 or so they don't feel that way. So I spend a little more money to get a quality garden hoe with some heft and durable materials.

A good garden trowel is also a necessity. I've seen cheap plastic ones, but I prefer a nice stainless model with some substantial weight.

Process

The next step in the process is the actual process itself. That may sound strange or weird, but the inputs are supplies are part of the process whole, but they only make up the setup for the process. In other words they are the things you need to get the job done. The process is the list of actual steps needed to get the job done.

Starting Seeds

If you need proof of how daunting some people consider this first process step, simply look at the started plant sections at any of the big box stores. The method of doing this is not terribly hard, but you will lose plants and you will have to pay close attention to what you are doing. I like to break things down in a when, where and how type of format. I'll even let you know the reasons why when it's applicable.

Where to Start

The first thing you have to decide about starting seeds is where to start them. I don't mean where in the garden or where in your house, although that is of sub-importance. I mean do you start them indoors or outdoors? Some seeds almost certainly need a jump on the growing season due to their subtropical natures. Tomatoes, peppers, eggplants and some herbs are good examples.

Conversely, some seeds will not transplant well even if they needed a jump on the season. Examples of this type are corn, beans, peas and some other grains and legumes.

Then there are the plants that work both ways such as cucurbits (melons, cucumbers, etc.).

When it doesn't matter and no major advantage is gained by starting indoors early I always err on the side of starting seeds directly into the ground. You will find less opportunity for mistakes and transplant shock if you just plant directly into the garden.

Indoors

Starting seeds indoors requires the same inputs as I listed above except you don't need nutrients immediately on the plant. The seed germ contains quite a bit of nutrients (that's why we eat so many seeds as food) and the seedling won't need a lot of nutrients until it gets some size.

You will find that most inputs must be replicated in some artificial manner indoors.

- Growing medium – pots with seed starting mix (not potting soil and not garden soil).
- Sunlight – fluorescent grow lights.
- Water – a mist bottle and water as needed.
- Temperature – household thermostat or artificial heat source.

Though we are talking about sustainable methods you will have to break a few rules by relying on electricity and store bought materials here. This is one of the few places I allow myself to break the rules because reliance here, reduces dependence later.

If you had to, you can get by without these things. Garden soil can be sterilized by baking it in the oven. Sunlight can be had at a south-facing window. Water is always available free as rain. Most houses are temperature controlled. If you had to, you could do this with wood heat or passive solar.

For growing medium I buy a seed starting mix from the store. These have no chemical fertilizers though they might have some derived elements that are naturally harvested such as lime or other ingredients. For pots I use disposable cups that I save throughout the year or simply buy some of the peat pots at the store. Peat pellets are also a great way to start seeds, but they outgrow them quickly and will need to be moved to a larger pot.

For those adventurous types you can always use a soil blocker. A soil blocker is simply a mould that can be used to press soil into compact cubes that will hold together and allow the seedling's roots to penetrate. These are great since they reduce transplant shock and the amount of materials you need to do this activity.

Some people plant scattered seed in a large flat and "prick out" or remove the individual seedlings and place them into pots or soil blocks. This must be done very gingerly with a small spoon or toothpick. Personally, I have no finesse so I don't do this, opting to waste a few seeds by planting two per pot.

Outdoors

Starting seeds outdoors is infinitely easier. However it is a little bit more unpredictable. Here's the problem, indoors you can control temperature, light and water. Outdoors you have much less control. Early spring monsoons, heat waves, cold waves, freak frosts and overly sunny days are just some of the things you will have to deal with. The worst conditions though are weather swings. Three days of rain and then two weeks of drought or two days of 60F plus and then a week of freezing temperatures can definitely set you back.

When to Start

Indoors

Knowing when to start your seeds indoors is simply a matter of counting backwards on a calendar. If your average last frost date is May 1 and tomatoes should be started 6 weeks before planting and can be planted anytime after that date then you just count backward to March 27.

Outdoors

Most seed packets will give you a general idea of when the best planting times are to get your seeds in the ground. However, as I stated before, Mother Nature can be fickle at best (see phenology below).

To deal with outdoor inconsistency it is necessary to be adaptable, observant and clever. You also have to know your plants and the proper germination temperatures. Once the temperatures outside match (and can be confirmed to match based on Weather.com outlooks for the next 10 days) then you can be assured that your planting will be at least some degree more successful than if you had simply "winged it".

For reference, here is a chart that describes best germination temperatures.

Phenology

As I've said before, I'm notoriously distrustful of the planting dates on most seed packets. I also only give cursory consideration to planting zone maps. I also don't like clothing that states: "One size fits all (or most)". In other words I think broad-spectrum applications of any rule or theory should only be used as a general guideline.

What supplements those general guidelines so one can form a more specific dates for garden events?

Having been raised in the country where farmers failed or succeeded by the dates they planted crops we used Phenology. Of course, at the time, we just called it "folk wisdom". Phenology, in basic terms, is the study of the correlation between events in nature that are dependent upon climate and weather.

Phenology is derived (like so many words) from the Greek word Phaino, which means "to appear" or "to show". Therefore the textbook definition of phenology is the study of appearances of natural events. Phenology is not a new practice, nor is it relegated to any one continent or people. The first writing referring to phenology was written in China in 974BC. The Japanese have been tracking the dates of cherry blossoms for around 1200 years. Native Americans and most early agrarian cultures learned their own phonological practices.

In more modern times, great naturalists such as Carolus Linnaeus, Henry Thoreau, and Aldo Leopold all studied phenology. However, it seems as more people have moved away from the country and into the cities this practice is quickly fading. This really is a shame since knowing how to read the signs is so very valuable.

There are two ways that phenology can be put to practical use. The first way is a general way and the second is a specific way.

The general way is by learning the natural correlations that exist in nature nearly regardless of location. These indicators are all based upon relative events. A few very basic lists follow.

Indicators of appropriate planting times:

- Plant peas when forsythia or daffodil blooms (or when you hear peeper frogs).

- Plant potatoes when the first dandelion blooms.

- Plant beets, carrots, cole crops, lettuce and spinach when lilac is in first leaf.

- Plant corn when oak leaves are the size of a squirrel's ear.

- Plant bean, cucumber, and squash seeds when lilac is in full bloom.

- Plant tomatoes when lily-of-the-valley plants are in full bloom.

- Transplant eggplant, melons, and peppers when irises bloom.

Indicators of pest activity:

- When chicory flowers open, be on the lookout for squash vine borer moths.

- Grasshopper eggs hatch at about the time the common purple lilac blooms.

- Japanese beetles often arrive when morning glory vines begin to climb.

- Mexican Bean Beetles appear when foxgloves flower.

Indicators of rain/weather:

- Tree leaves turn up.

- Toads appear in large numbers.

- Rocks seem to sweat.

- Red sky at morning, sailors take warning, Red sky at night, sailor's delight.

The specific type of phenology is one that is totally dependent upon your powers of observation. This is one reason why it is essential to keep a journal of every single garden activity and observation. For instance, you may not have access to observe chicory, but if you can correlate another flowering or event in nature to the arrival of squash vine borer moths you can successfully plant for subsequent years and make adjustments as needed.

How to Start Seeds

199

Regardless of whether you start seeds indoors or outdoors, for the most part the "how" is the same. Reference the seed packet for proper depth. The only real difference is that indoors you generally plant one or two seeds per pot (unless you are planting in a flat to "prick out" later).

Special Instructions

Some seeds require special processing. Normally on the seed packet you will be told what if any special considerations exist. Some seeds require stratification. Stratification is simply the simulation of outdoor conditions – cold weather. For these seeds you can simply place them in the refrigerator or freezer for a set amount of time.

Some seeds require scarification. Scarification, again, simulates natural conditions. Gnawing animals or digestive processes break the seed coating up a bit, allowing the sprout to emerge easier. For this you will simply have to use a file or knife to break the surface.

Other seeds may do better if soaked in water overnight prior to planting. This helps soften the shell and allows the sprout to break through, similar to scarification.

It's worth noting that these special instructions rarely exist in most common garden vegetable seeds. If this is necessary, the package will almost certainly let you know.

Indoors

Basically, to start seeds in a pot you simply fill about ¾ full with starting mix, drop a seed or two and lightly cover with the appropriate amount of loose mix. After doing this, I use a mist sprayer and mist the surface lightly with water. I also pour water in the tray the pots are in and allow the mix to soak up the water from the bottom. This is a gentle way of watering that ensures the seed won't wash deeper. Some seeds require no light while others require some light to germinate. The seed packets will let you know of these requirements.

You can actually forgo the use of pots altogether if you have a soil blocker. As previously mentioned, a soil blocker is simply a device that allows you to "mould" cubes of soil into compact packages. The seedling's roots penetrate into the block and between the compactness and the roots; the block stays together until it can be planted in the ground as one whole unit. This helps eliminate both circling and engirdling of roots as well as transplant shock from being ripped out of a pot.

If you do decide to use a pot, be aware that you will have to pull out any circled roots. In addition, NEVER set a peat pot into the ground without removing the plant from it. I've found that peat pots almost never break down like they are supposed to. This can seriously endanger a planting's survivability.

Outdoors

Whether you are planting seeds directly or transplanting seedlings before you plant outdoors you must make sure the soil is somewhat loose. Hopefully you've had a cover of mulch or a cover crop keeping the soil in this condition. If not you can simple loosen it a bit with a hoe. You don't need to go very deep, just enough to get the seed or seedling off to a good start.

Unfortunately, when planting root crops you have little choice, but to loosen the soil up very well or your crops will grow small and/or stunted. I do this very gently with a hoe or a device made by Fiskars called a Tiller (oddly enough). I never use a tiller. This is important because the hand tiller allows one to break the soil in a manner that doesn't churn the stratified layers.

One way I avoid all of the hoeing for non root crops is by using a planting bar. Planting bars are pretty uncommon, but can be made very easily out of scrap materials. Mine is a

201

series of steel tubes that I welded together. A planting bar is just a series of spikes on a central bar. The spikes are spaced equidistant and the bar is used to drive the spikes into the ground, forming divots. Then, seeds like corn, peas, or beans can be dropped into these holes. Simply cover the holes with a light layer of soil or compost.

Hardening Off

If you started all your plants outdoors you don't need to worry about hardening off. However, any plants started indoors now face this most challenging part for some people. Hardening off is the process of acclimating the indoor plants to outdoor life. At this point in the plant's development it is easily burnt by real sunlight. It also has a spindly, insufficient stem that can't stand up to much wind. And it very likely is not used to a varying temperature.

Therefore, it is necessary to begin (at short intervals such as one hour per day for a few days) to bring the plant or plants to a mostly sheltered place. Little by little they should be left out longer and in more contact with sunlight, wind and real temperatures. You can even use a coldframe in some cases.

I've found that the biggest challenge is the sunlight. Many of my plants do fine with the temperature and I can plant them deep enough to avoid the issues with the wind. However, I lose some to leaf burn from the light. I harden off religiously, but sometimes I jump ahead. Here's how I do that.

I bring the plants out for one hour on day one. Then two hours on day two and three. Then four hours on day four and five. Then I leave them out for between 6 and 8 hours on day six. I'm always keeping an eye on the leaves. If the tips start to shrivel, I'll add another day where I don't bring them out at all. I also keep a close eye on the weather. I'll skip any unusually hot, wet or windy days.

Location as I mentioned is also important. For this method, I keep the plants in mostly shady areas.

If all has went well, on day seven I will plant my seedlings. However, after I plant them I will use a small swatch of row cover cloth (a thin scrap t-shirt also works) and make a tent of sticks and this cloth. I make it in such a way that the sunlight still reaches the plant for a few hours at rise and set. After about a week I remove the tent.

This allows me to get the plants in the ground quicker and allow them to start growing. It also seems to take some of the sting off of the hardening off process.

Growth and Protection

Thinning

If you've direct planted (or planted more than one seed in an indoor container) you can begin thinning once the seedling has reached 2-3 inches in height. This is best accomplished by snipping off the smaller seedling at the soil level. Pulling the seedling can rip the roots off the desired "keeper" or pull it out altogether, as the roots will tangle.

For some plants, people will plant them scattered in a flat and early in their growth the plants can be pulled out or "pricked out". This is done with a small tool such as a popsicle stick. The seedling is gently lifted out and transplanted to another container. You have to be really selective about what you try this with. Some plants won't stand for it.

Companion Planting

Companion planting is purposely planting one or more varieties of some type of plant in close proximity to others for the sole purpose of gaining some advantage. That advantage can come in different ways. Some plants naturally repel insects or other pests. Some plants naturally attract beneficial insects that eat the insect pests. Some actually act as decoys to attract pests. And others can actually make certain varieties of plants grow better or some say even taste better.

I personally don't spend too much time worrying about companion planting certain flowers or plants that serve no purpose except as companions unless there is no other plant to serve that purpose. What I mean by that is simple. If there are two plants that I can companion plant with broccoli. One plant is edible and keeps harmful bugs away and the other plant is not edible. Even though the non-edible may keep the bugs away just as well, nine times out of ten I'm going to pick the edible plant. Also, I will purposely pick plants that are broad spectrum. In other words I want ones that do their job in the most broad and efficient way possible.

Reasons:

- Improve taste or effectiveness of a crop.
- Draw in beneficial insects.
- Fool plant predating insects.
    - Trap Crop
    - Shield Crop
- Physical advantages
- Nutrient advantages

The best companion plants may often times be a few weeds. Not enough weeds to choke out your young plants, but enough to draw in naturally the beneficials you want.

Improve Taste

Companion plants grown for this purpose are said to improve the taste of one of the companions. This – of course – is a highly debatable subject.

Plants high in volatile oils seem to improve taste of watery fruits and veggies. Tomatoes are improved by basil. Cucumbers said to by dill. The general rule is that plants that go together on the plate go together in the garden.

Plants high in volatile oils improved by plants such as nettles. I can't really discover why this is the case. Early mediterranean gardeners found that planting Basil (sweet) next to their tomato plants gave them larger, healthier, better tasting tomatoes. Perhaps the tomatoes' roots absorb some root exudate of the basil, or "breathe" some secretion of this sweet smelling herb.

Draw in beneficial insects

Also you can use plants to attract beneficial insects. The best plants that do this are any plant that forms an umbrella like flower head. These are plants belonging to the umbrelliferae family. This includes, but is not limited to, dill, sunflowers, chervil, cumin, parsley, anise, carrots, fennel, yarrow, lettuce (bolted), radishes, beets (in second year). All in all sunflowers are king. Buckwheat is good also, as is caraway.

These plants will attract just about every good insect you could hope to have. Ladybugs, lacewings, pirate bugs, hover flies, etc. Now not every plant will attract every one of these so pick and choose what you need. The reason that the good bugs like these so well is that some of these bugs need nectar and pollen at some stage of their life before they start eating your pests. These plants provide that.

You need a comprehensive flowering plan. Know what flowers when. Make sure you account not just for bloom times, but also colors.

Large plants are also great for this purpose. Sunflowers can do wonders as can corn. Corn has tons of nooks and crannies for lacewings.

Flowers mean bees, especially orange and yellow flowers. Calendula is great in this regard. Don't just think about insects. Tubular flowers also draw in hummingbirds which can decimate a whitefly infestation.

Trap Crops

Grapes take the cake as the best trap crop made. Aphids will go straight to grapes and they can't really harm a strong grapevine, but they will draw in tons of beneficials just by being there.

Eggplants seem to work pretty well as a trap crop for flea beetles, also groundcherries. Pick a plant in the same family of the one you want to protect, just make sure that plant is more appealing.

Shield Crops

Shield crops are plants with strong smells or the ability to release things predating insects don't care for. In my opinion, one of the optimum plants for doing this is the Nasturtium. Some people say that you can also use the French marigold for the same purpose, but I get conflicting reports on the edibility of the marigold. The Nasturtium, however, is quite edible. Nasturtiums have a peppery taste to the leaves. The flowers are also edible just more bland, but are a great way to give color to a green salad. You can even make poor man's capers from the seedpods. And the best part is that Nasturtiums repel aphids, beetles and whiteflies.

Other good companion plants for repelling insects are all of the strong herbs or plants such as basil, mint, oregano and garlic. If you plant Nasturtiums with these four, you are covering just about every insect you can hope to repel with plants.

Garlic – the aroma fools.
Nasturtiums – very peppery and strong.
Cilantro – stinks to me and to bugs.
Mint – easy to grow also.
Lemon basil and lemon balm – citronella

Physical

You can also use a plant to provide support. I've grew beans up grapes and corn. In addition, the taller plant provides shade reducing water loss and heat.

Physical companions also include co-planting and nurse crops. Co-planting is essentially planting two things so they grow at once (at some point). Like sowing clover and wheat.

Nutrient advantages

Things like alfalfa mine the soil for nutrients and help bring them to the surface. This makes them available for future plants as the alfalfa is chopped and dropped. You can chop the plant and use it as mulch or let the fungi work their magic. Dandelions are similar in this regard.

Bad Companions

There are bad companions too. Alliums are said to be bad companions to legumes. Fennel is said to be the worst companion.

In order to lessen effects of disease and pests, planting the same family plants close by is generally regarded as poor practice. For instance tomatoes and potatoes are subject to some of the same blights. Corn and tomatoes are both subject to rootworm. From personal experience I noticed that parsley next to carrots is a bad idea. The parsley drew in parsley worms (black swallowtail butterfly) and they also ate carrots.

Planning

One must have a plan for companion planting. The garden layout should basically revolve around companion planting.

"Pests"

My personal philosophy on pests has changed over the years. At this point I'm ready to eliminate the word pests from my vocabulary. I'm sure that will change again though. I feel like pest infestations are not a natural occurrence or Mother Nature, but rather a failure on the part of the gardener to properly plan. However I feel that it is worthwhile to cover, for new gardeners, some of the insect predation they may face.

I could not adequately cover every pest or situation you might encounter in your garden. I'm not going to pretend to know or to do that. However, I will give some examples of some common pests. I do this for two reasons. The first reason is that knowing these few common pests will keep you looking for them and aware. The second reason is that the things I list about them will give you the right mindset and questions to ask about new encounters.

Aphids

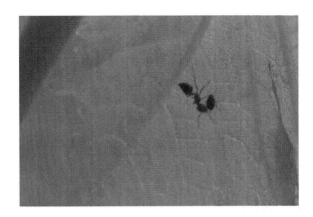

Harmful Stage and Damage: Nymph and adult - disease by sucking.

Complete or Incomplete: Incomplete - egg, nymph, adult

Appearance: Very small, many different types so different colors. Look like lice (called plant lice)

Order Hemiptera: True bugs having sucking mouth parts.

Eggs: Can't see them

Other Stages: Nymph- miniature translucent aphid

Eats Them: Many different predator insects

Eats: Almost any vegetation

Plant Controls: Garlic, nasturtium, mint, onions, oregano

Notes: Aphids form mutualism with ants. Ants will protect them to mine them for dew. They also will transport eggs and nymphs to food sources. They are often called ant cows. Crowding and food sources can force them as nymphs to change sex or grow wings.

Beetles

Harmful Stage and Damage: Adult -damage by eating leaves

Complete or Incomplete: Complete - egg, larva, pupa, adult

Appearance: Varied, but hard shells, sheathed wings.

Order: Coleoptera - sheath wings.

Eggs: Varied, but laid on the leaves or near plants that they feed on. Bean beetle on beans, etc.

Other Stages: Larval - grubs, pupa - hard rounded cocoon

Eats Them: True bugs, hoverflies (larval), ladybug (larva), spiders, ground beetles, parasitic wasps (larval)

Eats: Most anything, but most are type specific (bean beetles beans, cucumber, potato, etc.)
Plant Controls: Radish, alliums, mint, basil, nasturtium
Notes: There are over 1 million species of beetles. One must be careful when killing larva or pupa – it could be a beneficial beetle.

Squash Vine Borers

Harmful Stage and Damage: Larval - damage by eating vines
Complete or Incomplete: Complete - egg, larva, pupa, adult
Appearance: Frass from hole in stem of vine plants. Wilting for no real reason
Order: Lepidoptera - moths/butterflies
Eggs: Fat, brown and near stem base
Other Stages: Moth large, red and black with hairy legs.
Eats Them: Nothing
Eats: Cucurbit
Plant Controls: None
Notes: With this creature you are reduced to almost entirely mechanical controls. The moths lay eggs on plants at a temperature of about 90 degrees. Some options are: floating row covers, foil cover, BT (Bacillus thuringiensis), plant around seasons, plant resistant varieties.

Squash Bugs

Harmful Stage and Damage: Nymph and Adult
Complete or Incomplete: Incomplete - egg, nymph, adult
Appearance: Brownish or greyish with large body
Order: Hemiptera - true bug
Eggs: Bronze footballs found on underside of vine leaves.
Other Stages: Nymphs are small adults with white bodies and black legs.
Eats Them: Spiders, ground beetles
Eats: Cucurbits
Plant Controls: Radishes, nasturtium, mint, marigold
Notes: Mechanical control. Place a wooden plank in the garden and they will gather underneath it.

Beneficial Insects

Ladybug

Most Helpful Stage: Larva
Complete or Incomplete: Complete - egg, larva, pupa, adult

Appearance: Adult is orange. Grapefruit, lime, lemon color is a bad signal.. Larva is glossy grayish/orange with splotches, elongated with pinchers.
Order: Coleoptera - sheath winged
Eggs: Small yellow/gold footballs
Other Stages: Pupate - dark brown with two columns of dark dots.
Eats: Aphids, beetles, other sap feeders. Can eat more than 5000 aphids in lifetime.
Attractants: Umbreliferous - sunflowers, dill, corriander, caraway, fennel, dandelion, buckwheat.

Green Lacewing

Most Helpful Stage: Larva
Complete or Incomplete: Complete - egg, larva, pupa, adult
Appearance: Adult-a small bodied cicada, very shiny large eyes. Larva - brown and white, elongated with pinchers.
Order: Neuroptera - Net winged
Eggs: Tiny white footballs on hairlike filaments.
Other Stages: Pupate - light colored cocoon, egg shaped.
Eats: Beetles, caterpillars, aphids (known as aphid lion).
Attractants: Umbelliferous plants such as dill, caraway, corriander, sunflowers, fennel, dandelions

Hoverfly (Syrphid)

Most Helpful Stage: Adults for pollination. Larva for defense

Complete or Incomplete: Complete - egg, larva, pupa, adult
Appearance: Adult - small yellow and black "bees". Its eyes
are proportionately large.
Order: Dioptera - two wings
Eggs: Tiny, but deposited near aphid colonies
Other Stages: Pupate - tiny, brown with a row of dots
Eats: Aphids and other plant suckers
Attractants: Mints, umbreliferous, buckwheat
Notes: By imitating a stinging insect like a wasp or bee
(though it doesn't sting) this insect is an example of Batesian
mimicry.

True Bugs

Most Helpful Stage: Adults and nymphs
Complete or Incomplete: Incomplete - egg, nymph, adult
Appearance: Sucking beak or mouth parts. The minute pirate
bug is small with two black tears on its back. The assassin bug
has long legs and long beak.
Order: Hemiptera - true bugs
Eggs: Yellow with either a darker or lighter cap.
Eats: Anything it can shove its beak into. Most have saliva
that dissolves insides of other bugs.
Attractants: Hiding cover.

More on My "Pest" Philosophy

*The highest form of generalship is to balk at the enemy's plan.
The next best is to prevent junction of the enemy's forces. The
next in order is to attack the enemy in the field and the worst
policy is to besiege walled cities.* – Sun Tzu

I see a problem with the way pests are handled in the garden.

The question that is too frequently asked is: What can I spray
on my garden like magic juice that makes pests just – *POOF* -
disappear? Hardly ever does one ask if they should do
anything at all. I contend that in most cases you don't need to

215

do anything! Sometimes it's better to let nature take its course.

We are too quick to use the nuclear option. We spray everything in the garden with our favorite organic spray and hope it works. I call that "spray and pray". The organic label allows us to retain an air of nobility and justice. That's a little like beating someone with a stick and telling them they got an organic beating – at least I didn't use an aluminum bat. That would be unnatural!

There's an irrefutable law in nature that most people seem to overlook when dealing with pests. The things lower on the food chain are greater in number. I call this the rabbit to wolf ratio. There will never be more wolves than rabbits in a given area for a sustained time. The population of prey must support the population of predator. Thus, anytime you spray a pest you – by proxy – get rid of a few beneficial insects. It doesn't matter if they even come in contact with your "remedy".

This is the logic. Some people will point to the fact that they used an organic spray that doesn't harm beneficial insects, but you are depriving them of a food source. And if you remove their food from the equation you will either starve them out or give them the message that they aren't welcome in your garden.

Another general rule is that prey reproduce better than predators. If they didn't they would go extinct. Ladybugs make it from egg to larval (predatory) stage in about 5 days from as few as 3 eggs per "nest". It takes a ladybug up to 6 weeks to reach adult (egg laying) stage. Conversely, an aphid hatches from a nest of 50-100 eggs. The aphids that hatch only take about a week to reach adulthood (and thus egg laying potential). And that disregards the fact that if the aphid female cannot find a mate it can simply clone itself (in a process known as parthogenesis) and give birth to a live juvenile copy! So I ask you, if you nuke both insect groups, which will come back quicker?

And that's me assuming that the sprays are effective. Over time the target insect will likely develop immunity to the spray or just learn to hop away when it detects your movement.

216

Aphids don't develop immunity to ladybugs. They just get eaten.

It might be easy to disregard my barely coherent ramblings as pure theory and one might be smart to do so. However, I have seen these principles in action.

Just last year in my garden I had my first major aphid infestation. I watched in early spring before my grapevines had set a single leaf as ants packed little packages of aphidness up my bare grapevines. One single egg might have done the job, but the ants took no chances, packing up egg after egg after egg.

My wife: "Aren't you going to do something?"

The leaves were on the grapevine for about two weeks before I noticed they had large black blotches. The black blotches were in fact thousands of aphids, setting up shop. I had a lot of interesting afternoons sitting on the deck that I used for a trellis and watching the ants harvest the dew from the aphids.

My wife: "Would you do something?"

Eventually the leaves were so covered that some of them were no longer green at all just due to the covering of the aphids.

My wife: "I give up!"

Then a few days later the cavalry came and there were ladybugs everywhere.

At first it was just a few hidden on the back of a leaf or clinging to the stem. A week later all of the ants had abandoned their crop and went to ground. Before long I was watching full-scale attacks. The ladybugs were defiant – mating in full view of their aphid adversaries. I think they were sending a message!

Then came the lacewings. They made home base in my corn patch, but they were happy to fly over and place some eggs on the grapevine as well. A few weeks later and my grapevine was just a little worse for wear. Some of the leaves had holes in them, but my grapevine had grapes. The ladybugs had moved on to other plants and other prey. The lacewings stayed in the corn patch and propagated like mad. Not a single plant in my garden that season succumbed to pests.

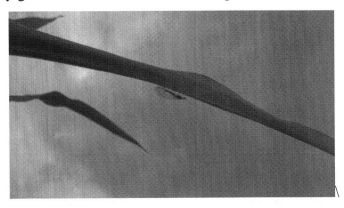

So maybe doing nothing is the wrong way to look at it. I didn't do "nothing" I just provided the habitat in the form of the big bright flowers on calendula and large hiding places in the corn and lots of nectar from sunflowers. I was going to plant those things anyway.

I might be extra lazy, but I say this spring, when the pests come – do nothing!

Pesticides

The good news is that there are now many "organic" pesticides on the market. These organic pesticides are made from natural ingredients such as bacteria that naturally occur or plant material. The bad news is that these are still pesticides and as such they upset the balance of a natural system.

These pesticides include BT (Bacillus thuringiensis) which is the natural occurring soil bacteria I mentioned, pyrethrin (made from dried flowers), Diatomaceous Earth (DE) which are the fossilized skeletons of ancient microscopic creatures and Neem Oil which is also a plant derived pesticide.

I admit to having used pyrethrin so it's hard for me to be so hypocritical about natural pesticides.

So here is what I recommend.

1. Plan your garden so you can avoid monoculture rows as much as possible and companion plant smart. Give beneficial insects a place to hide, leave a wild area and some "weeds" in the garden. Plant lots of diverse things.
2. Use preventive methods such as planting when it's smart, mechanical controls, etc.
3. When you witness a pest infestation, use more mechanical controls and allow at least a little bit of time (a week or so if possible) for predator insects to set up shop and take care of your problem.
4. If, at this point you decide to use pesticide, use the safest organic one you can find (for both food consumption and beneficial insect habitat) and conduct spot treatments. Spray when the pest is most present, but when you can avoid pollinating insects (late in the evening is usually best).

Mechanical Pest Controls (for Insects)

I spoke about mechanical pest controls and that term confuses many people. Mechanical pest controls are methods other than chemical. Some helpful methods include:

*   Row covers placed over plants before or during suspected pest activity.
*   Hand picking pests
*   Turning chickens loose to eat the pests.
*   Placing traps such as boards for squash bugs (recommended) or traps for Japanese beetles (not recommended).

Many of these methods will be successful in helping knock down the numbers of pests, but it's very unlikely that any of these mechanical controls will completely eradicate the pests, but that should not necessarily be your goal. These pests will eventually draw in beneficial insects and you will gain more by having them.

Non-Insect Pest Protection

Garden pests never attack the day after harvest or when the plants are young. They always seem to attack my garden the day before the big haul. A garden full of just ripened fruit and veggies must look like a neon all-you-can-eat sign to a hungry deer, or rabbit.

There are ways to effectively turn that sign off, but it will require perseverance and definitely some trial and error.

Deer

The most persevering four legged pests to ravage a garden are deer. Their sheer size and appetite can make for absolute garden destruction. Worse yet, many times they will simply ignore the things a gardener is apt to do to repel them. They jump all, but the very highest fence and eat right through a lot of treatments to plants.

Natural (or at least passive) repellants can be used, but it is a lot like using a pesticide. Eventually the pests develop immunity to the treatment. Repellants are theorized to work in two ways. The first way is by presenting the deer with something they associate with human activity. Deer in most places have learned to avoid humans at all costs.

There are a few repellants that fit into this category. The first is soap. A technique taught to me by an old Kentucky corn farmer was to actually put the soap in a sock and hang it from a stretch of fence. He hung them about every 40-50 yards. When asked if they worked he replied, "for a little while, then the damn things lose their fear". Some people rub the soap onto a pie pan and hang it from a string close to the garden. I've never tried this, but it should work in about the same way.

The second human related repellant is a little more revolting to most people. That repellant is urine. Collected over a period of time and poured in a perimeter around the garden, this will sometimes keep the deer away. Just be aware that urine in its raw state can burn your grass and crops. The theory here is that some deer just associate the smell with humans or that they can discern the smell of the urine of a predator.

Some people claim that human hair can also be used. Probably also best placed in a sock and hung from a fence.

There are also many plants that can be companion planted in your garden to repel deer. This second group of repellants works by odor as well. This group works by masking other odors. The theory with this group is either the deer won't go into places where they aren't able to smell predators due to the strong scents or that they simple can't smell the tasty vegetables due to the strong odors. The positive thing about this group of repellants is that they are completely natural and once planted should only require inputs same as the other garden plants.

Among the many plants that are purported to repel deer are yarrow, lavender, marigolds, rosemary, oregano, sage and thyme. The great thing about these plants is that most perform multiple tasks; repelling pest insects, inviting helpful insects, providing food or all three.

If all else fails, there are a few "last resorts". The first is making a pepper spray concoction from hot peppers and spraying the solution over the garden plants. The reason this is a last resort is that every rain requires a new dosing and it uses valuable peppers that could be best enjoyed as food instead of deer repellant.

Another last resort is the gun. Of course, this is not easy or foolproof in a lot of cases. For one, state laws (including hunting seasons, tags and permits) must be obeyed. Not everyone is allowed by local law to shoot where they live. Even then, it only takes care of the immediate problem and other deer are free to move in and continue the destruction.

The state where I live (Kentucky) in 2008 revised statutes to allow deer control tags to be issued in cases where:

- o Deer hunting occurred on the property during the previous deer season
- o Standard deterrent measures recommended by a department representative have proven ineffective or are impractical
- o A department representative certifies deer damage to crops, gardens, and property or wildlife habitat.

Again, please check local and state laws before discharging a firearm or hunting deer.

The final "last resort" is the fence. Fencing is costly to build to a height that deer won't attempt to jump and it can limit any garden expansions. However, a fence to a height of 5 foot or so will at least deter them somewhat. It is also an adjunct solution. A fence of that height can make it easier to trap them for a moment to shoot them. It also gives you a base from which to hang repellants.

Rabbits

Rabbits can wreak a lot of destruction on a garden as well. Pound for pound they are probably more harmful than deer.

Luckily rabbits can be stopped by most low cost fencing options. In fact, in the early 1900's in Australia, three fences, one nearly spanning the entire continent from north to south, were erected to prevent rabbits from encroaching further. Rabbits were an invasive species there. I bring up this odd bit of trivia to point out the fact that the larger the fence, the more likely that erosion and other animals will breach it and allow rabbits inside. This is exactly what happened in Australia. The fence must be maintained.

Most rabbit fences are made of chicken wire, which is a thin strand galvanized steel woven wire fence material. The shorter 36" height should be used and the first 6-8" should be buried in a pre-dug trench to prevent burrowing under or erosion from rendering the fence ineffective. Stake should be driven in the ground at appropriate distances to keep the fence in place. The wire can be stapled or tied to the stakes. This fence will also help with raccoons.

In addition, lavender (also mentioned above as a deer repellant) is also a rabbit repellant. With so many uses not just as a pest repellant, good insect attractant and more, it just makes sense to plant this one. Rabbits also hate garlic; so again, you can keep rabbits (and vampires) away and enjoy the multiple uses of a delicious plant. Foxgloves will also repel rabbits, but with only one use (other than being aesthetically pleasing) I wouldn't really bother with it unless it is a last resort before harming the animals.

For those who have no qualms about harming rabbits, a .22 LR or even a strong air rifle will do the trick. Rabbits are delicious to boot.

Pocket Gophers/Moles

Although listed in the same category, these two mammals are different in the ways that they harm a garden, but similar in how to deal with them.

Moles are a lesser concern as they do not eat veggies, but instead eat grubs, worms and other insects. This in itself is not a concern, but for the air pockets around roots that they leave which damage and kill plants. Moles rarely emerge from their burrows. Gophers will come out of their holes to eat your garden.

Some methods of prevention will require identification. This is not a difficult task. The first obvious sign of a gopher is that your veggies are eaten (see above). A mole will only leave wilted and/or dying plants. Both animals create mounds. The gopher creates a mound from which it pushes dirt and exits. The mound will have a hole (which may be loosely plugged) and the dirt will be pushed in a crescent pattern. The mole will push straight up and usually will not leave a hole. The dirt will mound in a nearly perfect circle.

Unfortunately, there doesn't seem to be a viable natural method of keeping pocket gophers and moles in check. Poison can be used, but I find this method wholly undesirable.

The first method is to simply build a barrier. This will require trenching down about 2 feet and burying your fence to that depth. If properly planned, this barrier could serve as a rabbit fence and gopher/mole fence in one. Just be sure that the wire weave on the fence is small enough to prevent the smaller ones from going straight through. An alternative is to fill the trench with rock or cement. The trench and rock could be used in conjunction with the fence. If you are building raised beds, the fencing can be nailed to the bottom of the frame or laid in.

The second viable method is trapping, but this will require more maintenance than even the fence. The traps will have to be emptied and reset and new tunnels will need to be addressed. Victor makes what is perhaps the most popular set of traps for gophers and moles. Just be aware that there are separate traps for each. So identification of the culprit is going to be necessary (see above).

Birds

I've never had a major garden problem with birds. Occasionally I will find a peck mark in a tomato or realize that they've dug up seeds I've just planted. In most cases birds actually help a garden by eating harmful insects.

However, I concede that there may be situation where they become a problem. In these cases, you can use a frightening device such as the aluminum pie pan you would use for deer. Owl and snake decoys only work for a short while. That is, until the birds realize they are immobile. You can also take countermeasures to eliminate nesting areas and perching areas.

Non-Insect Pest Summary

No pest control method is 100% effective. Fences break, erode, blow down or are jumped. Killing the pest only leaves a vacuum that is quickly filled by another. Pests will build immunities or otherwise ignore companion plantings occasionally.

The best approach is a multi-pronged approach using broad-spectrum repellants. The proper solution, of course, will vary with your particular pest problems, garden size and other factors impossible to list here. You could add pie pans with soap rubbed on to this setup to repel birds and add an additional layer of deer defense.

The important thing to remember is to use multiple options that address more than one pest to maximize your money and time.

Weeds

During one of my weekly podcasts I opened with the premise based on this quote from Ralph Waldo Emerson: "A weed is but a plant whose virtues have not yet been discovered". Surely this is contradictory to everything we know as gardeners, right? We've been told from the time that we could say vegetable that weeds were something to be destroyed without prejudice. Yet for the for the subsequent half hour I argued with myself out loud on Emerson's premise and was soundly beaten. The weeds had won again.

Reflection led me to discover some inherent flaws in what I was doing. Furthermore it allowed me to justify a little bit of laziness. That being said, I'd like to play the part of defense attorney and argue my case again for my client—the weed.

We are taught from a very early age that there are bad guys and there are good guys. The good guys wear white hats and always win and the bad guys wear black and are bad just for the sake of being bad. So much of our religions and stories and daily life are based upon this fact.

Therefore, when gardening, we seek the villain and along with pests and disease, weeds are one of our favorite enemies, but nature isn't as black and white as we believe. Everything, even the lowly weed, serves its purpose even if it is not always apparent. And like the best stories, we love to love flawed heroes or villains with a heart. Such is the case with weeds.

Support

We all strive to be organic in some sense or at least environmentally responsible. Yet even on smaller scales we learn very little from larger problems. The Dust Bowl of the 1930's in America was due to land breaking on a scale that had previously never been seen on Earth. This was the result of attempting to outsmart nature and make the land easier to plant.

Yet, what do so many gardeners do to plant a garden? Grab a tiller or other implement and rid the soil of anything growing. Thus begins the hopeless process of chopping earthworms, weeds, and mixing the stratified soil. After the seeds are planted and begin to sprout, some spend backbreaking hours keeping the surface around the desired plant as barren as the moon. This is apparent from so many gardens I see with nothing but rows and rows of plants and bare ground adjacent.

Nothing could be more unnatural.

I took this approach a few years back to a large patch of sweet corn. Before long, the soil around my corn plants was dry as sand and too loose to even hold in the corn. After a strong storm about half of my plants fell over, tired of fighting against me fighting against nature. You see, the root systems of various weeds allow good garden plants to grab hold and integrate into the network, providing them firm footing. This is a level of support that cannot be achieved by simply mulching the bare ground. Mulching can hold in the water and topsoil to a degree, but weeds can do those things as well or better in addition to holding your garden plants upright.

Nutrients

Some weeds may be unwanted plants, but that doesn't mean they can't benefit your plants in ways other than holding the soil and water down.

Take clover for instance. Clover invades my garden almost every year and I love it for that. That may seem crazy, but clover is a pea without pods. It is a legume that generates nitrogen within the soil due to the symbiotic relationship with bacteria called rhizomes that form nodules on its roots. It grows quickly which means that it can be chopped and the green growth can be used to nitrify compost or it can be worked into the soil as green manure.

Though its growth can choke out the plants it can help, Kudzu is also a leguminous plant.

Dandelion is another weed that we love to hate, but dandelions send out deep taproots that break up the soil and pull nutrients from soil layers that other plants can't reach. When we "chop and drop" the greens or compost them we add minerals that might otherwise never surface.

Nettles are another weed that can be used to activate compost.

Food

I mentioned the ability of the dandelion to help with the nutrients in your garden. Did I mention it could also help with the nutrients in your body?

228

Dandelion leaves contain tons of essential vitamins and minerals such as A, C, K, calcium, potassium, iron and manganese. Too boot, they also taste pretty good. I ordered a salad while having dinner with a client and found the small jagged leaves in my ten-dollar salad. I figure I got my money's worth, though I could have had them at home for free. Dandelion flowers (the yellow ones not the white fluffy ones) make a great wine if you can collect enough of the things.

Purslane is another edible weed green. It also contains vitamin C and antioxidants, but the real surprise is that it contains an Omega-3 fatty acid normally found in fish oil. Beat that lettuce!

Lamb's Quarter and Plantain are also edible weeds that can liven up a dull salad with essential nutrients and taste.

Companions

Many of the weeds I mentioned such as dandelion and clover also send out brilliant flowers that beneficial insects love to visit. Clover is one of the best plants to draw in honeybees that I am aware of. The flowers seem to provide easy access and are in close proximity most times. This helps the bees expend little energy as they gather up the pollen.

Some weeds are actually great companion plants in the garden. Dandelions repel armyworms. Other weeds are spiny and repel soft-bodied insects.

Weeds also help camouflage your garden. When a pest lands on your bare garden soil it simply has to walk, fly or hop to the nearest green thing and begin feeding to ruin your garden. Give them something to eat that you don't care to lose. Weeds around the borders will keep the bad bugs there in a lot of cases.

In recent experiments, stinging nettles were found to improve production of oil in peppermint and other nearby herbs increasing potency and flavor.

Or you can simply use the weeds to shade heat-phobic crops such as lettuce. You simply need to place them between the plants you want to shade and direction of the sunlight (southernly if you live in the Northern Hemisphere).

Medicine

Disclaimer: Herbal remedies should be prepared and taken under the strict guidance of a trained herbalist or physician.

Dandelion greens are a diuretic and can be made into a detoxification tea. The roots contain taraxacin (a bitter substance which may aid digestion), choline (a liver stimulant) and starch-type substances (that may help balance blood-sugar). In addition, the white resin that the dandelion parts ooze when broken can help dissolve warts.

Chickweed can calm skin irritations when made into a poultice.

Yarrow can be used to treat wounds or relieve a fever. In The Illiad, Achilles uses it to treat the wounds of injured Greek soldiers. It has been found to control bleeding, prevent infection and promote healing.

Nettle tea can treat bronchitis and bladder infections. Normally painful to the touch, topically it can be used to treat arthritis.

Even the lowly kudzu can be used to treat dysentery, high blood pressure and perhaps even alcoholism.

Summary

I've told you about all the virtues of weeds and while these are very true, too much of even a good thing is a bad thing. Therefore, to avoid competition it makes sense to work to suppress weeds where they won't serve any good purpose. Eradication should not be the goal (even if it were possible).

Colder Weather Growing

By now, it's fairly well known by most people that for most of the country it is possible to maintain a thriving garden though almost all of the year. Yet it is amazing how many people pass on the opportunity to garden though the colder times of the year. The fact is that fall/winter growing creates some of the best seasonal treats of the year. Combine that with the relative ease of working in an environment devoid of many of the challenges and heat of summer and it's hard to understand how anyone could rob themselves of this opportunity.

Challenges

Every problem is an opportunity for a solution. The simple truth is that many of the problems or challenges with fall/winter gardening simply require knowledge of the different conditions and ways around the roadblocks. You have to take the spring/summer gardening standards and throw them out the window. When gardening in the latter half of the year, a new rulebook exists.

The first challenge is the extremes of temperature. Notice I did not say the cold weather. That is not the issue, but rather the fact that the time between sweltering late summer heat and chilly autumn air is such a short duration. With short season crops such as radishes this is almost a non-issue. However, longer season crops have to be planted in the heat of summer where germination is tough in order to make it to the cooler temperatures where they may thrive, but before cold nights prevent any further growth. The obvious solution to this is to start seeds indoors.

The other solution is getting your timing right. Working back from the date we would expect the plant to die (usually first average frost date, but not always), you simply subtract the date to maturity for the plant. Be sure to include germination time as well. And be aware that germination under sub-optimal conditions may take longer.

Using temporary shade such as that created by tomatoes or corn plants in their last days can also help keep the soil cooler to promote better germination. If you are desperate, do what I do and use the weeds!

The second challenge is also weather related. Later fall in some climates can be very wet. During germination and early plant growth this is great (within reason). However, when temperatures drop, the wet weather will keep the soil cooler than it could be. Therefore, it is important to plant in well-drained soil. Pooled water is the enemy.

The Cast of Characters

It's true that you won't be growing tomatoes or watermelons through the colder season. However, you'll find that the replacement team is just as fun and delicious. In fact, you'll find interesting parallels in the types of winter crops versus the summer ones. Summer crops such as the aforementioned two are watery and acidic, perfectly suited for consumption during drier, hotter weather. In contrast, most winter vegetables are vitamin packed at a time when vitamins are needed most. Some are starchy and heavy, perfect for winter stews and meals in general.

I classify plants grown during cold weather into three main groups.

Brassicas are the group of plants derived from Brassica Oleracea or the wild cabbage. These plants include kale, cauliflower, cabbage, collards, broccoli, Brussels sprouts and kohlrabi. These plants do well with some heat, but love the colder weather as well.

Greens are the groups of plants that are non brassica type plants grown for salads. This means of course, the lettuces, spinaches, arugulas and other salad veggies.

The final group is the root crop group. These are especially intriguing for the cold weather gardener. Carrots, turnips, parsnips, beets, radishes all grow and thrive well in colder weather.

Planting

It is commonly suggested that the best time to plant for a fall/winter garden is the middle of summer around June or July. I simply find this not to be the case. Where do these people live, in Alaska? Every time that I've planted lettuce or spinach in June or July, the temperature has been so hot that almost no seeds germinate. I'd much rather plant in mid to late August or even September and risk having to overwinter my crops. The only thing that I ever got from planting in June/July was sweaty.

233

As I mentioned above, it's sometimes a good practice to start your seeds indoors. That is one way to get around the germination issues. However, this is a double-edged sword as hardening off will be twice as difficult with the summer sun beating down. So you can risk losing a few seeds to poor germination or risk losing a few plants to what I call "hardening off errors". I've got less invested in the seeds.

When direct sowing, I also do something that I believe helps the seeds germinate a little better and provides for the plant's continued survival. I plant a little deeper than the seed packet recommends. This allows the plant to set good roots deeper as protection against heat, frost and dry spells.

You will have to water the patches where you sowed your seeds more than normal during this time. This not only provides the water the seeds need for germination, but will help keep them cool. This will generally hold true for the plants once the seedlings have emerged as well.

I've already discussed how greenhouse and cold frames can help you. I will however mention other mechanical controls. Particularly at the beginning of the season or the end row covers can be helpful tools. This is especially the case if your plants are as close to harvest as they are also to the first frost. A good row cover can act as an umbrella in the heat or a blanket in the cold and can be added and taken away quite easily.

It is important to realize also that many of these plants can stand up to frosts and colder weather. Any carrots I leave in the ground, bounce right back first thing in the spring. I've also witnessed this firsthand with cabbage and turnips as well.

In summary regarding planting: Plant late and deep enough for good germination and monitor conditions, hot and dry needs water. Coming frosts or hot spells are good times to have protective devices at the ready.

Overwintering

A number of the plants I've mentioned in this article are so cold hardy that they can survive through the winter. Of course, survival is relative. In some cases, only the root systems will survive. This is the case with carrots, which not only survive at the root all winter, but also can be dug at just about anytime even after the tops die back (just be sure you can find them all).

Certain other vegetable varieties will overwinter if the right variety is chosen. Broccoli is just such a case. Broccoli comes in two varieties: single season and over-wintering types. Most of the purple types are of the latter variety.

The one thing you have to be aware of when overwintering is that some root crops such as turnips will want to bolt (go to seed) first thing in the spring. Like lettuce and spinach, once a root crop bolts it will no longer be generally edible, but this is a good way to get a crop of seeds.

Rewards

There is significant proof that harvesting vegetables after exposure to cold weather concentrates sugars and therefore improves taste. The first time I witnessed this firsthand was after harvesting some carrots for a carrot cake my wife made one November evening. I don't know if she was more surprised that I was able to harvest vegetables in the grip of winter or that the carrots made a superb carrot cake.

This doesn't just hold true for root crops, but also the other two groups—brassicas and greens as well. Some of the best salads were harvested with a bit of frost on the ground.

The other rewards are less tangible, but just as real. Once the mercury begins to drop, pests hole up and disappear from the visible garden. It's a little like making a fast break in basketball and finding yourself at your opponent's goal with no defenders in sight.

Likewise, most weeds find themselves on the way out as well. It should be known that I sing the virtues of weeds, but gardening is much easier when the roots of the weeds are there and the green parts are not so much. You get the network structure that helps support topsoil and your plants without the competition of the upright growth.

Cold weather gardening is never for the faint of heart or those with aversion to loss. It is exponentially trickier than spring gardening in some aspects, yet remarkably easier in others. Mistakes will be made and lessons will be learned and in the end you'll be a better gardener for the experience.

Domestic Animals in the Garden

Chickens/Ducks

You have to be scared of birds not to understand the positive impact that chickens can have on a garden. They provide a sustainable food source—eggs or an immediate one—meat. You can breed them and let them hatch their eggs and keep the cycle going. They can fertilize and clear a plot of land in no time and are like pest terminators. They eat any insect that moves.

The best use of chickens is containing them in what is known as a chicken tractor. The tractor is a movable pen. There are many ways to build one, but the purpose is all the same. The mobility allows the chickens to be contained over a specific area for all the purposes I listed above.

The downside is that everything eats chickens/ducks. They are also somewhat noisy if you keep roosters. Plus, many cities will not allow poultry within the city limits. A good alternative is to keep quail or bantam chickens.

Rabbits

Rabbits serve many of the same benefits as chickens. In addition, they have many of the same requirements and needs

236

and can be kept in the same manner.

Fish

Many homesteaders are beginning to realize the benefits of aquaponics. Aquaponics is a hybrid of hydroponics and aquaculture. I love this type of activity, but it is a system that recycles everything (almost literally). The fish produce waste in the form of ammonia and natural bacteria in the water can convert that ammonia into nitrates, which are plant usable forms (basically fertilizer).

The wastewater (from the bottom of the container of fish) is pumped into containers holding vegetable plants. The plants use the nitrogen and filter it out of the water. The cleaned water is pumped of funneled back into the tank full of fish, only to gather more nitrates.

If a fish like tilapia is used, garden waste such as weeds and green waste can be fed to the fish. Lacking good sources of greens, duckweed can be grown right along with the tilapia. You may still need to supplement with a bit of feed, but you can certainly save a lot of money.

On the downside, there is a high upkeep factor. The pumps have to work and a balance must be struck. If there is no balance then you can quickly end up with dead fish and dead plants. Plus these fish provide only a very seasonal harvest in most places in the US since they all make size around the same time and they have a limited growing season.

Pigs, Goats and Sheep

These animals are not a great idea for small urban settings. However, with a little more land, these animals can clear like nobody's business. Allowed to pasture on a plot of land they can clear, break the ground a bit and fertilize great.

The downsides are that they are smelly and they get loose easily. Plus, they require a lot of space and maintenance.

Once they run out of pasture (and in the winter time) they are going to require feed from other places on your land or from outside sources.

Bees

A beehive will provide a sustainable source of food and will pollinate the garden. Plus, they are great fun to watch. On the downside, they are a little finicky, sting and require quite a bit of investment.

Wild Animals in the Garden

Toads

One of the best wild animals you can invite into your garden is the common toad, which eats beetles and slugs like crazy. This is a widely known fact in Europe (especially England). Unfortunately, here in the US this is a lesson that has gone unlearned. Perhaps it is a function of the super neat, pesticide laced gardens that are so common.

One of the best parts about toads is that they are easy to draw in and keep. All that is needed is some type of shelter for the toad(s). To make a toad "castle" you can simply turn over a clay pot and partially bury it. You could also dig a small depression to hold some water and place rocks over top.

The toads mostly rest during the day, keep cool and hunt at night. You can also build a small pond to draw them in. They need moisture. They are very neat to watch and have in your garden.

The only real downside is the small amount of space you have to sacrifice to build their shelter.

Birds/Bats

The fact that some birds are voracious insect consumers is well known, but many people are afraid or concerned that those same birds will eat their hard-earned garden vegetables as well and pick off their newly planted seeds before the first one can germinate. While it is true that some birds have no beneficial effects or even detrimental effects, one must understand that birds are no different than insects. Some help, some harm. We try to invite the helpful ones in and accept the harmful ones as part of the ecosystem we've built.

Here are some things you can do to keep birds in your garden.

Bird Requirements – Food

Classifying birds by what they eat is a tough task. Most birds are though of as herbivorous, omnivorous or carnivorous or insectivorous.

The carnivores are easy to point out. These are the hawks, owls, eagles and falcons – the birds of prey. These would be handy to take out the occasional squirrel digging through the garden, but attracting these birds is a sketchy proposition at best. They are not the subjects of this article.

The omnivores and insectivores (which are of particular interest to the gardener) are the birds like purple martins, sparrows and robins. Many of the herbivorous birds that people point to (like geese and chickens) are actually omnivorous. Of course there are some herbivorous birds such as hummingbirds that are nice to look at, but provide limited help to the gardener.

Some birds are specialist feeders and the shape of their beaks speaks volumes. Short thick beaks are meant for crushing seeds and nuts. Some are smaller and sharper and are intended for catching insects. Others are longer and narrow and may be used for multiple types of prey.

Insectivorous birds require a high protein and fat content food; therefore, they are more difficult to attract with feeders.

However, fatty bird cakes can be bought at most stores or whipped up in the home kitchen. This provides an opportunity for specialist insect eaters as well as the omnivores to get a quick snack. Another option is to fill small bowls with mealworms or black soldier fly larvae. The offered food draws them in and if your garden is diverse with pests they will stay to help return the favor.

If fat cakes and insect foods aren't your thing or seem like too much trouble you can always feed the standard bird feeds that consist of seeds. The omnivorous birds will still come and enjoy your offerings and again, hopefully stick around to see to some garden cleanup.

Obviously the feed, whether it be fat cakes or seed, must be contained in a feeder and protected from the elements.

Perhaps the best option is a food source that requires little of your attention. Planting native plants such as elderberries, serviceberries, hackberries, dogwoods and other berry producing plants can give your birds an extra source of food in lean times. It just makes sense to include this in your comprehensive bird attraction plan.

It should be said that many people have an immediate objection to birds in the garden. That is that the birds will eat their lovely ladybugs and lacewings. What people do not realize is that predator to pest ratios exist which explains away this concern. The amount of pest insects in a garden could be four to five times as much as predator insects (like lady beetles). The amount of predator insects would then be three to four times as much as the higher-level bird predators around. It works itself out in the end.

Bird Requirements – Housing

The second part of the puzzle to attracting birds involves the offering of housing.

In nature, birds find, create or steal their own housing, but if you want to draw them in and keep them you will provide them some options. These options need not be limited to commercial houses or even built ones. Native vegetation, dead trees, brushpiles, etc. are great places for birds to make nests.

Of course, some are just going to prefer to have you set up an abode. Purple martin houses and bluebird boxes are just smart ideas when you can purchase or build them. The existing housing gives them little reason to wander away.

The most prevalent problem with housing is keeping out unwanted guests. The invasive starlings and other aggressive, less desirable birds can set up shop quickly and keep the birds you want from calling your land home. There are several ways to discourage this activity. Primarily you can add certain features to your houses to keep these out. This is also why entrance hole sizes are so very critical.

I list the optimal entrance hole for each bird type below. This is the first step in deterring invasive or aggressive native species of birds from either taking up dwelling in the house you create or worse-attacking the adults or the eggs of the species we intend to attract. Keeping the entrance hole at a certain size is not only helpful for the birds we intend to attract, but it will also make it difficult or impossible for the ones we don't want to enter. If you think this seems like splitting hairs I assure you it is not. Researchers have found that increasing or reducing an entrance hole diameter by as little as 1/16" can increase or decrease habitation by as much as fifty percent!

I mentioned that there were other ways to discourage such activity. The first method is simple inspection and there is no substitute. You must inspect your housing regularly and know when to inspect it. There is a right time and a wrong time. There is also such a thing as too much inspection.

The second method of deterrence is to add features that are known to repel invaders. One such feature that works for English Sparrows is to add fishing line to a bluebird box. Due to intricacies in the eyesight of the English Sparrow that are not well understood, they will fly into the line, feel it and fly away. Mylar strips also work well when placed on top of the boxes.

The final method is to trap the invasive species. This can be done by using your boxes as a trap by inserting a trapping device into the entrance hole. You can also set a live catch repeating trap. These can be found on the internet with a simple search. This is a more aggressive method and it must be said that you can't trap them all. It also must be said that you should always check local regulations in your area. Some birds are protected and cannot be harmed under penalty of law; while others are unprotected and should you feel it necessary they can be dispatched.

Bird Requirements – Water

The last challenge is providing a source of water. Actually this is no real challenge. A small depression dug in the soil or a bucket or pail that fills with rainwater will serve the purpose. The key is to monitor the level and ensure that when birds are there it stays full. Although some species are migratory, others in certain locations will be present year-round (bluebirds come to mind). Therefore it is important to ensure a drinkable supply of water is present at all times.

The Birds

Purple Martins, or *Progne subis*, is a large bird belonging to the swallow family. These birds are migratory and will live in crevices, tree cavities or when available large man-made boxes designed for the purpose. The migrants will often return to the same nesting site year after year. They are famous for eating flying insects such as mosquitoes. Standing water like nearby ponds draws in these birds. White gourds or houses on high poles are standard. The houses should be around 7x12 inches and at least 5 inches tall by compartment. The entrance holes should be 2 1/8". Placing the house in the center of the most open area possible and/or near water is the best location.

Red-Eyed Vireo, or *Vireo olivaceus* (it has large patches of olive green feathers), are beautiful little songbirds that feed mostly upon garden pests such as caterpillars and aphids. But they also feed on invertebrates such as slugs and berries. These birds are specifically drawn to berry plants such as Virginia creeper, elderberries and blackberries. I don't know of a house you can build for these birds, but keeping plenty of berry bushes around is your best bet for attraction.

Bluebirds, or *Sialia sialis (eastern), mexicana (western) or currucoides (mountain)*, are one of the few Thrush family birds found in North America, these birds are highly insectivorous. They nest in cavities of trees and nesting boxes when available. Bluebirds can be drawn by food in the form of berry suet cakes, mealworms and rarely seed feeders. They like houses that are about 5x5 inches and about 9 inches deep with a hole from 1 ½" to 1 5/8" placed toward the top of the cavity. Painting portions of the house bluebird blue can help attract them.

Orioles (*Icterus*) are a large family of birds with highly contrasting colors and are related to blackbirds. They consume both insects and fruit/nectar. They will not readily take to birdhouses so building one could be a futile effort. They are somewhat easy to attract with orange halves, orange suet, grape jelly or bright orange colored nectar feeders (similar to a hummingbird feeder).

I hope this article has demonstrated the many options to attract birds to your property and garden. Besides being beautiful and utilitarian with their pest controlling qualities I find birds to add a sense of peace and wonder to the garden setting. Perhaps it's the knowledge that the ecosystem I've nurtured is one step closer to fulfillment.

Snakes

Very few people really like them, but a snake will make sure that mice and gophers and moles never touch your garden. Many people kill them on site, but they really are beneficial for the garden ecosystem.

On the downside it's generally not pleasant to happen upon one!

Applying Permaculture Principles to the Garden

To the uninformed, a garden might not fit the permaculture idea of permanent agriculture. Annual crops, after all, die every year never (in most cases) to come back again without intervention on the part of the gardener. For many, perennials seem to be the best choice, but perennials in most cases take a long time to produce and let's face it, eating berries alone might keep us alive, but after a month of that, none of us would be too happy.

But an annual garden is one of the best ways to use to a great effect the permaculture design principles. Putting them to use in designing the layout of your garden can really have spectacular effects. And if you do it right and use the concepts every year and evolve and learn you can make it as permanent as you want.

The first principle is *Observe and interact*. I spend an incredible amount of time in the garden. My wife sometimes wonders what I'm doing out there all that time. It might just look to the untrained eye as if I'm wandering aimlessly, but my aim is quite clear. I spend a lot of time just looking and observing. I'm also interacting, training vining plants or filling in spots where seeds didn't come up. Interacting might mean just simply plucking squash bugs from your vines. Remember, you are a beneficial organism in your garden as well!

After that comes *Catch and store energy*. There are various forms of energy that pass through the garden that we might never really consider. For one, there's a lot of solar energy that hits our garden everyday. While we are able to take advantage of it and store some of it in the form of plant energy we don't take advantage of nearly enough. By strategically placing darker colored rocks, we can store the energy long after the sun goes down. The rocks will release the heat

244

energy for some time after dark.

There's something else rocks are good for as well and that is slowing down water and allowing it to soak into the soil. This can also be done by digging swales – level ditches on contour. Letting the ground store the water is the best plan.

The next principle is *Obtain a yield.* This might seem pretty easy, after all we grow things that we like to eat and that produce for us, but how often have you thought about the energy it takes to get some plants to produce? Obtaining a yield is about more than just getting something out of the work, but rather getting a return on it. If it takes 300 calories to grow one tomato and it only contains 200 then that is a net loss.

We must also *Apply self-regulation and accept feedback.* This is accomplished by not doing dramatically damaging things and recognizing when something is not working and making changes. When I started working with a way to tie up the urea in chicken manure so that it could be used nearly immediately on a garden I carefully watched the plants for reaction and adjusted my timing and ratios accordingly.

Use and value renewable resources and services is the next consideration. I mentioned chicken manure as a resource above. It is a completely renewable soil amendment. If I spend a small portion of my garden growing food for them and using the wild plants that grow there and in my yard naturally I know that I can maintain a high nitrogen amendment for virtually ever.

Oddly enough, *Produce no waste* ties into the previous consideration perfectly. In a garden there is no waste. When we do our "weeding" (I put that in quotes because there really is no such thing as a weed) we can drop the dead bodies into our garden as mulch or feed them to rabbits which in turn make manure for our garden. Our kitchen waste goes right to the chickens or worm bin or compost bin and gets reused to replenish our soil.

Designing from patterns to details is one of the principles that I've had the most trouble actually following. I obsess about details, but I think the point of the principle is if you just build to patterns the details are easy after that point. I'm finding that the layout of the garden contributes to this greatly and there are so many patterns to imitate. In many cases the patterns will allow you more space or more access or both. Keyhole gardens are a great example of this principle.

Of all the principles *Integrate rather than segregate* means the most to me personally. By inviting and keeping things in our garden (even things we might not directly see the benefit of) we build a more sustainable and efficient garden system. This is also one of the easiest principles to accomplish with projects. Birdhouses, bathouses, toad ponds, chicken tractors, cattle panels for hogs and goats will all allow animals – wild and domestic – to interact with the garden environment, improving it overall.

Using small and slow solutions is another key principle. Nothing should be ever done as an all or nothing situation. Test something out in a small controlled manner and then introduce it slowly, allowing yourself to see the full effects and measure the changes.

Another principle very near and dear to my heart in the garden is *Using and valueing diversity*. To some people this might simply mean not using a monoculture model where we plant our crops in straight rows and only plant a small variety of things. That is not a wrong interpretation, but I think it misses out on certain things.

For one thing, don't just view things narrowly such that a diversity of plants is good, but not a diversity of "pests" or "weeds" or birds. The most resilient system I've found is one that let's the ecosystem control the population naturally of all living creatures and, yes, that sometimes mean that tomato plant you nursed up from a seed gets tied to the proverbial stake and bashed with the proverbial shovel. The strong survive and the weak…well   you know what happens.

246

To *use edges and value the marginal* we have to look at where the life lives in a system. The edge of the woodline into my garden teems with life. I've managed to naturally attract mason bees, eastern fence lizards, toads and other creatures. The value is not necessarily in the edge itself, but the the ability of the edge to act as an interface between the two "not edge" portions. In my observation and work, this is best accomplished by providing links.

A lizard will rarely wander from the edge of my woodline and into my garden. My garden is too open and crossing into it could mean predation, but if I provide a small safe base for the lizards to run to it, allows them to have the best of both worlds, a place to hide from predation and a place to do some predating of their own.

The last principle of *Using and responding creatively to change* may very well be the most important and often overlooked principle. It's natural that many people fight change tooth and nail, but often change is the driving factor that makes things in the universe work. If the Earth hadn't changed many times in the past we would very well not be here today.

The Food Forest

I love to garden for so many reasons, but I also realize that almost all of the garden crops are annuals which only survive for one year (and in some cases two). Of course, saving seeds prolongs the ability to grow the crop.

I also love to build food forests. Food forests are a concept that is heavily supported by permaculture (which I will talk about later in this book). A food forest is a food system that isn't necessarily in a forest, but rather behaves like one. Plants – mostly perennials – support one another and work within the system together. The system is highly sustainable and a food production machine.

The food forest is adaptable to most any situation and for a prepper it makes a lot of sense to have dependable food sources. It doesn't matter if you are laid up in bed with the plague, an apple tree or blackberry bramble will produce food with little work once it hits a bearing stage.

The first consideration for a person in the midst of preparing for emergencies is simply where to find the funds to buy these perennial plants. A semi-dwarf fruit tree at the local big box store can run $25 or more, but there are options that many people are simply unaware of; options that can provide your food forest with perennial food bearing plants for pennies on the dollar.

What follows is a collection of techniques and methods that have developed over time. I don't claim that they will work for everyone or that there aren't better methods. These are just the best methods that I know of. These methods aren't solely mine and I owe thanks to the people who taught them to me. These people include my parents and grandparents, various Kentucky state employees working at the Fish and Wildlife Resources department and the State Forestry Division.

Planting Trees

Planning

Finding a Planting Spot

The first thing you must do is to determine where you will plant your trees. It's important that you do this first, otherwise you may find yourself with trees and no spot to plant them. In the northern hemisphere, the sun travels across the southern sky from east to west. In the summer it's high, in the winter it's lower. You must know this in order to determine if the spot you are eyeing has enough sun (or shade in some cases) to support proper growth of the tree.

You can watch the path of the sun at each solstice. That's the highest and lowest points. You may need to do some clearing. My advice is to always clear in the fall/winter, but identify the trees positively (which most times can only be done in spring/summer).

It also helps to know what the tree needs to thrive. Some trees need filtered sunlight or so much shade while others are not picky. The pawpaw is a tree with unusual requirements. It usually likes quite a bit of shade and damper ground. I could spend days and pages of this book listing what each tree needs and still never get done. So I'd advise to just look up your tree type on the web and discover its needs on your own.

Preparing a Planting Spot

When planting trees, the spot you pick generally doesn't need much preparation. If you know well ahead of time you can begin mixing in organic matter such as leaf litter or pine needles. If you can't find either of those you can use compost.

Getting the Trees

This is a common question because it's so tough to find a reliable source. I used Dave's Garden Watchdog (http://davesgarden.com/products/gwd/). The reviews seem to be very accurate. The only problem is that the company may change after a string of negative reviews. This is not the fault of "Dave" or the reviewers. Some companies just grow too big too quickly and service suffers.

Besides finding a reliable source it's also hard to find an inexpensive source. I seem to have found a solution to both of these problems. Below I list State DNR and Forestry Division nurseries, which will provide very small tree seedlings for a very minimal fee. These are all native trees grown in native soil so they are highly adapted. The only problem is choice, but you can always supplement these native trees with those you order from a nursery or grow yourself.

249

State	Link
KY	http://www.forestry.ky.gov/seedling/
TN	http://state.tn.us/agriculture/publications/forestry/seedlingcatalog.pdf
AL	
MS	
FL	http://www.doacs.state.fl.us/onestop/forms/11206.pdf
GA	http://www.gfc.state.ga.us/Seedlings/documents/SeedlingPriceList0910rev 010410.pdf
NC	http://nc-forestry.stores.yahoo.net/containerized1.html
SC	http://www.state.sc.us/forest/nur.htm
MO	http://mdc.mo.gov/forest/nursery/seedling/
CO	http://csfs.colostate.edu/pages/seedling-tree-nursery.html
IN	http://www.in.gov/dnr/forestry/3606.htm
VA	http://www.dof.virginia.gov/nursery/index.htm
WV	http://www.wvforestry.com/nursery.cfm?menucall=nurse
NY	http://www.dec.ny.gov/animals/7127.html
AK	
AZ	
AR	http://www.forestry.state.ar.us/
CA	http://www.fire.ca.gov/resource_mgt/resource_mgt_statenurseries.php
DA	http://dda.delaware.gov/
CT	
HI	
ID	
IL	
IA	http://www.iowadnr.gov/forestry/nursery.html
KS	http://www.kansasforests.org/conservation/index.shtml
LA	http://www.ldaf.state.la.us/portal/Offices/Forestry/Reforestation/SeedlingI nventory/tabid/242/Default.aspx
ME	
MD	http://www.dnr.state.md.us/forests/nursery/
MA	
MN	http://www.dnr.state.mn.us/forestry/nurseries/index.html
MT	http://dnrc.mt.gov/forestry/Nursery/default.asp
NE	
NV	http://forestry.nv.gov/ndf-state-forest-nurseries/
NH	http://www.dred.state.nh.us/nhnursery/
NJ	http://www.state.nj.us/dep/parksandforests/forest/nj_forest_nursery.htm

N M	http://www.emnrd.state.nm.us/FD/treepublic/default.htm
ND	http://www.ndsu.edu/ndfs/towner_state_nursery/
OH	
OR	
PA	http://www.dcnr.state.pa.us/forestry/nursery/index.aspx
RI	
SD	
TX	http://texasforestservice.tamu.edu/main/article.aspx?id=1165
UT	
VT	
W A	http://www.dnr.wa.gov/BusinessPermits/HowTo/LandownersIndustryContractors/Pages/lm_seedling_order.aspx
WI	http://dnr.wi.gov/forestry/nursery/

There is another way to get trees even cheaper. Unfortunately it's more time consuming, difficult and with less choice and reliability. Basically it's what I call "found" trees. Most of us know someone with some land holding or a friend or neighbor who does. It should be at least a possible task to get permission to go to that land and mark some trees for later digging. You should always dig while the tree is dormant. The only problem with that is that if you didn't previously identify the tree, it may be difficult to do so with no foliage.

When you dig it, dig a huge perimeter around it and prune the roots with the shovel as needed. Then lift the entire root/dirt ball and put into a burlap sack or large pot. You can see why choosing the smallest tree you can find and positively identifying is a good idea!

Propagation

I wish it weren't so, but one of the hardest things to do with trees is to grow new ones. In fact, this is one of the few things I'd rather spend hard-earned money to just buy. That's not to say it can't be done, but the fact is that it's hard, time consuming, unreliable and frustrating. Because it can be done, I will take you through a few of the processes that can make it happen for you.

The first way of propagating new trees is from seed.

Apples

With apple trees it's almost entirely possible that the apple the seeds came from and the tree that results from those seeds will be entirely different entities. Apples are notoriously crossed. Most times the tree itself is a hybrid. To boot, many orchards and especially commercial operations use crabapple trees as a pollinator. Crabapple trees are not used because they prevent you from growing new apples. Rather they are prolific blooming trees and there are plenty of native insects that will gladly carry their pollen. Therefore they are a cheap way to increase fruit production in orchards.

Needless to say, the apple tree you spend up to a decade getting to fruit bearing size may end up being just a good for pretty much nothing crabapple tree. If you have done this and are just now realizing it, don't despair quite yet.

There is some hope for your tree. Because crabapples are superbly adapted for most soils and conditions they form a hardier rootstock than regular apple trees. Since they are in the same family as other apples (Malus) they will readily accept grafted wood from any apple variety.

Stone Fruit

With the stone fruits or pit fruits such as plums, cherries and peaches you will generally get a better result from propagating from seed. If the results don't quite give you what you need then just proceed to the next section.

Grafting

When you've either propagated a tree from seed or cuttings and you realize that you didn't get quite what you wanted, you haven't wasted your time quite yet. The good news is that you've at least grown a good base for grafting.

Grafting is simply placing desirable plant material onto a less desirable one to achieve a result that is greater than the sum of its pieces.

Fruiting wood scions (pieces of wood intended for grafting) are not too difficult to come by. Most orchards would probably give you the scrap from their pruning activities if you just asked.

There are a few ways to graft wood:

Bud Grafting – Removing a bud from a desired tree and placing it in a small slit in a "host" tree. The bud will then usually take to the host and begin growth.

Whip/Tongue Grafting – A scion is cut at a 45 degree angle at the attachment end. A host branch is cut to the same angle and is roughly the same diameter. Then another small slit is put in each of the pieces of wood so that it matches up when joined. The angles are matched up to form a straight branch and the union is wrapped in electrical tape or another tape made for the purpose.

Split/Cleft Grafting – A scion is whittled into a wedge at the end of attachment and inserted into a split branch or trunk on the host tree.
Regardless of which route you take, remember to insert plenty of scions. In best cases you can still only expect about a 50% acceptance rate.

My Process of Planting Bare Root Seedlings

Most trees you have shipped to you will be sent as bare root. That means that basically no soil will accompany the tree. This is usually not a problem as long as the shipper takes measures to assure the roots stay moist during transit. Therefore, once you receive the trees, it's not imperative that you plant right away, but it is crucial that you soak the roots or at the very least keep them wrapped in moist newspaper.

My process for bare root trees can really save your back, but there are a few drawbacks. If you leave air holes the tree might not thrive or may even die. That's why it's important to make sure you leave no holes. I also use a sub-optimal tool in the pictures – a spade. A dibbler (also known as a Dibble bar or planting bar) works much better, but I can't make myself spend the money on one. If you buy enough seedlings from a Forestry nursery they may rent you one or loan you one for free. A regular cheap spade works just fine for me for now.

1. Pick your spot and probe for roots. You may need to move spots if the roots are just impenetrable. Drive the shovel as deep as you can. The depth should not be much deeper than the dirt spot on the seedlings.

2. Use your foot to get to correct depth if needed. Again, the depth should be slightly longer than the length of the root system of the seedling.

3. Pull the spade toward you. You are trying to open up a cavity in the ground to place the tree.

4. Wiggle the spade back and forth so you don't remove a chunk of mud when you pull it out.

5. Remove the shovel. You should be left with a crescent moon shaped hole.

6. Place the seedling in the hole and push until it hits bottom. If you made the hole too deep, fill in with native soil or a bit of potting soil or compost.

7. Moving the spade parallel to the previous hole come away from the hole about 4-6 inches and drive the

spade into the ground to a depth about 1" deeper than the original hole.

8. Being careful not to harm the seedling, pull the shovel handle down and toward the seedling. You are attempting to move the dirt to clamp up the original hole.

9. Remove the shovel.

10. Use the spade to chop the dirt in front of the second hole.

11. Use the heel of your foot to seal the second hole. You may need to drive your foot at an angle to help fill the hole. If this is just not possible you can fill the hole with loose native soil, compost or potting soil. You can actually add another hole to fill the second one and then use this step to fill that hole.

12. If you are able, use your foot and the properties of the final hole to create a depression at the root system of the tree. This depression will help trap and hold water at the roots of the tree.

13. Using loose mulch (to prevent runoff), mulch the root system of the tree well. Dry leaves work well, compost is ok and wood chips are less than optimal, but it is essential that some mulch be used.

Planting Potted Trees

For trees that come in a pot there is an old saying about planting. Dig a __ dollar hole for a __ dollar tree. The blanks of course are filled in with the number that suits the writer at the time. I haven't found any one rule to be the case. Here is the thing about potted trees, the more you baby them, the more they expect babying.

I generally dig a hole that is just deep enough to sink the root ball about 6 inches below the surface-being very careful to never bury the graft point (the large ugly knob near the roots). I dig the hole about 6-12 inches larger in diameter than the diameter of the root ball. I do this to get enough loose soil around the root ball to fill the air holes.

Here is my reasoning behind this and some may disagree with it. Circling and engirdling happens pretty frequently on potted plants. When people fill a hole with a ton of potting soil, the roots just swim around in this nice little protected area, soaking up nutrients and the water that the soil holds. By forcing them into non-loosened normal soil on your property, you force them to adapt and take a strong hold.

After I check my hole for depth and diameter I carefully remove the tree from the pot by gripping it just below the graft point and pulling. If this doesn't free it, you can cut the pot away (careful not to cut roots!). To avoid circling and engirdling as I mentioned above, it's also a good idea to loosen the roots a bit (cut them out only if you have to) and point them in all directions.

Then it is as simple as filling the hole in with dirt. I generally do this, not with a shovel, but by hand. It is easier to pack the dirt down in the hole to avoid air pockets. Once you get it filled well, you can probe with a spade point to ensure it's all down. Then, water the tree well, soaking all the surrounding dirt. This further fills the air holes. You will then most likely need to top up the dirt.

Other Perennials

Though I did not specifically mention other perennials such as blueberries, raspberries, blackberries and grapes – the same planting techniques and methods of planting trees apply.

The benefit to smaller perennials such as berry plants is that they of course keep coming back year after year when properly cared for and barring any disasters. They also actually need very little care or monitoring.

The homestead property I purchased in 2009 was 4 hours away from home and I was not there for long periods. I planted fruit trees such as figs and apples and plums, but also many raspberries, blackberries, grapes, blueberries, bush cherries, currants, etc. This turned out to be a good idea since they survived easily in the native soil and have grown in size ever since.

If there is any lesson I took away it's to the value of planting the small perennials now rather than later. Even if I'm not happy with the location I can move them easily and it gives me a plant I can propagate from.

Speaking of propagating – these small perennials make it easy for one to double or triple your plant stock in just a year or two.

In order to grow new grape plants simply save the cuttings during pruning. The red colored wood is last season's growth. Save it and cut it three nodes long. The nodes are the joints between growth sections where the buds appear.

Dip the node end that was closest to the plant roots in a rooting compound (or dip in water where a willow branch was soaked) and place them at least one node deep in good fertile soil. Keep them in a warm, sunny place and soon one of the upper two nodes will start forming leaves.

In order to propagate new raspberries or blackberries simply bury the tips of new canes about 4 inches deep and mark the spot. Once you see the new plant emerge and take off, clip the parent vine. A week or two after, you can transplant or simply leave the new plant where it is.

Care

Water

Although I briefly mentioned watering your plants above during the planting, it is warranted that we should talk about keeping water in the soil around your trees for future use.

If your trees are planted on a slope, swales can be dug on the contour just above your trees (hopefully you planted several on the same contour line), but truthfully it's hard to dig a significant swale without some heavy equipment. Small swales can be dug as a spot treatment, but to get a large effect you need the swale to be able to collect water from a large area.

I actually find it easier to take advantage of the surrounding land features. For instance I planted an apple tree at the funnel point of a small ditch. I know a lot of water will flow through this area, but how do I stop it or slow it down? Just beyond where I planted the tree, I dug a small swale and stacked the dirt on the opposite side to create a berm.

The berm now will allow the ditch to hold a small supply of water.

The situation won't work for every planting because every planting is on a different spot on a different piece of land. The point is to know the land features and use them to your advantage. Build or remove features that don't make sense according to your water plan.

Mulch

I'm not sure it needs to be repeated, but I love mulch. Mulch will not only hold moisture close to the root system of your trees, it also decomposes fairly quickly to get nitrogen and carbon into the soil in a usable form. Adding more mulch keeps the topsoil that you are making with the first layer from blowing or washing away.

There is some controversy over which mulch to use. I'm not sure why people fight this one other than they want to use what is cheapest and most available. Usually that would be wood chips. I like wood chips only as a last resort. It's not because I believe they harbor disease (though there is some evidence that is true). Rather, wood is rather absorbent and has a tendency to suck moisture from the soil and bring it to the surface where the sun can evaporate it. And that is exactly what we are hoping to prevent. Now this absorption is still less drastic than bare soil, but it's there in some form. You can see this for yourself a few days after a rain.

I like straw as mulch. It is less absorbent than wood, but it does tend to let air flow. This generally causes evaporation too.

My favorite mulches are compost and leaf litter. I like the leaf litter to be as finely chopped as possible, but I'm not above placing whole dead leaves as I did above. The leaves absolutely will not absorb any moisture so they are like a plastic tarp at holding water in. They are also natural and expected to be at the base of trees. When comparing to wood chips can the same thing be said? When a tree falls in the woods does it fall at the base of another tree? Well leaves do.

Compost is mulch that simulates natural conditions as well. Compost is simply decayed carbon and nitrogen. It's just leaf litter at a further stage.

Fertilizer

If you've properly mulched your tree's root systems with compost or leaf litter (or even wood chips) then you've done a great deal to provide nutrients to your trees. Sure, if you dumped tons of nitrogen fertilizer on your tree's roots you could probably improve your harvest, but you'd also do a lot of harm to your soil's ecosystem. It's better to let things happen naturally for the long run instead of thinking of only short term gain.

Other "Growing" Choices

Mushrooms

For someone looking for a perennial crop that's easy to grow, nutritious and delicious it's hard to beat mushrooms. Yet the first reaction you often get from others is surprise when you mention that you can grow your own mushrooms. At least that's the case for me since most of the people in my area (including myself) grew up hunting mushrooms in the woods.

In addition to the great wild varieties I described finding in the wild in the Gather portion of this book there is also a wonderful range of mushrooms that the home gardener or homesteader can grow on their own.

Though the wild types like morels can be propagated the production is variable and unreliable at best. The standard domestic types are mushrooms such as button mushrooms (common grocery store mushrooms), portabello, oyster and winecaps (which can be grown directly in the garden). However many people are finding the best luck with the very old domesticated Japanese varieties Maitake and Shiitake – which I describe growing below.

Shiitake

As I mentioned there are many choices but I believe the obvious choice for growing on your own is the Shiitake mushroom. For me it's even more obvious for other reasons.

For one, I have in my state, the lady who wrote the book (literally) on Shiitake production in woodlands – Professor Deborah Hill. Professor Hill works out of the University of Kentucky and has answered my questions on many different occasions even when they were at times annoying beginner questions.

The other reason is that Shiitake is derived from the Japanese *shii* which is commonly thought to mean oak. However *shii* is actually an evergreen tree related to oaks. The word *take* means mushroom. Shiitakes are for the most part, oak mushrooms. In that case you could call my four-acre property in Western Kentucky shiiland because every third tree is an oak.

History

Shiitake mushrooms, like all mushrooms, belong to the fungi kingdom. Its proper name is **Lentinula edodes.** Shiitakes are native to China, Korea and Japan (of course). The first written record of shiitake cultivation is attributed to the Sung Dynasty of China. That writing was made several decades before the Normans conquered England.

The mushroom has been gaining more and more popularity in the US as it becomes "hip" to eat Japanese and eastern cuisine. In a way, the popularity of sushi has probably spread the shiitake more than anything. Not that shiitake relates in particular to sushi, but the same Japanese restaurant that serves sushi usually has a few udon type soups that contain some quantity of shiitake mushrooms.

Appearance

The shiitake is a large mushroom. The color can vary from white and tan to white and dark brown. The brown part at the top tends to exhibit a crackle pattern exposing the white beneath. However it should be noted that the mushroom itself is only the fruiting body of the mycelium. If the mushroom is the "fruit" then the mycelium is the "root". The mycelium is an invisible thread-like mass that invades the rotting log, soaking up nutrients and moisture by breaking down the wood with an excreted acid. A sheath protects the threads from its own acid.

Growing Them

Inoculation

The process of introducing mushroom start to the wood is called inoculation. It is essentially infection of the log. It consists of a few steps. I will attempt to explain the steps and why it's done the way it's done.

Wood Selection

I'm making an attempt by experimentation this year to determine just how much both type and size of wood matters. Conventional knowledge states that oak is the way to go. However, I theorize that using different types of wood could affect not only yield, but also speed of fruiting and duration.

I've got access to and will try oak, sweet gum and hickory. There are only a few types of wood that are said to not work. First of all you should not use any coniferous trees. Some do not rot well and others contain chemicals such as terpenes that are found in pines. Most hardwoods are acceptable fodder for shiitakes. However, it should be said that there are better and worse types to use. The harder types of wood are better. Oak is primary followed by maples, hickory, sweet gum, birch, sycamore and poplar. Walnut and black locusts are not desired because they are too hard and rot resistant due to chemicals in the wood. Aspens and willows are also not desired because they are too soft and will allow contamination.

Selecting the wood should be done before fall. Paint or tape off trees you want to fell later. The best size is said to be 4-8" in diameter. However, it's impossible to harvest a tree that is 6" in diameter all the way up. In addition, a stack of logs of exactly the same size is going to fruit for the same duration and in the same manner. I think it's best to have a variety of sizes.

I've cut trees with main trunks that are about a foot in diameter. That way I can harvest a good deal of the limbs as well as the main trunk. The size guidelines are mostly in effect to help the user deal with the wood. An oak log a foot in diameter and 3 feet long is a chore to lift. Simply cut them shorter.

It is a good idea to fell them after the leaves have fallen, but before the trees bud in the spring. During this time the moisture content is said to be ideal in theory. Apparently the problem with cutting trees during the growing season is that the bark is looser than during the dormant times. The bark is essentially the armor for the log and by association – the mycelium. Without the armor of the bark, all kinds of outside organisms can contaminate the log.

Speaking of contamination, it's essential to inoculate the logs within 2 weeks of cutting. While making sure the bark stays on is a long-term protection, getting the inoculation done is a short-term protection for closing the wounds you've inflicted by cutting the tree to begin with.

Drilling

The next step to the inoculation process is drilling the holes. If you've chosen sawdust spawn then the hole size is 7/16". If you've chosen plug spawn then the hole size is 5/16" generally speaking. It's important to keep the depth at about 1 inch if you've chosen plugs. The plug needs to contact the bottom of the hole to avoid forming air pockets causing the mycelium to have difficulty taking.

Plugging

The next step is inserting the spawn. With the plugs it's easy. Just insert, hammer in and you're done. If you are using sawdust its helps to have a tool to take up and deposit the spawn.

Waxing

Cover the plug or sawdust and entire hole with a dab of cheesewax. The goal is to simply seal the "wound" and allow the moisture to stay inside the log.

Stacking

After the logs are fully inoculated the next step is to stack the logs in a shady moist area. In the north this is commonly done by leaning them against a standing fence. In the south the log cabin stacking method is commonly done. This is simply stacking the logs in a square configuration similar to a log cabin.

Watering

If the logs do not stay sufficiently damp then the fungi mycelium may succumb, suffer or not produce well. In certain cases the grower may need to intervene by watering the logs.

Flushing

The actual fruiting of the mycelium by producing edible mushrooms is called flushing. Shiitakes usually fruit in force, sending up mushrooms in quantity. The timing all depends on the spawn type, log type, weather, moisture levels, etc. It's important to watch the logs after changes in rain amounts and temperature.

Apparently sometimes thumping the logs with a hammer can force them to fruit. It is not known why this happens, but theory is that the vibration sets off a mechanism telling the mycelium it's time to reproduce.

Saving Seeds

The truly self-sufficient gardener saves his/her seeds for replanting during the next season. In most cases this is a simple task that will reduce costs of the garden (when combined with the other techniques in this book) to almost nothing. The bottom line is that you can spend the labor yourself or pay someone else to do it. If you pay someone else, expect to incur shipping costs. Worse yet, you may not get what you've paid for. F1 hybrid tomato seeds look exactly the same as Roma VF seeds to most if not all gardeners. One year, eight Roma tomato plants I started from purchased seed turned out to not be Roma tomatoes.

Saving seeds from hybrid plantings can be done for some plants. However, be aware that hybrid seeds may be either sterile or the resulting offspring will not produce true to form.

Here I will address saving techniques for some common garden plants.

Tomatoes/Cucumbers

1. Scoop or squeeze the seed and jelly from a fully ripe fruit out into a container. This can almost always be done in a way that saves the rest of the fruit for consumption.
2. Add water to bring the mixture to twice the starting volume.
3. Let the mixture ferment for 2-3 days in a warm place.
4. Add water to loosen the debris. The seeds will settle quicker than the debris. Anything floating should be discarded. This includes non-viable seeds that float. Keep adding water and pouring off the debris until what remains is almost strictly seeds and water.

5. Pour the seeds onto a paper towel or screen and let them drain. Place the seeds in a warm place to dry for a few days.

Peas/Beans/Okra

1. Let the pods dry on the plant until you can shake the pods and hear the seeds rattle. Monitor closely as the pods will open and spill the contents.
2. Remove the pod carefully.
3. Open and remove all seeds.

Peppers

1. Open the fully ripe pepper carefully.
2. Gently scrape the seeds and collect on a paper towel.
3. Let dry.

Lettuce

1. Let the lettuce plant bolt and form the stem and dandelion like flower head.
2. Once the head is somewhat dry, remove it and place it into a plastic bag or other container.
3. Shake the head to remove the seeds.
4. Let the seeds dry for a few days.

Squash/Pumpkin

1. Scoop out seeds.
2. Let dry.

Carrots/Beets/Onion

1. These plants must be left in the ground over the winter to produce seeds the second year.
2. Cover the plants with mulch and/or leaves.
3. Uncover in the spring when you would replant the variety.

4. The plants will form seed heads. Remove the heads when the seeds are somewhat dry.
5. Shake the heads to remove the seeds.

Longevity

Seeds from onions, corn, parsnip and peppers should be used within a year or two.

Seeds from beans, carrots, broccoli, asparagus, celery, leeks, spinach or peas are viable for up to about 3 years.

Seeds from cucumbers, lettuce, eggplant, radish, chard, cabbage, beets, watermelon, tomato, squash and pumpkin are viable for about 4-5 years.

Viability is only an indication of proper germination. Seeds may still germinate after these deadlines, but the rate may decrease. The seeds have no internal timer and no two seeds even from the same variety are alike. Your mileage may vary.

Teaching Children

It is noteworthy that an output from gardening can be a result such as a learning experience. The only way to make gardening sustainable is to teach your children how to do it so they can do the same as you – provide their own food independence and enjoyment by gardening.

After all, who wants their kid to grow up believing that tomatoes originate at the grocery store, or that they come off the vine with a "made in Chile" sticker attached?

Yet I find that most gardening + kids articles address the reason why, but seldom do they address the reasons how. It's true that some children are born with an innate interest in gardening. I was lucky that way. My son Jackson comes running when he hears the rattle of a seed packet or glimpses the reflection of spring sunlight off a garden trowel blade.

However, I suspect that some children simply do not care much for the garden. Interest is not all genetic. Some things I like, my son is simply not interested in learning…until I find new ways of presenting them.

Make Gardening Fun

The first way to get children into the garden may seem obvious and it can be, but it can also be overt. That is to simply make gardening fun in ways that kids can understand.

My first memory of being in the garden was when I was six. We were planting a large patch of potatoes. If my memory serves, every one in our family had some type of digging implement, trying to "hill up" the dirt in preparation for planting. The work was tedious and I was quickly losing interest until I uncovered a snake egg.

Of course I did not know what it was, but after my dad explained it to me I could not move dirt quick enough, looking for more or trying to uncover some other buried treasure. I didn't find digging in the hot sun to be very much fun, but when it became a game or a scientific adventure my interest was secured.

So when Jackson and I dig in the garden we aren't just working the dirt or making a furrow. Sometimes we are digging for worms or trying to find buried treasure. I just listen to him and let him make the story up. Most times nowadays he's a construction worker, excavating a road or a hillside. When he's older I suspect we may be archaeologists in search of lost fossils.

Grow Interesting Things

It's true that children can get bored quickly. Therefore it is important to keep things interesting. One of the best ways to do this is to find interesting things to grow.

The most obvious way of doing that is by planting varieties of common plants in wild and vivid colors. There are several varieties of carrots being grown now that are purple, red and white. There is a type of beets that grows alternating rings of white and red, aptly named Bull's Eye Beets. Striped Roman tomatoes and Moon and Stars watermelons are just a few other examples.

Another way that is often overlooked is to grow things that your kids are interested in *eating*. My son has little interest in eating lettuce so he could care less when I go to harvest it, but he's right there with me when I'm harvesting plain peas or plain carrots. That's because I can relate them to the act of eating them. He likes eating them and associates the eating with harvesting.

Give Them Responsibility

Early last spring about three feet from my neat rows (for once) of peas was a row in my garden that meandered like a drunken snake. The plants were spaced strangely, some too close, and some too far, but I couldn't tell you how proud my son was when I was letting him drop seeds in and tamp the dirt down, him chanting "GROW!"

But from that moment on, that was his patch of the garden. Whenever we went to the garden I made sure to point out how his patch of peas was doing. It was important to give him positive reinforcement along the way. Of course when he gets older it will be important to teach him the "right way", but when they are young it's more important to instill interest.

He also knew that his spot in the garden was his to maintain. I admit it didn't always go smoothly, but he was given the responsibility to water and weed his patch.

Give Them Tools

For someone like myself who's trying to become more minimalist I was a little perturbed when my wife bought a cheap set of "toy" garden tools for my son. It wasn't that I didn't want him to use them in the garden, but I didn't see what use they would be when he commonly commandeered my trowel anyway.

Hat in hand, I had to admit how wrong I was though. I severely underestimated my son's need to imitate Mom and Dad. Now, when I grab my tools and go to the garden, he grabs his and follows.

These tools are great. They are real metal (no sharp edges) with nice heft and they are durable. The entire set, trowel, rake, hoe and shovel were less than five dollars, but they have provided a ton of entertainment, but of course, we could never put a price on the amount of time he's worked with us in the garden, his own tools in hand.

Be Positive

Now I am probably the wrong person to preach about patience – at least according to my wife anyway, but I'll say it anyway. Patience is essential. You can quickly drive your kid away from the garden, ruining all the progress you've made quickly with just an angry word.

Something that I found quickly is that you should write off about 5% of your crop to "stompage". I wonder how many plants I trampled as a kid in our family's garden. I know that as a parent I see every one that Jackson has laid foot across in my nightmares. It's hard to deal with that loss, but you have to just push it down.

I've also learned to do things to help us both coexist in the garden easier. For instance, laying a stepping stone path in my garden for my son to walk on, keeps him off the plants and directs his path in and out of the garden.

Another common problem that can cause garden blowups is the issue of the child pulling weeds and the occasional non-weed – in other words, one of your treasured plants. A story that my grandparents love to tell perfect strangers is the time I weeded my grandma's roses. Apparently I had to get all those ugly red flowers off the pretty thorny stems.

My son has pulled more than a few plants and brought them to me proudly. I've learned to keep my mouth shut...and plant extra. Let's face it; it's hard for us to tell our plants from weeds sometimes. A three year old will fare not much better.

When you do lose your temper-and it's bound to happen-you should apologize quickly and explain your actions calmly, but plainly. I speak from experience here.

Whatever your reasons for wanting to include your children in your garden (and there are many good ones) it's important to realize that they may need some incentive to get there in the first place. By taking extra steps and putting in additional effort up front you can yield great returns in the garden well before your first harvest.

Process Conclusion

Although I use the word, it's a misnomer. No process ever really concludes. It merely ends a cycle to begin again.

Putting It All Together

So, when we garden we take a series of inputs such as seeds, soil, sunlight and we use our tools to move to the process which is the actual seed starting, planting and nurturing of plants until we get to our output, which is a harvest, more seeds and a learning experience.

That's not the end of the cycles however, just one cycle. The new seeds, the things we've learned-even the dead and decomposing plants-all go right back into next year's garden. Like the mythical phoenix, the life of the garden arises from the death of the previous one.

Section 3B – Animal Husbandry

Introduction

Though it's completely and totally possible to garden without livestock involved it is my firm belief that any and every gardener should have his/her own companion animal or animals to help with gardening chores. It's a good idea to start out with one type of animal, although you will usually want to get two of a type because most animals do better with companionship.

Besides the food products that livestock provide there are so many more benefits that remain unseen by most people. Animals provide free organic fertilizer for the garden. They can help you work in the garden - taking care of pests or rooting up the soil. They can become another source of income as they reproduce. In addition, they provide a great deal of fun and entertainment.

But they can be a lot of trouble and a huge headache if you don't plan ahead and do things right from the start. This involves thinking things out and thinking ahead, not to mention observing your certain situation and making the right choices. In this section I'll lay out the benefits, as well as the potential problems, so you can avoid them in your particular journey.

As a homesteader, I believe it's important to nurture systems that give multiple benefits. If I put effort into something I expect that effort to yield more than one reward. It is in this way that the system becomes sustainable.

I for one am not opposed to, but rather tend to look beyond one off livestock methods. For instance, if I raise an animal and slaughter it I've put a certain amount of energy in and gotten a certain amount back, but that animal will never reproduce again and usually the one or two meals is not an excellent return on the time and feed I spent to get the animal to slaughter size.

For this reason I like to devote a greater deal of my resources to raising animals that provide a less finite source of protein. I'm fond of raising smaller animals so in this book I will not cover the largest of livestock – cattle and I'll explain why.

For someone just delving into the world of animal husbandry it's easy to look at only the end result. I've talked about that a little above, but we can delve deeper. Livestock animals require feed – that's an irrefutable law. One can pasture the animals or allow them to free range. This reduces the amount of feed costs immensely, but it takes work and it requires room. Conversely, one can feed purchased grain or hay or other transported feed. This is less labor intensive, but it is costly and it's not sustainable in the traditional sense.

Regardless of how you feed the animals, some animals are better at converting that feed to protein sources. A certain amount of energy is just spent keeping the animal upright. Larger, heavier animals require more energy than small light animals. Poultry, for example, have hollow bones and hollow feathers – they are evolved to fly (mostly) anyway. Therefore they convert feed better. The calculation that explains this is the Feed Conversion Ratio (or FCR).

Poultry have a 2:1 feed conversion ratio. Which means for 2 pounds of feed you get 1 pound of body mass (some of that is actually the eggs calculated in). For a goat, sheep or cow the feed conversion ratio is much higher at 7 or 8:1. In other words, poultry converts feed better.

Plus, with cows you tie up all of your feed in one animal. If that animal gets sick and dies you lose hundreds of pounds of feed (and consequently protein). If one chicken, rabbit or pygmy goat gets sick and dies you've lost a couple of pounds of grain or feed.

Any animal, harvested for meat, becomes a one off proposition. Cows can reproduce of course, but the gestation period for one calf is 285 days. For a chicken, an egg hatches in 28 days, almost exactly $1/10^{th}$ of the time. Plus a broody hen or an incubator will hatch more than one egg. A rabbit's gestation period is 28 – 31 days as well.

Of course a dairy cow will produce milk continuously, providing protein over an extended amount of time. A cow produces about 25 pounds of milk per day. So essentially we have a thousand pound (or more) creature making 25 pounds of milk. Take a laying hen, weighing about 5 pounds ($1/200^{th}$) producing an egg weighing 0.125 pounds ($1/200^{th}$). So essentially the chicken and the cow produce the same amount of protein, but the chicken (or similar sized bird) does it with 4 times less feed.

The point is not to tell you what you want to eat, but rather to provide data and facts to help you make the best choice on how to properly utilize your land.

Poultry

The good thing is that when considering poultry you have a wide range of choices from quail all the way up to ostriches. You simply have to pick the one that fits your situation best and interests you the most.

The real consideration is room and obtrusiveness. If you have very little room or you need to keep your new hobby somewhat secret then you want something small and quiet like quail or even some bantam chicken hens. Chickens are probably the most tame and reliable for eggs. Turkeys, guineas, pheasants and the large flightless birds (emus, rheas and ostriches) are all good choices for people with lots of room.

Choices/Breeds

Most people will invariably pick chickens and for the first timer this is a probably a wise choice. They are probably the easiest to keep, but there are a wide variety of breeds, which begs the question: Which is best? Well there is no right answer. Everyone has a favorite breed. If you are looking for meat then you want a Cornish cross or other fat breasted meat variety. For dual purpose (meat and eggs) it's hard to beat a leghorn. For egg production the Rhode Island Red, Wyandotte and Brahmas are good choices. If my recommendations seem narrow, it's because I believe in keeping docile friendly breeds at first.

After the breed is chosen I recommend a new owner to buy juvenile birds. These are birds with most of their feathers. If you buy them in the spring they can very likely go straight outdoors. Buying one day old chicks require all new equipment and skill sets. Juvenile birds, as opposed to adults will imprint to you easier.

The new chicken owner can also get day-old chicks straight from the hatchery (and shipped) or from the local co-op or farm supply store. Doing this requires a new set of equipment and skills. You will need a draft-proof brooder structure and chick feeders and waterers. You will also need a heat light. The setup is illustrated well below with some chicks I recently purchased.

If you intend to just harvest the eggs for eating, you don't need a rooster of course. A rooster won't make a hen lay any better or worse. If you intend to hatch the eggs, that is a different matter and you must have a rooster amongst the hens. Usually one rooster to four hens is a good ratio. The rooster will also help protect the flock. Having a rooster doesn't make the eggs taste any different, but he is one more beak to feed.

After you introduce them into your housing (which you should have complete before you purchase) you will need to keep them fed and watered. Feeder, feed and waterers are all available at your local Tractor Supply Company or local feed store.

Shelter

Another consideration you might have is where you will put or keep your birds. Again, you have a wide range of options. Some birds are so wild they have to be caged (quail, pheasants) and some can be allowed to roam (guineas and chickens). Regardless, you need to have a spot where your birds can go to get away from predators and lay eggs.

Cages and coops can be elaborate structures or simple. My latest chicken coop is a ten-foot by six-foot coop with a twelve-foot by ten foot run. The one before that was a two-foot by four-foot cage, in which I kept 4 bantams in my garage. The fascist city where I lived at the time did not allow chickens in the city limits, but they couldn't regulate what I kept in my house.

Each type of bird needs a certain amount of room. For instance a good rule for chickens is 15 square feet per bird.

The main consideration for me in the rural area where I am now is predators. Foxes, weasels, mink, coyotes, bobcats, raccoons, rats, snakes, raptors; everything likes chicken (or any other bird). My coop has a full wooden floor and the wire on my run is buried at least a foot deep all the way around. Most people do not put a top on their run if keeping chickens, instead choosing to leave it open. Chickens will not usually fly out (other birds will), but predators will get in, especially birds of prey.

My secondary consideration is comfort. I want my birds to be comfortable and warm in the winter. The coop is located in the woods a bit. It gets sun in the winter and shaded in the summer. It has decent ventilation, but it keeps sufficient heat. This is a delicate balance. The proper site has a profound effect.

The main consideration in the city was sanitation. Since the cage was in my garage it had to be easy to clean. The droppings fell through the wire floor and into a bin with wood chips. I then aged them in my composter and onto the garden they went.

The author's garage pen

Another good option is to use a chicken (or other poultry) tractor. A chicken tractor is simply a moveable coop, touching the ground. The chickens have access to healthy ground, able to scratch and peck around and with access to insects and grass. Moving the coop allows them access to new areas. They also scratch up the ground and defecate on it, fertilizing and tilling a bit.

Food/Water

A significant amount of the total time and money spent on poultry will be tied to feeding and watering.

One thing I've found great about poultry is that kitchen waste goes directly to my birds. This reduces the cost of feed and begins the composting process. Don't waste calories by composting them! Run them through a bird first. They will eat just about any vegetative kitchen scrap. Some of the best items are bread, tomatoes, melons (they won't eat the rinds) and strawberries to name a few. I don't feed them meat or anything that's too hard to peck.

But even with a good deal of kitchen waste you will find your poultry still need additional feed. If you've got room to grow wheat, barley or any other cereal grain you will find this makes great poultry feed. You will also find that many birds will eat weeds such chickweed, clover, dandelions, etc. It's best to let them have access to fresh greens as much as possible whenever you can.

If you simply can't grow enough food for your birds you will have to supplement them with storebought feed. There are three types of storebought feed and each have their distinct purpose. Chick starter is obviously used when brooding chicks. Generally after they get fully feathered you can back off of this feed (it's more expensive). Laying hens and young adults you want to fatten quickly should be fed layer crumbles or pellets. This is a high protein feed at 15% or so (but not as high as chick starter at 20%+) that will help ensure good egg production. Roosters and other birds including free ranging broilers or even laying hens can be fed simple scratch. Scratch is a combination of cereal grains and cracked corn. It's called scratch because the birds have a lot of fun scratching through to find choice kernels.

One consideration is that you should keep your feed and water as high as possible. Poultry aren't super smart and they will defecate into their food and water. Whenever possible I like to use nipple waterers as they make it impossible for contamination to occur. For juvenile birds, a high protein chick starter or layer mash is sufficient and recommended.

Another consideration is how birds eat. I fabricated custom limiters for my feeders out of Tupperware. If you do not take this extra measure you will find that birds (as I mentioned above) will scratch out four kernels of food to find one they want.

Health and Maintenance

If you buy chickens or turkeys and you plan to allow them to free range or at least forage you will want to leave them in the coop at least until they gain all their adult feathers and they have imprinted to the coop (as home). It's also a good idea to feed at a regular time and schedule.

Maintenance/Health

As far as maintenance goes, keep the housing as clean as possible. If you notice any bird with a runny nose (beak) or a sneeze or cough (yes they do!) or acting lethargic you should pull them into quarantine as quickly as possible. There are bird antibiotics that can be administered in the drinking water if necessary.

Outputs

Food

The primary goal of keeping poultry is the food they provide – at least that's the case with most people. The great thing about poultry is that they provide a delicious protein source in the form of eggs 200 days or more per year in most climates. This is a protein source that does not require any butchering or killing and it stores better than its alternative as well.

Extra birds, old birds or hens past peak laying ability at 2-3 years can also be harvested for meat. It's tougher meat at this point, but the good thing about poultry is even tough poultry is pretty tender.

In addition some people raise poultry called broilers for the sole purpose of meat. These birds take food fast and put on weight quickly, coming to slaughter size in a month or so. This is a healthy alternative to caged or "free range" chickens from large poultry operations.

Manure

One of the greatest gifts from poultry to the homesteader is manure. Poultry manure is considered by the uninformed to be a toxic waste. It is true that poultry manure can burn your plants. It's because of its high content of all three essential plant elements – Nitrogen, Phosphorus and Potassium. To see that illustrated, take the following table for example:

Manure	N	P	K
Poultry	33	48	34
Beef	21	14	23
Swine	11	8	5

This commonly leads to the correct assumption that chicken manure is "hot", but I find this to be an advantage rather than a disadvantage. Wood chips have high carbon content and just about the only thing that can compost them in equal amounts is manure. I find that the wood ties up the elements as they soak in. So for the bedding in my coops and pens I use wood mulch or wood chips. I then let the mixture age for a few weeks and add it to my garden bed. I haven't found this to burn my plants at all. They grow like wildfire.

Other Benefits

Gathering eggs for hatching requires that you collect them daily or better. An incubator is a good idea and a whole chapter could be written on using such a device. If you have a hen that is broody (willing to hatch eggs) then you can even move another hen's eggs to the broody hen's nest. The Asiatic breeds such as silkies, brahmas and cochins are infinitely better setters than the Mediterranean breeds such as leghorns.

Most people do not desire a broody hen as a broody hen wishes to sit on eggs that could be eaten, but having one is like having an incubator that doesn't require electricity, monitoring or worry. The hen will also raise the chicks, taking another step out.

Other than those few tasks, keeping poultry is not difficult. It is also not terribly difficult to keep the system going. Feed and water the poultry and take care of them. Receive eggs and manure. Eat the eggs and use the manure to feed plants that will in time feed the poultry.

It is not hard to see why raising poultry is so desirable to so many homesteaders and people intent on self-reliance. No other form of livestock offers so many options and variations while at once offering efficiency and reliability.

Rabbits

Like poultry, rabbits are a great choice for the homesteader. Unlike chickens, which require quite a bit of room to be happy, rabbits need very little space. With a 4:1 feed conversion ratio (four pounds of food to get one pound of meat), a short 28-31 day gestation period and high reproduction rate rabbits make a great choice for self-sufficient protein.

Choices/Breeds

For meat rabbits the requisite choices are the whites – New Zealand and California Whites. These two breeds have been molded into choice meat producers by decades of breeding. They make a fine choice for a beginner. However, one has to examine what features may have been bred out or perhaps might not be desirable.

For one thing, the whites take on feed quickly getting to eating size quickly, but often the sacrifice is more feed for the speed. And an experience rabbit breeder may find another breed such as a Satin puts on the same amount of weight with less feed, albeit at a reduced speed.

Ultimately the choice, like most, is a personal decision that should be built upon the needs and conditions of the individual and their situation.

Shelter

There are two ways to raise rabbits effectively for meat purposes. The first way, which is good for beginners, is to raise them in a hutch style method. The second way, which is great for experienced or full time homesteaders, is the colony method.

The hutch method consists of individual rabbit cages. These can be built in series with the individual cages or condos sharing a side. Each individual breeding adult gets his/her own cage. In addition, the offspring or litter can be housed after weaning in their own large hutch or they can be separated by male/female if they will be kept for longer periods. Each breeder needs about 6 square feet. There should be a mesh bottom where the waste can drop through as well. The sidewalls of the hutch should be covered with "baby saver" rabbit wire that is smaller at the bottom to prevent the offspring from falling through the wire and out of the cage.

In this configuration the female is brought to the male's cage for breeding – never vice versa. The individual rabbits get quite territorial and although I've never witnessed it, the female can fight the male too aggressively and bite off certain necessary male features. After the doe is in the buck cage they can be left overnight to take care of business or they can be watched until successful. If you watch and then remove the doe it might be a good idea to repeat the process the next day to ensure success. Remove the doe and place her back in her cage.

You should never inbreed (sibling breeding) your rabbits. You can line breed (offspring to parent) and you can breed cousin rabbits.

At between 10-14 days after breeding you can test the doe for pregnancy by pushing gently on the doe's stomach and feeling for the embryo (which feel like small marbles). At 28 days or before you can introduce a nesting box to the doe's cage. At right at 31 days she will kindle a litter (give birth).

It's very important to monitor the doe at this stage. You have to be prepared to place the baby bunnies into the nest should the doe unfortunately give birth on the cage floor. They also have to be secure in the nest and not able to easily fall out. You should check the litter and if you find any deformed or runt babies it is usually best to dispatch them now quickly and humanely. If for some reason you desire to transfer the litter to another mother, this can be done before the bunnies are 12 days of age, but not after.

On about the 15th day the nest box can be removed if all has gone well and the weather is acceptable. A small piece of plywood should be added for the bunnies to stand on until they are used to the cage. At between 4 and 8 weeks of age the bunnies can be removed from their mother's cage. The rabbits at 8-11 weeks are considered "fryers" and can be harvested for meat.

Food/Water

Like chickens, rabbits are great at converting kitchen waste, weeds and crops you grow into delicious protein. I always look to these sources first and foremost when feeding rabbits.

Like most animals there is a known list of safe foods and a known list of unsafe foods that can be fed to a rabbit. Just because something seems to fit don't make an assumption. You could be left with dead rabbits. A fellow blogger friend of mine says that Queen Anne's Lace is toxic to rabbits in the right dose. You would think that a close relative to carrots would be safe, but alas, it is not.

Some good things to actually grow for rabbits are:

- Mangelwurzels (cut up of course).
- Alfalfa
- Buckwheat
- Carrots, Turnips, Beets
- Clover
- Sunchokes
- Oats
- Plantain
- Wheat

Even if you grow some of their food you will invariably at some point end up at the feed store buying feed for your rabbits. Just beware that you are almost certainly buying GMO products. If you want to keep your rabbits fed then you will have to live with this and try to limit it as much as possible. There are certain formulations for certain ages and conditions of rabbits. Ask a person at the store and they should be able to help you pick the right food.

Feeders and waterers for rabbits are quite simple. Feed hoppers work just fine (make sure the bottom is screened). Bottle waterers with the rolling ball are the best choice for watering. Keep feed and fresh water in the cages at all times with the rabbits. If you feel them and you can't easily feel shoulder bones then it may be time to back the rations down a bit.

Maintenance/Health

Rabbits are susceptible to quite a range of ailments. Listing them all here would be akin to listing common human diseases – it simply would not be possible. Diagnosis is best left to an experienced breeder or a veterinarian, but I can help you with a few simple rules.

1. Observe the rabbit's defecation habits, behavior and feeding. If you notice a halt to all bowel movements, sniffles or malaise or simply a rabbit that won't eat you have a problem.
2. Quarantine the affected rabbit if at all possible.
3. At the very least, research the symptoms to discover a cause and make adjustments if you can.
4. Take the animal to a veterinarian if the symptoms are severe or if adjustments do not work. Small animals succumb quickly so it's important to be vigilant.

Outputs

Food

The killing and processing of rabbits for meat is not a pleasant job, but when done with respect and in a humane manner you can feel a little better about eating something it took work to raise and care for.

There are two schools of thought when it comes to killing a rabbit. The first is bludgeoning. This is simply striking the rabbit behind the ears with a blunt object. It will render the rabbit unconscious and it can then be bled out and processed.

The second method is cervical dislocation. This method breaks the spinal cord immediately killing the rabbit. This is commonly done by placing a broomstick behind the rabbit's head, applying downward force to the broomstick and pulling backward on the rabbit's rear legs. This method is more humane in my opinion, but it takes some practice.

At that point hang the rabbit up by its hind legs from someplace at working level. Remove the head. Remove the front feet. Then you will skin the rabbit and eviscerate it at the same time. Skinning the rabbit is a pretty straightforward process. You slit it from where its neck it to its anus, cut around the anus. Make a cut to the end of each leg from the main cut. At that point pull the skin and it should separate easily. After the skin is off, the organs and blood are easy to remove. Be sure to reserve the heart and liver. The organ meat is the most nutrient dense part of the rabbit. From there you can freeze and prepare the rabbit whole or dress it out. Remove all legs at the body joint. You can also quarter the torso into four easy to prepare pieces.

Rabbit meat is very tender when the rabbits are harvested young and it is meat that is easy to prepare and preferred by chefs as it takes on flavor easily.

Manure

Rabbit manure is even better than chicken manure for the main three essential plant elements. It has more nitrogen, phosphorus and potassium by weight than any other manure. Yet, because rabbits eat a lot of pulpy fibrous things whereas chickens do not, and the moisture content (and urea) is low the manure is benign enough to use for vermicomposting or application directly into the garden without using any bedding or other carbon source.

In addition, rabbit manure is a lot easier to handle than just about virtually any other manure. As I mentioned above, the moisture content is low and the manure comes in little pellets that are easy to find and move.

Other Benefits

While most people do not raise rabbits for anything other than food and the byproduct of manure they do provide other outputs that the homesteader can use, profit from and enjoy.

The pelt is the obvious benefit. Many rabbits can be bred for meat and still produce a beautiful and marketable hide. It's important to find the market and talk to them about what they expect. Most buyers will simply want the hides either frozen or salted and dried.

If you choose to keep the hide yourself you can tan it quite easily. Brain tanning is the least resource intensive, but it's not easy. It's said that every animal contains enough brains to tan its own hide. I won't go deep into the process here, but essentially you get all of the flesh off of the hide, put it into a water solution and add the mashed brains.

There are commercial tanning solutions on the market that do a great job. The process is easy, but the materials cost a little money. You remove the flesh then pickle the hide in a solution of vinegar and salt. Rinse thoroughly. Then you soak in the solution. It's that simple.

Bees

Although they are typically not thought of as livestock (or even a tame animal!) bees are great homesteading companions. A hive is unobtrusive, easy to build and relatively maintenance free. Despite the fear of stinging and the need for specialized equipment bees can be done cheaply and effectively.

Choices

There are really only two variations on the bees you can buy from an apiary, but there are other choices I will discuss here as well not relating to the type of bees. The two types of bees are Italians and Russians. Both are a fine choice, the Russians are said to be a little more aggressive though.

I recommend that if at all possible the beginner should attempt to find a local source of bees. Local bees are adapted to the climate and specific conditions of your area. Plus, if you use a local source you might just get a little free and helpful mentorship from the proprietor.

The second alternative choice is to trap your own bees. Traps are actually not terribly difficult to make, but if you don't have wild bees in your area you might have very little to show in the form of results.

The trap is essentially a modified part of the hive complete with frames full of comb. The bees can enter or leave freely, but once the scouts find it they will set up shop and the entire swarmed hive will enter and stay, allowing you to take them and transfer them to a permanent hive. It helps to use a lure. The best lure is lemongrass oil. It gives off a scent similar to queen pheromones.

If you are left with no choice, but ordering from a commercial apiary then don't despair. Commercial apiaries offer quality products and best of all they ship direct to your door. They are not cheap however. Packages with queens usually cost me right around $100. The queen is still in process of being imprinted onto the hive, but this will complete right after installation.

The real problem is making sure the hive doesn't abscond. This happened to my first hive and many times it's near impossible to diagnose the cause.

Shelter

There are three types of hives that can be used for keeping bees. One type is the Warre hive, but I don't find it to have any benefit not clearly covered by the other types. The most popular type for commercial use is the Langstroth or Lang type hive. This hive is a stack of boxes full of frames. The bees use the frames to make comb. They can put two things in the comb – provisions or brood. Brood is the egg cells (which eventually become larvae (worms)). Provisions are honey of course, but bee bread (a concoction of honey and pollen used to feed larvae) is also stored in combs.

The bees will typically use the lower larger box (called a deep or brood chamber) to store the brood and bee bread. Because the larvae will eventually pupate and become adults these cells can be used again and again, but beware the box and comb will limit hive size and may eventually cause them to swarm, dividing the hive and leaving it quite depleted.

Many times, just above this box is a 'selective barrier' called a queen excluder. The purpose is to keep the queen from leaving the brood chamber, but to allow the workers to do so. Thus you ensure no brood into your honeycomb. This is usually not a problem, but if the hive expands the queen will have to lay eggs in upper chambers.

The bees will store their immediate food in the form of honey above the deep box in the supers. If you add more supers ideally the bees will add more honey. You should always keep one super full of honey. This leaves enough food for the bees. Anything above that chamber can (again ideally) be harvested for the homesteader's use and enjoyment.

The second type of hive is called a topbar hive and is both easier and more complicated at the same time. While the Langstroth is relatively modern, the topbar is quite old. This type of hive has been in use in Africa for centuries. It has several distinct advantages over the Langstroth, but also several distinct disadvantages. It is easier to use, more natural for the bees and easier to build, but it is less reliable (in the experience of those whom I know) and you have to destroy comb to harvest honey. Destroying the comb forces the bees to spend time and energy rebuilding instead of making honey.

Put off by the difficulty of building or the cost of buying a Langstroth setup one winter I decided I would build my own top-bar hive and I would do it in the most economic way possible. That meant scrounging materials, making use of what was available in creative ways and resisting the urge to run down to the hardware store to buy things.

To build one like I built there is a simple material list that I will provide. Almost anything on the list is optional even the lumber. This can be built in so many different ways that I won't even give detailed drawings besides just some crude line sketches. Looking at my pictures and researching on the web will show that no one builds two alike and even though I am happy with mine, I'd build the next one differently.

Materials List:

Wood (sizes are dependent on what you want)
    Free
Hinges
    ~$4
Exterior coated screws (dependent on wood thickness)
    ~$3
Metal screen (commonly called hardware cloth)
    ~$5
Some type of roofing material (I used corrugated plastic)
    Free
Carriage bolts, nuts and washers
    ~$5

I had some wood in my workshop, but I knew where I could get tons of good solid oak boards for free. I work at an automotive factory and everyday we pack dumpsters full of nice pallets. Most of the wood is cheap, but a few that hold steel coils are solid and that's where I found my oak. The boards are roughly 48" long, 10" wide and about an inch and a half thick. Luckily they are tough enough to withstand being taken apart from the pallet. As skids beneath these boards there are heavy 4x4 inch beams. I'm not sure what they are made of, but they are hard as the dickens and heavy.

So for the bottom board and the sides I decided to use the oak planks. I decided that the 4x4 beams would be great for legs (something not all TBH have). I used some leftover plywood from a train table I built for my son for the ends and the roof.

Basically you simply take the end boards and mark an angled line on each side. The angle should be the same on both sides, but I guess if you were off really bad it wouldn't really matter. Make the same line marks on both end pieces. You can actually make the size of the end pieces work for you here as you determine the angles. My end boards are about 2x2 feet in dimension. The angle I chose is about 25 degrees. If I had it to do over again I would have chose a much more acute angle. Once you have the lines marked, pre-drill and run your screws in to join the ends to the planks. Depending on the size of your ends and planks you may need to place two planks per side. I joined my top and bottom planks on each side with a small piece of 2x4 scrap. This also gave me another surface to hold screws.

Once I had what I called the general frame built I added a bottom board on two hinges spaced equidistant from the ends. Then I added the metal screen over the bottom. The screen allows ventilation in warmer times and the varroa mites that infect the bee colony will fall through the screen instead of being able to climb back up. The bottom board is on hinges so it can hang free most of the year, but can be reinstalled come colder weather. There are about a million ways to accomplish the same thing. This may not be the best.

For the roof, I cut a piece of plywood big enough to overhang the top opening by some distance. Then I placed runner boards that were just big enough to slip over the box itself. The fit is tight and snug. Bees will tend to glue things together if they are letting in too much cold or weather. They will also stand at entrances and fan if things get too hot. I then took and stapled and glued a few pieces of black corrugated plastic that was thrown away at work as well. It is completely weatherproof and lightweight. Roofing metal and many other materials work great as well.

At this point you can drill your entrances, add the bars and you are done if you intend on hanging the hive from a tree or sitting it across stumps. For me, I really wanted it to have legs. It brings it to a height where working is easy and you don't want to be working with bees and having to bend. You can get them caught in some bad places.

I simply took a few of the beams and cut them to equal lengths and bolted them to the end pieces. They are in very snug and should I find them a problem, I can quickly remove them.

Most people recommend you drill one set of entrance holes. I am a belt and suspenders type of guy so I did two. One is a simple slit at the front where the bees can slide in and out. ¼" is apparently the best size from my research so the slit is ¼" tall and about 4 inches long. The length isn't greatly important. I then drilled in ¼" and ½" holes about every 4" along the side. This should give them some ventilation and extra spots to enter if one becomes crowded. If they have too many, they can always seal one up.

The top bars were the easiest part. I simply removed the roof and installed a few runner boards near the top of the frame on the inner sides. This allows the bars a place to seat. I'd like to have secured them better. I had a little room at the back so I put a spacer board to fill the gap.

From my research I determined that 1 3/8" bars are the optimal size so after accepting a donation from relatives of some scrap 2" thick pine boards I slit them to 1 3/8" wide and just long enough to fit on the runners, which ended up being about 16". I then set the table saw blade much shallower and made a 1/8 inch groove about half an inch deep down the length of each bar. The groove was precisely in the middle (3/4" inward from each side). This groove will aid the bees and give them a foothold when they build the downward hanging comb. If you don't cut them in the bees will not only have a hard time, but also so will the beekeeper. I then placed all the bars in and made sure they were reasonably snug and replaced the roof.

Regardless of which type of hive you use, you should place the hive in a location shaded during the summer and sunny in the winter with access to water and pollen-laden plants. Then with a quality queen, a package of bees and some simple equipment you can start along the path to producing your own honey, pollination and tons of entertainment.

Food/Water

It's a mistake to think that bees don't need food or water and are a carefree form of livestock. While it's true that you won't be buying a bag of feed at the feedstore or stocking a waterer you will need to make sure they are getting their needs met.

Though the bees will get their food from the pollen and nectar from flowers you will need to be prepared to feed them during periods where flowers are not present. For this reason it's a good idea to plant things that flower at various times. Bees like brightly colored flowers full of nectar. Plants like clover, dandelion, blackberries and tulip flowers grow wild and make great bee fodder. Garden plants like sunflowers, calendula and borage are great for bees as well.

In lean times you will need to feed the bees either sugar water or candy. Sugar water is just a simple syrup placed in a baby chick feeder (add rocks to keep the level just a few millimeters deep to keep drowning down). The candy is made from sugar, water and cream of tartar (sugar can be substituted with Karo syrup). It is cooked to 235 degrees F and then let it cool. Once it is cool, it is kneaded by hand. I like to add dried mint or mint oil at this point (mint is an anti-parasitic). The block is then put in the beehive for the bees to consume.

It's generally not necessary to add any water to the hive in any form. However, it is the responsibility of the beekeeper to ensure a small pond or puddles are nearby where the bees can drink. If the bees cannot find water easily they will move the hive to a place where they can. A small birdbath or 5 gallon bucket of water will also work well.

Maintenance/Health

Colony collapse disorder (or CCD) is a real concern and threat for even the small scale beekeeper. The simple truth is that beekeeping has become a bit of a gamble these days. The prevailing diagnosis is that pesticide use is the major cause. The fact is that you can't control if your neighbor uses the worst concoction imaginable on their land. Your bees cannot be corralled. The important thing is to give them plenty to eat and drink nearby.

Another threat (which may be a CCD contributor) is varroa mites which are also called varroa destructors – and for good reason. These mites are tiny little arthropods that wound the bee between the exoskeletal plates on the bee's abdomen. Once inside they suck away the bee's vital fluids. This leaves the bee susceptible to infections and weakening.

The safe and organic solutions to the mites include essential oils such as mint, thyme or lemon. Also powdered sugar or talcum powder prevents the mites from getting a grip on the bees. Also, whenever possible, screened bottom boards will allow the mites to fall out of the hive when they lose grip.

As bees are not like other livestock, they do not respond to health issues in the same manner. A goat or chicken may get sick and succumb leaving the rest of the animals untouched. It may die or get better. Individual bees die constantly, but when the hive – as an organism – is unhealthy the bees will simply move on and you'll be out money, time and effort.

Outputs

Food

Honey is the primary reason for keeping bees and it's a great food source. It is a little bit seasonal in the harvest. You can't go get it right before the bees overwinter, but it stores great and can be sold easily or bartered. Not to mention it is medicinal and delicious.

Other Benefits

The bees produce honey because they take nectar from plants you plant and from the wild. While this is a great benefit in and of itself the act of the bee 'stealing' the nectar pollinates your plants. Though the result may not be evident rest assured that increased pollination means more fruits and vegetables.

Pigs

In general and in my experience the larger the homestead animal the larger the problems the owner can expect. The one exception to this rule seems to be pigs. I have found pigs to be extremely care and trouble free. Pigs are one of my favorite animals on the homestead. I don't even find their stink offensive.

Choices

There are essentially two choices when raising pigs: Small and regular size.

It's generally considered a faux pas to talk about it, but for the homesteader with very little room pot bellied pigs are great to keep, but I've literally seen urban legends repeated on the Internet in an effort to keep people from eating them. In eastern Asian countries these pigs – that we consider pets – are actually raised for food.

The regular sized breeds are also a great choice and in actuality don't take up a great deal of room. There are several common breeds that make good choices. The white (pink) pigs like the Yorkshire, Hampshire, American Landrace and the red/brown Duroc are all great choices for the homesteader and proven producers.

Shelter

Providing a place for pigs to live and breed and be happy is not terribly difficult either. A fenced enclosure with a simple shelter works just fine.

It's important to consider your fencing type well before you get the pigs as well as the special considerations for each. Electric fencing in the form of electrified netting or strands (either wire or electrified rope) are all decent choices. Pigs are very smart animals and once they get shocked it will be terribly difficult to even force them across the line where the fence was.

The only problem with electric fencing and pigs is at the onset. Young piglets, startled or otherwise will run headlong into the fence and if it's the least bit penetrable they will crash right through and beyond. The good thing is that they are easy to train and you simply need to put a barrier just beyond the fencing. As long as they are given enough time to make contact with the fence and get a jolt they will learn.

Another type of fencing and one that I prefer is the simple galvanized after welding mesh wire fencing. This fencing is tough and durable and good looking and as long as it's properly installed it is impenetrable. There really is no disadvantage to it. It doesn't require electricity or really any upkeep.

The location of the enclosure is also important. Most people do not understand the origin of pigs as a woodland creature. Wild hogs on this continent and others are naturally born and content in the forest foraging for food such as nuts, plants, etc. Therefore, it's important to keep this in mind when picking an area to enclose.

Food/Water

There are a few reasons for the ease of raising pigs. For one, pigs will eat anything. Whereas other animals get picky or hurt with the wrong food, pigs will eat the worst stuff and just love it. This means they can eat basically byproducts.

Byproducts include waste food products from kitchens, restaurants, supermarkets, businesses, food factories, distilleries, etc. Pigs are omnivores, which means they are one of the few homestead animals that can eat your meat waste.

Corn is a great crop that can be raised for the sole purpose of feeding your pigs. A common method on larger farms is to harvest the full plant when it's still green and store it as silage. The wet debris ferments and can be fed to pigs as a very nutritious feed.

Watering pigs is a fairly straightforward task and the water can be mixed with the food waste and the whole mess. This is referred to as 'slop'. A trough can be made of wood or purchased and used to contain the whole mess.

Maintenance/Health

Again, listing all of the diseases that could be possible would be quite a task. The best bet is to make sure your hogs are fed and watered well and given access to forest land, shade, pasture and shelter. Signs of a healthy pig include healthy appetites, sleek coats, active vibrant energy and curly tails. If you see any evidence to the contrary of the healthy signs take the animal's temperature. It should read about 102.5° F.

Outputs

Food

The primary output of pigs in the form of food is, at least to me, quite unique. Sure a pig at slaughter time becomes a collection of edible parts. The uniqueness is the ability of most of these parts to take smoking, salting and preservation not just well, but outstandingly.

Hams and bacon can be salted, cured and smoked and can last for quite some time. Pork roasts are mainly eaten immediately. The lard that can be harvested is outstanding for cooking with or even actually using as a preserving device itself. My grandpa has quite fond memories of eating deer or beef tenderloin that had been preserved in a crock of lard.

The only problem is that slaughtering a pig is no easy task. Speaking generally the pig must be dispatched. It's almost imperative that this all be done on a cool winter day. This is usually done by shooting it between the eyes at least where I'm from. The pig must then be hung and bled. Bleeding is accomplished by using a long sharp knife and severing a large artery close to the heart. This must be done as soon as possible to get as much blood out as is practicable.

At this point the pig must be lowered into a large barrel or tub full of very hot water. The carcass is soaked briefly and then removed. The bristles (hair) and the thin layer of outer skin are scraped off. The carcass is then washed.

Then the head and innards are removed. Wash the body again. After this is accomplished the carcass should be hung in temperatures between 30 and 40 degrees for 24 hours. Finally it can be sectioned and preserved as desired.

Other Benefits

Swine manure like the other livestock manures is a great choice for use to grow things. The only real problem is that sometimes it's tough to contain the manure to remove it and use it. In these cases the best bet is to grow things near the pen or areas where you keep the hogs.

Hogs that are tame enough are also great to use for rooting up the garden. They will dig and eat any tubers and roots they can find and you will be left with nice fluffy soil.

Goats

Though their ability to convert feed into edible products is less efficient than that of the smaller choices in livestock, goats provide many benefits that may be more difficult to realize in smaller animals.

Choices

When picking a breed of goat there are basically two main types and then breeds that fill out each type. The two main types are meat or dairy. The meat goats pack on pounds quickly to get to slaughter size. Good meat breeds include Kiko, Boer and Fainting Goats.

The second main type is the dairy goat. Good dairy goats include Nubians, Nigerian Dwarf, LaMancha, Alpine, Saanen, Toggenburg, Oberhasli and Pygmy goats. These goats are in general smaller (especially the dwarf and pygmy varieties) and produce copious amounts of milk.

Shelter

A goat shelter is fairly simple to construct and can be as simple as a woodframed structure with a tarp covering or as complex as a metal barn. The type of shelter should depend on your climate, needs and particular situation.

With the miniature varieties of goats some people actually use the large commercial dog houses and these work just fine, but it helps to have a shelter you can use to milk in.

Food/Water

The great thing about goats is that they pasture well and will eat types of vegetative growth that other pasture animals won't touch. This makes goats a perfect choice to mob-graze (or intergraze) with other animals on the same pasture.

In the winter time, like most undulates good roughage like hay is an essential part of a good diet. Goats also do well with regular grain rations. This will also serve to enamor the goats with your presence, taming them and making your work easier.

For water, a simple trough full of clean water will serve the purpose well.

Maintenance/Health

Keeping a goat healthy is done through good prevention, diet and observation. Goats and playful and active animals and any injury, cut or otherwise should be treated immediately. Food should be appropriate for the season and good rations should be given. The animals should have access to grass and pasture whenever possible. Water should be clean and changed whenever it is not. The goats should also be given access to soda (the white powder type) as well as a good mineral lick.

Because they are rampant grazers, through accident or intention, invariably goats will eat something that is not agreeable to them. There are lists of plants online that should be avoided with goats. A good healthy pasture, rotation and supplemental feed can solve a lot of these problems, but some weed infestations make putting a pasture in certain places an issue.

Here, again, the important thing is knowing when you have a sick animal and being able to take the appropriate action (usually calling someone in to look at your animal). Goats – as I mentioned – are playful and active. If yours suddenly slows down or becomes lethargic it may be time to worry. Excessive noise (bleats) is another sign that there may be an issue.

Lack of appetite or thirst, changes in droppings are also signs of a sick goat.

Outputs

Food

While there are multipurpose breeds, as I mentioned, most people choose goats based on their ability to produce meat or milk efficiently. While goat meat is a great choice, having a dairy goat is where the real benefits are realized. For one, the dairy goat doe must be bred and impregnated in order for her to produce milk. In this way the goat owner gets a two for one. For one the kid can be an additional dairy goat or a source of meat (depending upon its sex of course).

The benefits of a dairy goat are long term. There's no one-off harvest. As long as you can keep a regular milk schedule (1 to 2 times per day every day) you can keep coming back to the "tap" so to speak. This is a sustainable source of protein for you and your family.

Many people are not familiar with goat's milk. Goat's milk is actually more easily digested and similar to human milk than that of a cow. It's produced in good amounts, but you can more easily control the output from a sixty-pound goat than a six hundred pound cow. My grandparents remember this about goats: Frequently a new mother who could not nurse a child would be told to either buy a goat or a coffin. Goat's milk could be digested and utilized by an infant while cow's milk would cause trouble in this regard.

Goat meat is – according to some sources – to be the most consumed red meat in the world. That figure includes beef! Goat meat is commonly barbequed and is by all accounts tasty and nutritious.

Other Benefits

Goat manure, like all of the waste from the animals I've mentioned, is of great benefit to vegetative growth. However, there are some unique attributes that make goats special to the homesteader.

Goats are renowned for their ability to eat anything. The old cartoons with a goat eating a tin can are not accurate, but they are close! Goats can be used by the thoughtful homesteader to help clear land that is full of thorns or land that is overgrown and weedy. In the modern world we take this for granted because we have power tools and tractors and land clearing machines. However, these tools require inputs such as gasoline and maintenance. Goats simply require you to take them to the land so they can do their job. They convert marginal land and objects into useful ones.

Larger goats can also be used to pull a cart or small plow!

Conclusion

I purposely left out the larger forms of livestock or ones that are overly complicated or input needy. This is because the person intent on providing a sustainable food source will have less difficulty with smaller animals and smaller steps. The permaculture principle of small and slow solutions applies here. Consider the smaller or less complicated animals to be a training plan for the others. Take your time and set up the system that fits your life and personality.

Section 4 - Eat

Introduction

Eating is an agricultural act. – Wendell Berry, On the Pleasures of Eating

It is also an ecological act, and a political act, too. – Michael Pollan, The Omnivore's Dilemma

I firmly believe that if we knew the true effects (as the quotes above point out) of what and how we eat that many of us would immediately change our habits, but the truth of the matter is that we are insulated from our food supply. We are insulated and isolated in the ways I pointed out previously as the inspiration for this book, but we are also in a way insulated in a cocoon we create.

I submit that not only is eating an agricultural act, an ecological act and a political act, but it's also an emotional act and a spiritual one to boot.

Emotionally, food makes us feel good; it connects us to a place and time and in many cases to our heritage and our faith. There's a reason for Sunday dinners and kosher foods. In my grandparents house you don't eat ANY food until it has been prayed over.

But for every good and positive thing that emotional and spiritual connection with our food has brought, there are an equal number of wrongs.

The real truth about eating is that it is an act of survival. We would do well to remember that and that we eat to live and we do not live to eat. We are not entitled to food, but rather entitled to seek it out and produce it. The emotion we feel for food should be relegated to happiness and pride in producing it and the faith we feel in it hopefully is faith in ourselves that we can produce more to enjoy.

Harvesting

It has been said that knowing when to harvest your vegetable crops from the garden is as important as knowing when or how to start them. I'll go a step further. It is *more* important. I ask, at what stage are more energy, time and mental anguish invested if not at the culmination of one's efforts?

Seed packets contain many pieces of information about how and when to plan, but rarely do I read when to harvest. As I really get good (better anyway) at saving seeds I'll soon find myself without packets anyway and at that stage anything can happen.

Fortunately for the budding gardener, many common garden vegetables give good indications of ripeness. For the sake of brevity, this writing assumes that the gardener reading it knows that tomatoes turn red (or sometimes yellow or purple depending on variety) when they are ready. In other words, if a plant makes it obvious when harvesting should occur I wouldn't touch on it here.

Aparagus

When: Spears are 6-8 inches long and thick as a pencil or your pinky finger.
How: Snap or cut off at ground level.
Notes: Sources aren't clear, but you should only harvest spears for anywhere from 4-8 weeks. Otherwise the plants won't be able to produce enough food to thrive.

Beans (Green/Snap)

When: Before the seeds start to bulge and the outline becomes visible. Don't take any chances here. Pick them small if in doubt and adjust from there. Strings develop and the beans take on an odd flavor.
How: Pop them right off the vine.
Notes: I harvest all the beans at once regardless of smaller ones. The size difference makes a unique product when canned. It's just my idea of a secret stab at industrialized food.

Beets/Onions/Carrots/Turnips

When: Check the shoulders of the root and decide how you like them.
How: The first time I tried to pull a carrot out by the tops Bugs Bunny style I ended up on my butt with a handful of greens. A fork is ideal. Come in at an angle and pry up. A spade or trowel will also work.
Notes: Mulching roots and letting them overwinter will concentrate sugars and produce a unique and tastier product.

Broccoli/Cauliflower

When: Well before the flower heads (the part you harvest) starts to blossom or flower. This is a crop that won't get riper, it will flower and you'll be left with nothing.
How: Use a sharp pair of scissors or a knife.

Corn (Sweet)

When: The silks at the end of the husks will turn brown and will feel dry. The juice from the kernels should be milky white when you bust one.
How: Pull and twist.

Cucumbers

When: You will have a limited window. When the variety you are growing gets to a decent size for your purposes (pickles or slicing), but well before it turns yellow.
How: Pull off the vine.

Garlic

When: The tops will fall over and die.
How: With a fork or a spade, dig out the bulb and let dry.

Melons

When: Books could be written on this subject. The stars must align right and several of the indicators should be present. The melon must smell ripe; the vine must break off easily. The bottom will begin to change color to a yellow instead of white.
How: It should slip off the vine.

Preserving the Harvest

Part of the fun of dealing with your garden harvest is preserving it. Because in doing so, you have guaranteed that you'll be eating your garden output for months to come.

There are some options for preserving the harvest. Among those: freezing, canning, drying, making a wine, or making jellies (a form of canning). Of course, everyone has an opinion, but each method seems to produce a different result when tried on the same produce. For instance, I do not care for canned tomatoes, but the same tomatoes, dried or made into a sauce and canned are divine.

Blanching

In many (if not all) cases, vegetables will have to blanched prior to freezing or drying. Blanching is a simple process; nothing more than steaming or boiling the produce and then flash cooling the produce.

For instance, carrots call for slicing into uniform pieces and then boiling (or steaming) for three minutes and then flash cooling in ice water. This is necessary to stop the enzyme action in the vegetables that causes them to break down. Basically they begin rotting almost immediately and cooking ends that process. That means, no off flavors, colors or squishiness.

The following vegetables require blanching and for the listed time (in minutes).

Artichoke	7
Artichoke - Jerusalem	3-5
Asparagus	2-4
Beans, Snap, Green, Wax	3
Beans, Lima, Butter, Pinto	2-4
Broccoli (flowerets 1½ inches across)	3
Brussels Sprouts	3-5
Cabbage or Chinese Cabbage	2-3
Carrots	2
Cauliflower (flowerets, 1 in. across)	3
Celery	3
Corn	7-11
Kernel Corn	4
Eggplant	4
Greens	2-3
Kohlarabi	1-3
Mushrooms	3-5
Okra	3-4
Onions (chopped)	Flashed
Parsnips	2
Peas - Edible pod	1-3
Peas - Green	2
Peppers - Sweet (Rings)	2
Potatoes - Irish (new)	3-5
Rutabagas	3
Soybeans - green	3
Squash - summer	2
Turnips	2

Freezing

315

Freezing is a simple task. After blanching, place the produce into freezer safe bags or containers and freeze.

Canning

Canning is an older technique than most people think. The process was invented by Nicolas Appert in order to win a 12,000 Franc French military contest in 1785. The purpose was to preserve food for armies. It was, after all, Napoleon who said "An army marches on its stomach".

In essence, the process pasteurizes the food (taking it above a temperature in which all harmful organisms are killed) and then seals it inside a vacuum (no air in or out). This provides a sterile environment in which food can be kept safely. In fact most literature recommends canned food be eaten within a year or so, but most people have a story about food that was perfectly safe after five years or more, but I don't recommend taking this chance.

The only confusing thing about canning for most people is which method to use – steam or water bath.

The water bath method involves completely submerging a filled jar (with lid and ring) into water. The water is then brought to a boil for a prescribed time period. The jars are then cooled and stored after checking for seals. The water bath method is suitable only for food with high acid contents. This high acid keeps a lot of the harmful organisms from thriving in the food. Foods that are suitable are most fruits and some tomatoes (depends on variety and acid content). Lemon juice is added to some of these foods to ensure an extra level of safety.

Steam canning involves using a special steam canner. The filled jars are placed in a few inches of water and then the lid is placed on the canner. A gauge on top notes the pressure. Once the proper pressure has been met, the jars are left under this pressure for a prescribed amount of time. Since steam under pressure raises the temperature inside above boiling point you can guarantee no harmful organisms are left alive inside the food.

Drying

Drying vegetables after blanching is a little bit more difficult. Refer to your dehydrator handbook for proper drying times and temperatures. You can also sun-dry your produce in a solar dehydrator or under a metal mesh screen or muslin cloth. That should tell you how I feel about equipment. My thought is this. A dehydrator is nice to have, but the people who tell you that you have to have one are mistaken. If you buy one, there are brands that do a fine job with a modest price tag.

The process of drying is fairly simple. Some foods must be blanched or treated before drying, others can go directly in. The dehydrator (if one is used) is turned to the appropriate setting and the food is left for the appropriate time. It is always a good idea to check a sample of the food for moisture and "doneness". I like to check the thickest piece and use it to judge the rest. One bad piece can impart moisture after storage.

Once the food is dry and cool you can pack it into airtight jars (with or without some type of desiccant) and store it for future use.

Wine

One of the most enjoyable ways to preserve food – both during and after the preservation process – is by making wine. "Vinting" as it is sometimes called is the process of taking high sugar and acid content fruits (and sometimes vegetable) and allowing yeast from natural or manufactured sources to convert the sugars into alcohol. Alcohol in its own right is a preservative and the wine is strong enough to have an alcohol preservative effect (yeast die at ~15% alcohol), but it still captures the flavor and much of the nutrition of the initial produce.

Making wine can be done with a lot of equipment and very very fine detail, but it can also be done well by amateurs with little to no experience or equipment. My first wine was a strawberry wine I produced in a clean plastic milk jug with a purchased airlock and small packet of yeast. It was delicious stuff!

To make wine you need:

- A container that can be made airtight.
  - Paid solution: Glass carboy purchased
  - Free solution: Milk jug or plastic juice bottle (good for one use!)
- Yeast
  - Paid solution: Packaged yeast
  - Free solution: Natural yeast collected from the air – unreliable though.
- An airlock
  - Paid solution: A plastic airlock
  - Free solution: A ballon with a small pin hole.
- Fruit (most commonly)
  - Paid solution: Bought from the store/producer
  - Free solution: Grown yourself or overripe produce from the store
- Bottles
  - Paid solution: Purchased from a wine shop.
  - Free solution: Collected for free from the local bar.

There are other small ingredients you may choose to use or leave out. These include: Extra sugar, yeast food, clearing agents, wood chips (for flavor), etc.

The process is simple:

1. Sanitize all equipment. This can be done with a commercial sanitizing agent or can be done with diluted bleach in water.
2. Crush fruit and add it to your primary. The primary is a bucket or small bowl that holds the must (crushed fruit) for the first few days. Pitch the yeast in. I really

do recommend commercial yeast!

3. Let the yeast work for a few days.

4. Drain the young wine from the must (fruit peels and solids) into a secondary fermenter which is your jug or carboy. It must also be sanitized and must be made airtight with the airlock you will add at this point. The airlock is best purchased from the store as well. It is filled with water and lets air out, but none in.

5. Let the wine continue to work and settle for a month or better.

6. Bottle.

7. Enjoy!

Cheese

Legend tells of a merchant traveling across the desert sometime after the first civilization took root. At his side was a skin (dried calf's stomach) full of milk to sustain him on the journey. The calf's stomach was full of an enzyme called rennet, which helps calves digest mother's milk. The "breaking" of milk divides it into two things – curd and whey. Curd is a globule of fat and protein and whey is the leftover protein that could not be incorporated into the curd. The curd is somewhat solid and the whey is liquid.

Upon stopping, the traveler discovered that his milk had become essentially curds and whey. When he tasted it he found it to be pleasant and this is how – according to legend – cheese was discovered.

The truth we may never know, but cheese is old and has been made by cultures around the world for many many years. Everyone has their own techniques and recipes, but cheese is fairly simply to make. It is simply milk, rennet and salt. A starter culture is sometimes used to make the process easier, but it's optional. The milk is aged (set out to start turning) heated gently and rennet is added. The rennet starts to separate the cheese from the "not cheese". The curd (a solid mass) is cut into smaller cubes to allow the whey to more easily separate. More heat is added and the whey is poured off (and can be retained).

Essentially cheesemaking is getting as much of the whey out of the curd as possible. After that point, salting and pressing occurs.

Cheese Press

Materials you will need:

1. (2) stainless or galv 6″ shoulder bolts

2. (2) matching nuts (not the aircraft type with the locking plastic!)

3. A handful of matching washers

4. A small chunk of PVC (4″ diameter is a good place to start)

5. One 4″ knockout cap for the PVC

6. A wooden cutting board (about a foot long)–normally this will make the pusher board and the base surface.

7. A few smaller pieces of PVC, or wooden dowels of about 1″ in diameter

You should be able to pick up all of that for less than 10 bucks. You may find ways to substitute things, so read the directions first and then modify (like I did).

1. Draw the inside circle of your large PVC onto what will be the unused surface of the cutting board or other suitable chunk of wood and cut it out with a jigsaw or other appropriate power tool. Cut your large and small PVC to length. Further ahead you will find out that I cut the smaller ones way too long and had to cut them down again. I am really bad about measuring things and usually I just cut to fit. The PVC pieces must be completely flat on one side. That is the side that will be against the base or the follower. And the larger piece should be about 4-5″ tall. You can also cut your cutting board down to a more compact size. Since you probably have cut your round out of it, you may want to cut off the sharp corners. If there is enough left, cut out your pusher board or find a suitable replacement.

2. Note the rasp, next step is to clean up the edges.

3. Check the fit–doesn't have to be exact.

4. Take the knockout cap (because in plumbing jobs it's temporary) and remove the flange. If your wood block fits perfect you don't really need it, but it's so hard to get the wood follower just right. Check the fit on the cap after you are done.

5. Drill 1/16" holes about an inch apart up/down and around the circumference of the big PVC. I also like to file in weep notches on the bottom surface. Resist the urge to cleanup the holes on the inside with sandpaper. You want to protect the inside surface from scratches which harbor nasties. Use your thumbnail instead.

6. Drill holes with matching spacing through your pusher board and your base cutting board.

7. Begin assembly. From the bottom up. Two bolts–>two washers for each bolt—>into the cutting board base—>large PVC on top.

8. Add the followers.

You may have to recut the small PVC pieces. You can see here that this is about the exact distance you want. The PVC pushers must be just shorter than bolts when the followers are in place and at TDC (top dead center).

8. Add pusher board, washers then nuts.

Want more options? You can build mold and follower sets for various sizes. Here's my mack daddy-sized set. After the build, put all of your stuff here that touches food into a dishwasher and blast the heck out of it.

The great thing about this design is that it allows you to utilize one of two methods of pressing. You can either use mechanical force by tightening the nuts and bolts or you can place a weighted object on top. Some recipes call for a certain weight to be added so it helps to be able to adjust to the learning curve.

Odd Preservation Methods

Preparing for hard times is not terribly difficult if your heart is in it, but after the freeze-dried and canned food runs out what will you do next? People with certain skill sets will always be able to find food, but the real problem may not be how to get food, but rather how to make it last. A large kill such as a deer will not be eaten in even a week and we may not be able to count on the weather cooperating.

It's likely that things will never get so bad that we won't be able to use a freezer, pressure canner or a dehydrator. And even if we can't, making jerky is not terribly hard either. But for some time now I've been asking myself when I harvest an animal or sit down to a dinner from prepared food —*what would I do if I had to make this food last for a week, a month or even a year and I didn't have the resources I do today?*

So I'm constantly curious about what people did before we had all of our modern conveniences. What was it really like not knowing if you could keep your food until you really needed it?

Disclaimer: This writing is for informational purposes only. Do not try this at home!

The first method of preservation I'd like to talk about is just simply growing things that don't require preservation. Growing grains like field corn, wheat, barley and rice make preservation easy. You just let it dry and you're done. Of course there are some hazards. Ergot is an organism that affects wheat in storage.

Of course any animals on the hoof or foot are preserved until the moment they die or are harvested. As long as you keep them that way you are preserving them. Large catches of fish or turtles could be caged and kept alive until ready to eat. That makes it easy to gather the food source one time and use it over a longer period.

The second method is more historical and that's learning to do what our ancestors did.

If we go way back to the Paleolithic days we'd see our distance relatives harvesting the stomachs and intestines of the animals they killed. They would then clean out those organs and pack them with the meat they could not consume immediately. They would put a rock in as well, tie off the ends, attach a cord and sink the meat-packed organ. Anyone who has dove 15-20 feet down into a lake knows that the deeper you go the colder it gets. This was a natural method of refrigeration even in warmer times.

People have recently tried this and reported that the meat wasn't tasty, but it was safe. I personally would not want to try it, but it's always good to know.

Much later, in frontier America, before freezers, people got even more inventive in regards to meat preservation. In order to store large halves and chunks of meat from recently harvested livestock, they would basically pickle the meat. They did this by salting it well to draw out all the blood. Then they would make brine consisting of salt, saltpeter and water and sink the meat into a barrel filled with the brine. Of course, it had to be thoroughly desalted when it was pulled out.

Another method that is better known is curing of hams. This is a fairly simple process, but the knowledge is quickly being lost. The process is a lot like brining, but you take the hams out after a couple of days of brining and smoke them.

Now smoking is another method unto itself. Many people think smoking is what you do to make barbecue. While tasty, that method will only cook and not do much to preserve the meat. To preserve it, you have to cold smoke it.

Cold smoking is not too difficult, but you have to have a metal container to contain the smoke from the fire, and another wooden container that's fairly airtight to hold the smoke. A piping system moves smoke from the metal container, cools it and flows it into the smokehouse (the wooden container I talked about). This can be done on smaller scales as well.

People on the frontier also packed meat such as bacon, beef or venison in airtight containers filled with lard. The lard prevents oxygen from getting to the meat. Without oxygen the meat doesn't ruin. My grandfather tells me that this was a method commonly in use in his house in the era of the great depression. He had fond memories of fighting his brothers over the tidbits packed in the jars of lard.

One of the oddest preservation methods may be the Century Egg. In the time of the Chinese Ming dynasty there is a story of a man who found a two-month-old duck egg covered in lime (the powder) used for masonry work. I guess curiousness got hold of him and he tasted the egg and found it to be somewhat palatable. Thus the century egg was born.

The traditional method involves salt, quicklime and wood ash. The secret is that the alkaline mixture changes the chemical content. The modern method is a brine of salt, calcium hydroxide, and sodium carbonate for 10 days followed by several weeks of aging while wrapped in plastic.

These eggs look very nasty, essentially turning black and gelatinous. They are supposedly very odoriferous and an acquired taste. I've never had the opportunity to try one so I can't comment. A similar treatment by Norse peoples with whitefish creates Lutefisk.

I believe it is important to learn all we can about how things have been done in the past. Primitive technology is only primitive in the sense that it is reliable when modern amenities are removed.

Diet

My views on diet and food are pretty radical. I think when you put yourself so close to your food and you know "too much" about it you tend to take a different view.

There are, in my opinion, too many idealists when it comes to food. There are people who eat based on what another culture eats, based on what their ancestors (way back) may have (or may not have) eaten. There are diets based on excluding one thing or another or adding more of some thing or another.

Humans are omnivores. Plenty of evidence exists for the human as a vegetarian. For example: Our hands are poor at tearing flesh. We have no claws or "killing" teeth. Our intestines are "too long" for meat, but plenty of evidence exists that we evolved as carnivores as well. Our brain is capable of higher intelligence – compensating for no claws or killing methods. We have teeth that are good for tearing and biting as well as crushing and grinding. Meat tastes good.

No, humans are not carnivores and we are not vegetarians. We are opportunivores. If you place us on an island with small amounts of protein (maybe fish) and large amounts of fruit (bananas, coconuts) and some leafy greens and we'd probably do just fine. Inuits live in the Artic with essentially no vegetable sources at all. The real evidences point to the human diet being a diverse and wonderful thing and the human body as a finely adapted machine capable of converting varying types of diets into energy and muscle.

People ask me what the perfect diet is and I really believe it's dependent upon the individual.

My views on obesity and health issues are similarly radical. I believe that processed food is not optimal food. I believe it is capable of taking a person who is quite inactive and quickly destroying their health, but I do not shun grains and sugars for all people. The problem is not so much that the processing is bad (it is to a degree), but rather where the processing was done. Was the processing done a thousand miles away in a factory or in your kitchen? The processing of food has taken cheap oil and turned it into calorie packed food that people no longer have to work to achieve.

Processing food is tough work and you burn calories doing it. Turning the crank on a handmill or slicing apples and preparing them to can. These things take work. The proper balance of work (energy output) and calories eaten (energy input) should be as close to 1:1 as possible. This is also why people spend time and money in gyms, on treadmills, lifting weights. If you have to fence a pasture or build a chicken coop or hoe a garden row you no longer delegate your work responsibility to oil and it's hard to consume more than you put out.

Although I believe meat should play a big role in a person's diet I do not believe it should be the centerpiece. Making a meal of just a big slab of meat scares me in more ways than one.

Meat has tons of benefits. It packs protein, fat and minerals into a compact package. If you raised the animal and worked for the meat and enjoy it, there's a ton of benefits. If you bought it from the grocery store with your oil money to pay for the oil money that was used to grow it (provided it's not grass fed organic and even then there was oil involved probably) then you aren't doing yourself any good.

The problem with meat is that the current way of operating with CAFOs and input intensive agriculture makes meat not only unsustainable, but damaging to the environment.

It takes, on average, 28 calories of fossil fuel energy to produce 1 calorie of meat protein for human consumption, [whereas] it takes only 3.3 calories of fossil-fuel energy to produce 1 calorie of protein from grain for human consumption.
—David Pimentel, Cornell University

Nutrients in animal waste cause algal blooms, which use up oxygen in the water, contributing to a "dead zone" in the Gulf of Mexico where there's not enough oxygen to support aquatic life. The dead zone stretched over 7,700 square miles during

the summer of 1999.
—Natural Resources Defense Council

According to John Revington of the World Rainforest Report:

In Central America, 40 percent of all the rainforests have been cleared or burned down in the last 40 years, mostly for cattle pasture to feed the export market—often for U.S. beef burgers.... Meat is too expensive for the poor in these beef-exporting countries, yet in some cases cattle have ousted highly productive traditional agriculture.

Sustainable meat is possible with intensive rotational grazing, intergrazing, mob-grazing and smaller animals, but not at current levels of consumption and current levels of population growth and arable land. About 272 pounds of meat per year.

If everyone who raised cattle did it with intensive rotation methods they'd be able to stock 10 cows per acre so we figure 1/10 acre per cow. At slaughter the useable meat from each cow (about 1000 lbs) is reduced in half (about 500 lbs) so it's really 1 "net" cow every 1/5 acre (meat-wise), but intensive rotational grazing requires each acre to be grazed for 3-4 days and then "rested" for 30. So we have to multiply each 1/5 acre by 10 (10 1/5th acre paddocks, each grazed 3 days and rested 30). Now we are up to roughly 2 acres per 500 lbs of beef. Eaten at 25 pounds below the rate at which we currently consume meat, that's 1 acre worth of cow per year per person. Each person is sustained meat wise by one cow/acre.

The U.S. has 470 million acres of arable land which is holding roughly 311.5 million people. Thus every man, woman and child in the US has a theoretical 1 ½ acres of food producing land. You just gave up 1 acre to grow your cow so you've got ½ acre left for a house, parking areas, etc. Of course 72 million acres were used to grow corn in the US – 58% of which we can deduct since we no longer need livestock feed since we are ONLY eating grass fed beef and no other terrestrial meat products. That's another 1/5 acre you just lost. Roughly the same amount in soybeans is grown (minus its share in livestock feed). That's another 1/5 acre. This also does not account for the land used to grow cotton for your clothing. That takes another 1/10 of your land. Wow, your remaining half acre went pretty quick. Of course this makes no account of the land used also for dairy, for poultry and eggs (which COULD be mobgrazed on the cow pasture). It also makes no account for breeding. This land is a one-off thing - there's no cow left in the US after this is done ONCE!

Is there any wonder that CAFO's exist?

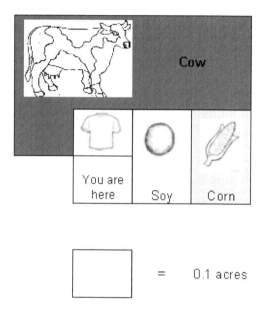

This also makes no accounting of the 1 million acres of arable land lost to desertification, development, etc. through the very processes that make producing meat possible and necessary in the first place! So if the population were stable and all we did was stress the land with more development, in 150 years that ½ acre would be lost to time. And again, that's not taking into account the additional 51 million additional "new" people in the US by that time – all expecting their share of the food as well!

I think in the next 50 years we can expect resource wars, mass contamination of food, waterways and oceans, dead fisheries, starvation, thirst, death. That is unless we change our way of thinking.

So what is the solution? Do we all become vegetarians? Well as I stated before I don't think that would be a healthy diet for the majority of people reading this book (though some will find success with it). The solution is much more complex. There is an immediate and crucial culture shift that needs to occur quickly. This shift must be toward consumption of less meat and what meat we do eat needs to be varied and as sustainable as possible. And we need to grow as much food as we can – meat or otherwise.

Buying from local producers who pasture their beef is a necessary first step. Encourage them to intergraze and intensively graze. Eat lower on the food chain – smaller animals. Instead of tuna or beef eat more herring, salmon and goat. Grow your own food – not just meat based, but vegetable based as well. Hunt more – there are many squirrel populations in need of control and squirrel is delicious and nutritious.

In the end, your diet is your own. You have to own your choices and the consequences. We can certainly continue on a business as usual path for a little while at least or we can make conscious decisions to change things for the better while we still have a choice and the transition will be easier.

The Ideal Diet

Diet is finally starting to take on its right meaning in our culture. Diet is not something you go on, it's something you live. So what would the ideal diet be to me?

First of all, you'd not eat the same thing very often and definitely not in the same form. The food would be as varied as you could possibly make it. One day you eat beef, the next chicken, the next maybe no meat at all. And the meat would not be the centerpiece. The meal would be "the meal" not a pork meal or a roast meal. The meat would take up less room on the plate. Instead of a pound of beef it would be a 6-8 ounce steak. Grains would not play a primary role either.

Good whole grains would play a part, but there wouldn't be bread every single meal. The majority of the plate would be good vegetables and salad with some fruit.

The meal would consist of both fresh and preserved foods, but at least something on the plate at all times would be seasonal – fresh tomatoes or just harvested spinach from the garden. Yogurt made from fresh milk.

There's no need to use artificial colorings and flavorings. You'd use the herbs in your garden to create unique flavors.

The meal's appearance would be appealing because it would be real, good food.

Conclusion

Putting It All Together

Collectively everything I've written about in this book will work independently – each element can function as long as the appropriate inputs and work occurs, but together the individual elements, when connected, form a powerful food system that is resilient, sustainable and efficient.

By looking at the outputs from the SIPOC I taught you to do in the Introduction of the book you can now start to see not only outputs that can go toward the inputs for other elements, but you will realize new outputs that you previously could not see or you considered "waste". You will start to see every item, material, and movement as a resource that can be used to further the entire system.

Because every piece of land is as different as each person, I cannot give a blueprint that works for everyone. Nor should I – each system is designed to cater to the individual family or person's needs wants and desires.

But I can tell you how my homestead will work when it reaches its full function.

I capture a lot of rainwater and most of this goes toward watering the animals. The garden needs very little to no water because the soil is full of rich organic matter. The manure from the animals is dropped into the garden directly by the animals, by me carrying it or it's conveyed downhill by gravity. The animals are fed kitchen waste in the form of fruit, vegetables and meat. The animals are bred and the stock used for food are slaughtered – everything is made use of that is possible.

In the spring, the greenhouse fills up. The kitchen garden is planted and the crop garden comes last with more frost tender crops. The berry bushes and fruit trees start to put on leaves and bloom. The beehives buzz with activity as they reawaken. The livestock give birth to new offspring who are each destined for a purpose. We fish for crappie and bluegill in the lake just down the hill from the orchard. We search for wintercress and dandelions and morel mushrooms.

In summer and late fall we harvest fruit, vegetables and other crops. We start canning and drying and preserving what we harvest. We fish for catfish using trot lines and other techniques. We milk the goats and collect eggs from the chicken coop. We decide what animals we want to feed through the winter and which we will harvest. Persimmons and pawpaws and hickory nuts start to ripen. Chanterelles start to fruit.

In the winter I hunt just 100 yards from my house, hopefully putting squirrel, deer, rabbit and duck into the freezer or jar. We keep some greens going in the greenhouse and coldframes for salads and fresh vegetables.

My hope is that by reading this book you now understand why it's imperative to start taking some of the steps toward independent food production, but I also hope that you see it's not terribly difficult to implement at least a few of these activities into your everyday life. I believe it's important enough and that the knowledge is being lost so quickly that not only must you know how to do these things, but also you should be teaching your children as you learn.

I'm inspired by the stories I hear everyday from people who are starting their first garden or learning how to hunt, kill and butcher their own meat. It gives me hope for the world yet.

14829124R00179

Made in the USA
Charleston, SC
03 October 2012